A Political Economy of Banking Supervision

Damir Odak

A Political Economy of Banking Supervision

Missing a Chance

Springer

Damir Odak
Zadar, Croatia

ISBN 978-3-030-48546-7 ISBN 978-3-030-48547-4 (eBook)
https://doi.org/10.1007/978-3-030-48547-4

This Springer imprint is published by the registered company Springer Nature Switzerland AG
The registered company address is: Gewerbestrasse 11, 6330 Cham, Switzerland

Preface

Banking is the cardiovascular system of our society. As in the human body, its functioning enables the smooth operation of the economy. Likewise, if it malfunctions, it becomes a doomsday device.

Such a position creates an asymmetry of the impact banking could have on the real economy. The asymmetry between the grim consequences of accepting risks and the modest rewards emerging from such action.

The asymmetry has two sources: economic and political. The impact on the economy is a consequence of the fact that adverse developments in finance create shocks disrupting the normal flow of economic activity. In contrast, positive developments do not create "positive shocks".

The political is more dangerous, and it is a consequence of desperation. When financial shocks adversely impact a high number of people disrupting their lives, they lean towards extremist populistic policies.

Finance was one of the critical technologies enabling the creation of modern society. However, today, it contributes little to economic growth. On the other hand, its malfunctioning has a profound and lasting adverse impact on society.

This book explains why, what and how. Why is it essential to maintain a tight supervision of banks? How can banking supervision improve stability, not only of the financial system but also of the entire human society? What went wrong with the regulation in the past?

Banking is, in today's EU, still a source of increased risks for the society. Although it is clear what needs to be done, a widespread misperception that the growth of banking credit sets the pace for economic growth so far disturbed efforts to do it.

Facing the negatively biased asymmetry between risks and benefits, banking supervisors must understand and keep that in mind: if we err, we should err on the safe side.

Because of the mentioned misperception, that is easier said than done. Due to fear of recession, politics usually very carefully listen to the bankers' arguments and hold regulators' hand to prevent "too harsh" treatment of the banks.

Therefore, when the asymmetry shows its ugly face, before blaming bankers and regulators, we should first look at the role politics had.

Zadar, Croatia

Damir Odak

Introduction

Abstract In late 2008 the disorderly failure of an investment bank shook the world, bringing the financial system to the edge of collapse. Our society cannot withstand financial system failure. Therefore, the political decision to intervene is a reasonable one. While trillions of dollars and euros are in the game, the final cost is just a small fraction of the sum involved. The framework of the new regulation, compared with 2008, changes things for the better. Some high expectations are nevertheless let down. In a situation when risk-taking creates small benefits for society, while its consequences could be disastrous, the undivided focus of the regulation should be risk reduction. We still need to make a few steps to get there.

The year was 2008. Bad news and bad feelings accumulated in the financial markets during the first three quarters. The outlook was grim, and markets expected adverse developments.

Still, almost no one expected what followed. The ensuing developments caught all of the once confident analysts, economists, bankers, central bankers and ministers by surprise. The understanding that we had learned enough to be sovereigns of our destiny had vanished.[1]

The demise of the single bank shook the world. It dispersed the mirage of cornucopia created by endless financial magic. It suddenly replaced it by a treacherous storm threatening to harm the world economy in, during our lifetime, an unknown way. Hope for great moderation, and permanent economic advancement proved to be an expensive illusion.

As the world was being shaken, the financial meltdown brought banking supervision up into the limelight. More than a trillion dollars and euros were globally injected in banking systems to keep them afloat. Supervision, the activity, until then dull and almost invisible, became immensely popular.

[1]"As the clouds of recession started looming over the US economy in 2007 and early 2008, economists were often asked whether another depression or even deep recession was possible. Most economists instinctively replied NO!" (Stiglitz, 2010) Kindle, loc. 195.

Conventions and regulations, practically unreadable to anyone but a handful of specialists,[2] became the hot topics in drunken pub discussions. So hot that they temporarily pushed aside football, fast cars and beauties.

People got confused and angry. While governments poured endless piles of money into the financial system to stabilise it, bankers received sizable bonuses for their excellent work. To a lot of people, the rules regulating the operation of banks were beyond the realm of common sense and their perception of decency.

In late 2008 and early 2009, it appeared that, if left to its own devices, the system could collapse. Today, having the benefit of hindsight, it is clear that, despite all controversies, the political decision to intervene and stabilise the financial system was a reasonable one. Not "only" the financial system was threatened. As the crisis unfolded, a hidden threat also loomed over fundamental values and the way of life of the free world.

Fortunately, the financial system was not (and it should never be) left to its own devices. An implicit government guarantee firmly stands behind the banking system. Individual banks may fail, but the government should use whatever it takes to keep the system running. Our society cannot withstand the consequences of the financial system failure. Therefore, the governments reasonably jumped in with "our" money and saved the day.

The final financial outcome also proved them reasonable! Today, the whole operation appears as some kind of alchemy. While trillions were in the game, the final cost was just a small fraction of the sum involved. Some countries even earned money for their budget from those salvage operations. On the other hand, others ended up with a double-digit increase of the public debt to GDP ratio. However, even those unlucky ones spent less than the pending financial collapse could have cost them.

The disorderly failure of a single investment bank triggered all that clutter. Economic problems and accumulated risk would unavoidably cause a slower growth or recession, but without that trigger, there would hardly be any comparison between 1929 and 2008.

The public outrage and concern aroused by those events focused politics on banking supervision. Politics publicly demanded an explanation from competent authorities and required assurances that such things would never happen again.

Regulators commenced work on new documents, creating rules that would make the financial landscape radically safer. Nonetheless, the documents implementing the regulations, once prepared and presented, were extremely slowly approved and

[2]"The jargon of bankers and banking experts is deliberately impenetrable. This impenetrability helps them to confuse policymakers and the public…" (Admati & Hellwig, The Bankers' New Clothes, 2014) Kindle, loc. 85.

implemented. In principle, everyone agreed with the objective but required further polishing of details.[3]

EU politics clarified its request. They defined that the reform should not "obstruct the credit flow to the real economy." It means that the improvement should be gradual and slow, aiming much below the initial "never again" goal. The request was caused by fear. Fear that the banks, faced with stiffer regulatory requirements, would rather initiate a credit crunch by radically deleveraging[4] than raising new capital.

Today, despite all delays, the framework of the new regulation has been completed. Without a doubt, after its full implementation, compared with the situation before the crisis, the safety of the system will be significantly improved.

Having said this, we must also say that it was not a great achievement. Compared to the situation in 2008, any change could only be for the better. The fundamental idea of the then prevailing internal-rating-based approach was deeply flawed. A system in which each bank decides alone how much capital it needs was so wrong that it is almost impossible to think of anything "wronger".

Some high expectations were nevertheless let down. While a serious book proposed limiting the total assets of a bank to three to five times the equity,[5] the regulation limited it to 33 times equity. A report recommending a division between investment and commercial banking[6] made no impact on the regulation.

Time passed, and the subject gradually faded away from public interest. These days no one discusses the Basel Accords in pubs.

In the early twenty-first century, we learned what consequences could be caused by neglecting banking supervision. Therefore, it would be advisable to retain some public focus on the issue of supervision in good times. Things could take a wrong turn again.

The primary obstruction to do it is a language of the regulation. The banking regulation is practically unreadable even to highly educated people, and at the same time, it is difficult to find texts explaining it to the unprofessional reader. This book is a modest attempt at filling that gap and enabling the interested reader to get some high-level understanding of past regulatory developments and present regulatory issues concerning banking supervision.

We will try to explain why it is necessary to supervise banks (it is not as obvious as it appears). What should be the task of the supervision and what it requires to achieve the set goals? How does it operate, what are its capabilities and limitations? Can it prevent future crises? Why does the financial system create such risks for the economy and the society? In the end, we will discuss the existing EU banking regulation and possible ways to improve it.

---

[3]"Yet, despite the wreckage, serious attempts to reform banking regulation have foundered, scuttled by lobbying and misdirection." (Admati & Hellwig, The Bankers' New Clothes, 2014) Kindle, loc. 94.

[4]Glossary "Deleveraging".

[5](Admati & Hellwig, The Bankers' New Clothes, 2014) p. 179.

[6](High-level Expert Group on Bank Structural Reform, 2012).

The approach presented here focuses on the risks that banking could pose to our society. We will analyse why those risks appear and propose strategies for their mitigation and control.

An alternative approach to the subject prevails today in the EU regulatory community. It is an attempt to maximise the social benefits created by banking. To achieve it, regulators balance between a "too harsh" and a "too lenient" approach. The purpose of such balance is an attempt to combine classical supervisory tools with policy tools guiding the banks' activities towards socially desirable outcomes.

We will see why such an approach could be risky. While the benefits of such encouragement are limited, neglected banking could disrupt the fibres not only of the economy but also of the entire modern society.

The asymmetry between risks and benefits is the primary reason why this book proposes focusing exclusively on risks. In a situation when risk-taking brings little benefits for society, while its consequences could be disastrous, it seems clear that the focus of the regulation should be on reducing risks.[7]

References

Admati, A., & Hellwig, M. (2014). *The Bankers' New Clothes.* Princeton University Press.

High-level Expert Group on Bank Structural Reform. (2012). Report of the European Commission's High-level Expert Group on Bank Structural Reform, (Liikanen report).

Kay, J. (2015). *Other People's Money.* Profile Books, ISBN 978-1781254431.

Stiglitz, J. E. (2010). *Freefall.* W W. Norton & Company ISBN 9780393077070.

[7]"A country can be prosperous only if it has a well-functioning financial system, but that does not imply that the larger financial system a country has, the more prosperous it is likely to be." (Kay, 2015) p. 3.

Contents

Chapter 1
Why Banks Must Be Supervised?

Abstract The banking provides the perfect breeding ground for the moral hazard. Banks create externalities called "financial or banking crises". When crises occur, they cause immense damage to everyone. A critical feature of banking is its interconnectedness. It causes spread of the failure through the system and creates the "forest fire" effect. Control over the risks accepted by banks preserves financial stability. The financial stability is the precondition for economic growth and political stability. The market proves inefficient in achieving it. As a consequence, the government organises banking supervision. Fulfilment of the task requires the balanced regulation which keeps the banking system free enough to be competitive, while sufficiently restrained to prevent it from causing a mishap.

> It was not created to bring us to heaven, but to save us from hell.—Dag Hammarskjöld[1]

The essential foundation of modern market economy is free entrepreneurship. Under the assumptions of the standard microeconomic theory,[2] the best outcome of market activity lays in unrestricted free competition without government intervention. In theory, regulation obstructs entrepreneurial activity and decreases output. The resulting rule is simple: the more the government intervenes, the poorer we are. The economic collapse of rigidly regulated communism empirically proved such a conclusion.

Still, this theory has a fundamental flaw. While it nicely illustrates the forces behind the market economy, it does not deal with a crucial issue—the externalities.

Externalities are part of the costs created by economic activity. They are different from other expenses, as they do not burden the entrepreneur. They are paid or borne by other people.[3] Obvious consequence: the better the entrepreneur uses the externalities, the more competitive and more productive he will be. With more money to invest,

---

[1] A famous Dag Hammarskjöld quote, although he was talking about the EU, is applicable to banking regulation as well (Geert, 2012).

[2] Glossary: Standard microeconomic model. For details see, e.g.: (Marshall, 1890; Samuelson, 1948).

[3] Lin (1976).

D. Odak, *A Political Economy of Banking Supervision*,
https://doi.org/10.1007/978-3-030-48547-4_1

and other people copying his success, his business model will unavoidably prevail. Consequently, the exploitation of externalities is a self-replicating system. There is no possibility of an "equilibrium" before exhausting the resources in question.

A classic case of externalities is air pollution. Letting raw exhaust gasses directly into the air is the cheapest solution. So, everyone will do it as long as we have any air left to breathe. Although the standard microeconomic theory would not recognise it, we would all willingly agree that having much money, a beautiful house and a car is not the economically optimal solution if we cannot breathe.

We are willing to pay the cost of the intervention to prevent such an outcome. The regulation needed to decrease pollution would impact us initially through lower economic growth, lower salaries and higher prices of goods. We accept such costs, as we like having breathable air and drinkable water. This argument quickly gets consensual support. With such support, the regulation becomes "legitimate", meaning that the majority would recognise it as reasonable, despite its costs.

The agreement that regulatory intervention could be advantageous triggers an important question: "How much regulation is sufficient?" A too harsh approach would severely hamper economic activity. Alternatively, a lenient approach would make excessive pollution very attractive. So, the right answer is somewhere in the middle.

The process of finding an answer is called "politics". The paradox of the politics lays in the fact that on the one hand people (i.e. voters) like having jobs and money, whereas, on the other hand, people having jobs and money are susceptible to stinking air. Of course, they blame the politicians in both cases: if they don't have jobs and if the air stinks. So, if politicians want to be re-elected, they should propose striking a proper balance. Otherwise, they will lose the elections and make a career change. This is, of course, also an idealised model, but still much closer to reality than the "standard microeconomic theory".

At this point, the story becomes more complicated. We distinguish between two classes of externalities. We can call them "visible" and "hidden". Visible externalities, such as smoking chimneys, are generated daily by economic activity. The government can effectively regulate them and can measure whether those factories observe given limits.

Hidden externalities are much trickier. There is no way of measuring them as they occur irregularly. Usually, a lower frequency of their occurrence means they could cause more catastrophic consequences.

For example, the "visible" externality of air transport is noise pollution. It is easy to measure dB and to tell which planes are allowed to operate and when. This drives operators to cooperate with the regulators by buying quieter crafts despite their higher price.

In addition to visible, there are also "hidden" externalities within the same industry—crashes. Crashes occur randomly and have catastrophic consequences for the people involved. The government then creates rules based not only on actual investigated accidents but also on maintenance and air traffic control records. Such constraints increase the cost of air transport in an attempt to avoid potential accidents. Some could assume that ideally, such increased costs could be maintained indefinitely, preventing the occurrence of any real crash.

However, if that were the case, you would pay much more for your flight. In the real world, the absence of accidents indicates to both suppliers and buyers that the cost of an intervention is unnecessarily high. Therefore, they would find ways to influence the regulators to decrease the costs.

Politicians are influenced by aircraft producers, promising them more jobs, meaning voters, if the government softens the rules. Operators offer not only more jobs, but also cheaper tickets, meaning happy voters. The politicians then turn to the regulator, asking why they are prevented from having happier voters. The regulator explains his, complicated and very technical reasoning which the politicians do not understand. To avoid any doubt, the politicians request a recent example of such an accident—a situation the regulator is trying to avoid. Fortunately, there is no such example. The politicians go home satisfied that the rules are unnecessarily cautious, depriving them of happy voters.

When the regulator's term of office is coming to an end, the politicians appear again. A week later, the regulator meets with industry representatives to identify those rules that are the costliest and the least risky. They agree to change them, and the regulator gets re-elected.

The cycle repeats itself until an accident happens. Then the politicians criticise the responsible agency for its recklessness, the industry happily implements the new rules, and life goes on until the next long period without a crash.

In such a way, political feedback keeps the cost of intervention reasonable. Nevertheless, the mechanism cannot always go that way. In some industries, the cost of hidden externalities could be such that even politicians would not dare meddle with it. Take, for example, nuclear power. Politicians and the public would readily agree to keep high regulatory costs for that industry regardless of a long period without an accident behind us. It is enough to take a brief look at the surroundings of Chernobyl to grasp why.

Still, there is one industry having potentially costlier hidden externalities than nuclear power. It is banking, here used as a synonym for the financial sector as a whole.

Banks do not create "visible" externalities but are very prone to create "hidden" ones. Such "hidden" externalities are called "financial or banking crises". They indeed cause immense damage to everyone.

The mechanism of creating those externalities is simple[4]: in daily business banks take risks, turning them into income. They accept liquidity risk and get an interest margin for it. They accept performance risk and get some extra margin for that. Accepting risks is what banks are supposed to do.

The financial industry does the same. It is supposed to take and control higher risks than banks: risks of accidents, illness, the future performance of companies. Risks managed by the financial industry are connected with the risks managed by banks.

---

[4]Bandt and Hartmann (1998).

Banks finance the financial industry, and problems in one industry could quickly affect the other.

Both industries can handsomely earn by taking those risks as long as they properly recognise and manage them. But there is a trick. When a bank accepts more risks, its short-term profitability increases. As the system of awards connects salary and profit, it creates a strong temptation for bankers to earn more by implementing a more flexible risk policy.

Bank governances, protecting shareholders' interest, should establish a balance between short-term profitability and the long-term consequences of the accepted risks. Today the shareholders' influence on bank governances is usually quite limited. Without their interference, the bank's management tends to adjust the policies to its interest. That could result in more liberal risk policies than shareholders would prefer.

If such an approach is widespread in the industry, risks accumulate. They accumulate silently, increasing the likelihood of the worst peacetime human made calamity—a financial crisis.

An interesting by-product of risk accumulation is frequently a reassuring widespread deception that everyone wins. In the late 1920s, everyone was earning lavishly on the stock market. In the late 2000s, the increase in real estate value made everyone richer day by day. In 1637 everyone was happy with the rise of tulip bulb prices. The "general impression" limits the ability of regulators to react in such a situation. People perceive that such an intervention would take "safe gain" from their hands.

How could the failure of a bank create more damage than a nuclear plant failure?

If we consider only immediate consequences, the failure of a single bank cannot cause anything comparable to the Chernobyl disaster. Should a bank collapse, everyone would survive. The effects could be mopped up in 2–3 years. So, life would go on, despite the size and importance of the bank.

But such judgement could prove very misleading. There is an important difference between nuclear power and finance. As opposed to the Lehman brothers, the Fukushima accident did not render all the Japanese and global nuclear reactors uncontrollable. A critical feature of banking is its interconnectedness. Failure could spread through the system and create a "forest fire" effect.

When the fire spreads from finance to the real economy, it causes unemployment and insolvency across the board. That is bad enough, but it is not the worst part.

The worst things would happen once a lot of unemployed and insolvent people would get together sharing the misapprehension that they have nothing to lose. Then things can quickly get out of hand, and risks threatening society could become unpredictable in the worst possible meaning of the word.

The primary tool for the prevention of such development is the control of risks accepted by banks. To control their risks, banks make reports. Reports recognise risks and their connections. Those reports finally integrate into the periodic report where bank shows its financial standing and exposure to risks. This report enables shareholders and clients of the bank to understand and price the level of risk bank, on their behalf, accepts.

Those reports are created by management and checked by auditors. Auditors should be an additional check, hired by shareholders, preventing management from misreporting both—financial and risk position of the bank. Despite all that precaution, reports frequently prove to be less than comprehensive. They sometimes omit evidence decisive for a bank's future and destiny of those relying on the bank.

There is also a widely spread misperception about reckless auditors. That perception is certainly wrong. They are not reckless. They are very detailed and reliable—for those who pay them. Besides, they are painfully diligent in the most critical art—protecting their own back.

To understand them, we should look into their motives. They are entrepreneurs on the market, looking for a client willing to pay for their services. So, as every reasonable seller does, they try to provide the paying clients with what they desire.

First, let us look into the definition of their task. The auditors' responsibility is to check whether the accounts are true and fair. The word "true" is not a synonym for "realistic".[5] Its meaning is that a company's accounting is done based on valid documents and according to International Accounting Standards known as IAS[6] or IFRS,[7] other applicable accounting rules and the company's accounting policies. All those standards enable a standardised disclosure of the value of assets and liabilities to the diligent owner.

Let us take an example. If a bank accounts for the value of its loans based on historical cost, then the auditor should examine whether the loan documentation is complete, whether the bank disbursed the loan, whether payments were made in due time, and whether the bank performed all standard procedures of quality monitoring. It is not their obligation to check whether the business plan of the borrower makes sense. To recheck all credit decisions would be too much work.

The owners are those who hire auditors. The critical assumption is the owners' diligence in the process. They are most interested in having realistic accounts, as those accounts describe their ownership.

There are efficient checks against management abuse, and an auditor is one of them. Unfortunately, there is no protection against the owners' indolence or abuse. A common assumption is that the owners will hire an auditor with the request to check whether management has hidden some money or risks from them. The auditor will do a good job, and everyone will be happy.

However, let's imagine that the shareholder representative hires an auditor and tells him: "Please, allow an optimistic valuation of our assets. Permit management to tell me that I am richer than I am! That would make me happy![8]"

Such an offer is a temptation for the auditors. If they accept, they could compromise their reputation. If they reject, they lose a very well-paid job to a more flexible

---

[5]www.wikiaccounting.com (2019).

[6]www.iasplus.com (2019).

[7]www.ifrs.org (2019).

[8]Such conversation, of course, would never really take place. Such wish would Supervisory board, as representative of the shareholders, send to the auditor through modification of the accounting policy.

competitor. So, if they are reasonable and having a competitive mindset, they will try to find a way to incorporate the reports into the structure of the accounting standards. They will also hire top lawyers to develop such an arrangement of disclaimers, letters to the management, and representations to make them legally immune. Then they will audit the financial statements the way they are supposed to—in line with the owner's request. They will be, indeed, careful and reliable.

Those assumptions seemingly do not make sense. Why would people want to cheat themselves? Why would the owners instruct management and the auditors to tell them lies about their ownership? If they would request the auditors to misinform them, they would never know how valuable their property really is.

Such behaviour usually occurs in one particular case. If the owners, by "rule of thumb", guess that their company went broke, they could decide to hide it from others. They could hope to reverse the company's fortune in the meantime or, more practically, sell shares or get some more dividends, salaries or expenses before you-know-what hits the fan.

To do that, they need others to believe the company is alive and kicking. Therefore, they instruct the management and the auditors to report that way. A fancy name for such behaviour is "moral hazard".

Having typically passive shareholders, the management frequently de facto takes full control of the relationship with the auditors, increasing the consequent risks.

Of all the industries, banking is the most susceptible to moral hazard. A murky balance sheet packed with items still tens of years until maturity, unprofessional creditors unaware that they are creditors, all spiced up with an unlimited government guarantee and an even bigger implicit guarantee,[9] creates the perfect breeding ground for a moral hazard. That is the reason why it just loves finance.

If governances of a bank got plagued by moral hazard, a large gaping hole could suddenly appear in its balance sheet, swallowing its entire net value and a substantial part of the creditors' assets.

Other bankers are aware of such a possibility, and it is easy to frighten them with bad news. But even when such news reaches them, the decision to abandon the affected bank is not easy. If it fails, that could also trigger some unforeseen "domino" or "forest fire". So, banks will think twice before leaving their colleagues behind.

Therefore, between the horrendous scenario of the spreading forest fire of a financial crisis[10] and a gentle breeze filling the banks' sails with extra profit lays just a single phrase—mutual trust. Here banking supervision jumps in.

Despite all the risks and problems they can cause, banks are good for us. They enable us to buy all those beautiful things before our hair turns grey. We can buy a home and a car before we have saved for them. Or we can invest in a business when we do not have enough money to start up. That is nice and convenient. Still, while

---

[9]"A remarkable feature of the global financial crisis is that most people in finance seemed to regard it as self-evident that government and taxpayers had an obligation to ensure that the sector ... continued to operate in broadly its existent form. What is more remarkable still is that this proposition won broad acceptance among politicians and the public." (Kay, 2015, p. 4).

[10]Mukunda (2018).

granting those loans, banks tend to periodically cause events depriving numerous people of the ability to repay their debt orderly. The close supervision of banks decreases the likelihood of such unpleasant developments.

As we will see, in the present institutional framework, the market alone repeatedly demonstrated a lack of efficiency in directing finance.[11] As a consequence, the government has a responsibility to organise banking supervision. Besides the inefficient market governance of banks, there are three strong reasons why the government should do so.

The government provides an unconditional guarantee for all depositors having less than 100.000 EUR in a single bank. Therefore, the supervision protects the government as an insurer, checking whether each bank follows good business practices.[12] Also, based on the authority granted by the Parliament, the supervision issues and withdraws banking licenses, deciding who can and who cannot use such a guarantee. Due to the government guarantee received, small creditors of licensed banks bear the same risk as a creditor of the government. Therefore, the bank obtains funding much cheaper than its creditworthiness would otherwise allow. Furthermore, those funds are more stable, as the guarantee radically decreases the likelihood of a bank run. Banks, of course, profit from that,[13] and to earn that profit, they must accept the regulator's prerogative to examine and restrain their business.

Thus, the regulation and supervision of banks is not something forced upon banks by the government. Each bank and banker, voluntarily applying for the licence, explicitly requires all the benefits and obligations arising from the arrangement.

Besides, supervision provides other banks, uninsured creditors and investors with additional comfort when dealing with a bank. Earlier, we said how vital mutual trust between banks is. All banks are familiar with the way that supervision observes them. They know that the supervision measures are the same for all banks. If those measures are convincing, each bank can be confident in the creditworthiness of the others. So, by doing their job right, the supervisors provide confidence to the market and make interbank dealings cheaper and faster. Most importantly, as a lender of the last resort, the central bank uses the supervision findings as a basis for deciding whether to provide a loan to a bank in distress.

On the other hand, if the banks and investors are aware that supervisors are powerless or slack and superficial, then their activity will not be the reassuring factor.

The third reason is the ability of licensed banks to create money. They generate currency, other than cash, as good as the one created by the central bank. The central bank, being in charge of price stability, keeps the quantity of the money in check using monetary measures. Supervision observes the consistent implementation of those measures throughout the banking system.

---

[11]Nier and Bauman (2006).

[12]Once the government provided this insurance, it had to make sure that it was not exposed to undue risk.... The government did this by regulating the banks (Stiglitz, 2010, p. 81).

[13]From the perspective of the banks, therefore, borrowing is cheap. But this is true only because costs of bank borrowing are partly borne by taxpayers (Admati & Hellwig, 2014, p. 8).

We can simply say that supervision takes care that the vast majority of depositors get their money timely and in the full amount without the involvement of the government.

By doing its job well, the banking supervision creates an environment supportive of financial stability, i.e. the situation in which all monetary flows are unobstructed, financial instruments reliable and there is no fear that the payment system could suddenly fail. The best definition of financial stability, attributed to the ex-Governor of the Bank of England, Mike Carney, is that financial stability is an ability of the financial system to absorb shocks without creating them.

Financial stability, of course, does not mean that a bank failure cannot happen, or that the prices of financial instruments would remain stable. There is always the worst bank on the market, and it may fail. In a financially stable environment, this would be an isolated case not causing systematic shock.

Financial stability is the primary precondition for stable economic growth and the orderly functioning of democracy and the legal system. Therefore, protecting financial stability should be an essential political consideration for the authorities. Unfortunately, very frequently that is not the case.

In reality, politics tends to tolerate an increased level of risk in the financial system. It becomes more and more tolerant of risks when the financial system goes a long time without a significant hiccup or when steps leading to a stable financial system interfere with its political agenda. We will not be mistaken if we say that a political approach to financial stability is somewhat closer to the one applied to air transport than the one applied to nuclear plants. Politicians perceive that a happier financial system will deliver them services making the electorate happier. Economic growth and affordable loans are the most desirable among them. From everything we know today, they are wrong.

But if banks would be able to grant more and cheaper loans, why would risks bother us? If things get sour, the government and central bankers will once again do their financial hocus-pocus and save the world. They have proved capable of it. We all survived the last crisis, and it was the worst in almost a century. Why wouldn't we accept the risks of a smaller one? It can't be the worst every time! In the meantime, we would live better and pay less interest.

There is no doubt—if banks are less restrained, they create more and cheaper loans. Nevertheless, it is a dubious blessing. We do not usually consider highly indebted people as very prosperous. Furthermore, periods of fast credit growth are typically followed by periods when a significant number of debtors have problems with repayments. Such periods we call crises.

Someone could still claim that it is worth risking a crisis now and then to get cheaper loans. If we would only consider direct damages caused by a financial crisis, then maybe it would be a reasonable dilemma. But after taking political risks into the equation, the conclusion appears crystal clear—all efforts must be made to avoid them or to minimise their impact. We must keep in mind that financial stability is not a means to an end, but a tool to preserve social stability.

The source of such dilemmas is a misunderstanding. Most of the people would without hesitation take this as a plausible statement: "Economic growth depends on the growth of banking credit." It seems self-evident. Nonetheless, it isn't! Therefore, we should be careful and, after such a statement, require proof. No one has presented such evidence as yet.

If we compare countries by the average mid-term growth rate and by the level of indebtedness of the private sector, we notice a negative correlation.[14] That means that a higher average level of overall debt in the economy is associated with slower average growth. We say associated instead of caused, as some economists claim that there is a third factor—the level of development. There is a positive correlation between the level of indebtedness of the private sector and the GDP per capita and a negative relationship between the GDP per capita and the average growth. So, they claim that slower growth is caused by a higher level of development, not by higher debt.

We cannot be sure about that, but we can certainly claim that a higher level of indebtedness, with other variables remaining constant, increases risks in the economy.[15] Despite all that fuzz about the importance of credit, there is no proof that the growth of banking credit explains oscillation of economic growth. In the short term, the growth of credit alone does not significantly explain the change of the GDP growth rates.[16] In the mid and long term, much less. Even if the correlation is statistically significant, which usually is not the case, its influence is small and explains only an insignificant part of the growth rate oscillation.

Let's touch another misconception for a moment. The claim that banking regulation distorts the market and decreases its efficiency. So, the more we deregulate banks and rely on market discipline to keep them on track, we will have better results.

Market discipline means the cautious behaviour of banks caused by their clients' reactions. When banks do something undesirable, their clients' response forces them back in the right direction.

Market discipline was historically the critical factor steering the banks' behaviour. It worked well for centuries, so why wouldn't it work today?

The introduction of deposit insurance made market discipline much less effective. The introduction of deposit insurance was the only way out when "market discipline" became so intense and over-sensitive that it almost caused the collapse of the entire US banking system. Once introduced, insurance proved to be difficult to withdraw. As long as we have it around, market discipline alone cannot steer the banks' behaviour.

Nevertheless, we should also keep in mind that, while it was a major steering factor, market discipline was also very volatile and sometimes an intimidating force. Periods of optimism periodically abruptly swapped with general pessimism and caution. Banks either suffered a shock when it happened, or they permanently kept excessive reserves and generated much less credit than they could.

Furthermore, the existence of deposit insurance significantly influences the behaviour of market participants. The idea to remove or decrease it substantially would require shifting between two very different market equilibriums. In the new

---

[14]Kulu, Randveer and Uusküla (2011).

[15]Lehmann (2016).

[16]Takáts and Upper (2013).

equilibrium, less credit would be available. Making the road map for such a transition would be demanding, and following it would be extremely unsafe. Finally, is it worth such an effort and risk only to restore once failed and abandoned system? Nota bene, all reasons for its demise are still present, and it would most likely be abandoned again.

Deregulated banking has existed for a long time, from the fifteenth until almost the mid-twentieth century. Its regulation was not something that politics did happily. Banks were firmly regulated only when there was no other way of keeping them going.

Therefore, especially if we want banks to be reliable credit generators, the combination of deposit insurance and strict supervision is a better solution than market discipline. It enables banks to better plan and much easier to withstand shocks. But to fulfil its intended role, supervision must be rigorous.

The crucial weakness of market discipline emerges from the apparent fact that the market can only react to information it knows. Primary sources of information are the bank's reports. A lot of risks and factors influencing risks are not visible from the reports. Sometimes they remain hidden because the reports are not extensive enough, and sometimes because bankers do not want to show them.

That is, in fact, reasonable behaviour. Market discipline means pressure on funding for riskier banks. Disclosing the risks would lead to increased prices and decreased funding stability. Of course, a reasonable banker would try to avoid that if possible.

For example, capital adequacy is not meaningful information without the proper disclosure of risk density. Banks tend not to disclose such details in a fully transparent manner, to say it politely. Also, where a bank provides a fully open disclosure, it usually makes it so extensive and complex that most of the market participants are unable to read it. They do not have enough time.

As market participants cannot have the full information needed to assess the risks, they act based on prevailing sentiments. Therefore, they tend to oscillate between two emotions: overly optimistic and overly cautious. When being too confident, they behave based on market incentives without calculating risks. Therefore, they bring money to the banks offering the best rates. By doing so, they usually stimulate the accumulation of risks. In case of a shock, their behaviour would change, and they would recognise only the risks. Vulnerable banks did not declare risks before, and depositors now assume that other banks also present incomplete disclosures. Assuming so, they tend to become extremely sensitive and volatile in their decision-making.

Unlike market participants, Banking supervision is professional, educated and experienced in understanding banks and the risks they undertake. More importantly, it has full authority to access all documents and information relevant to the stability of a bank. Therefore, the supervision can understand the situation better, react timely and more rationally than the market would. In the case that a bank cannot continue its business, supervision removes it from the market with much less stress than market discipline.

Without severely limiting or cancelling deposit insurances, it would be illusory to declare market discipline as a predominant factor guiding a bank's behaviour. The limitation or cancellation of deposit insurance is not a realistic possibility. Even if it were a practical option, most likely it would not be a good idea. The world learned the hard way what kind of instability "market discipline" could cause. Therefore, it is both more efficient and safer to have the present arrangement. But it cannot be overemphasised how important the firmness of the supervision is for the arrangement's stability.

The shortcoming of the arrangement is ample incentives for bankers to engage in activities involving moral hazard. The moral hazard is unlikely if everybody expects that the supervision will soon learn what they are doing and initiate corrective measures.

For all the reasons explained, it is not possible to truly deregulate banks. Left to their own devices, and steered only by market discipline, they cause too much damage. If the government does not intervene in the banking business before, it will be forced to act after things get bad. As the government is aware that the ultimate responsibility for stability lies on its shoulders, it should also keep things under control. Such control is what we call banking supervision.

Nevertheless, the need to regulate and supervise the banking business firmly should not be understood as a request to provide sophisticated and detailed regulations for every aspect of the banking business. While drafting regulation, the regulators must keep in mind that banks are institutions having all the money in the world (literally) at their disposal to pay lawyers. Complex and overlapping regulations allow them to perform "regulatory arbitration". That means using rules without breaching them to do the things the supervisors would not like them to do.

Firm supervision is much better off if it relies on simple rules. Simple rules reinforced by significant capital.

Still, let's not make a mistake by discarding market discipline. Together with the transparency of banking operations, it remains crucial for the successful business of a bank.

Though the core of a bank's liabilities is protected by deposit insurance, still a significant part remains uncovered. Investors in a bank's shares, the bank's junior creditors, senior creditors[17] and all depositors holding unsecured assets still expose the bank to market discipline. Nevertheless, those investors are usually much better informed, and consequently, their reactions should be more rational than the reactions of the general public.

The confidence of the investing community in the competence and ability of the banking supervision aligns the actions triggered by market discipline with supervisory activities. If investors are confident in the supervision, their reaction to attempts of the supervision to harness emerging crises will be supportive.

We should not forget that no one, except for the supervisors, has full access to the original bank documentation. The supervisors are better informed than the investors, and the investors know that. We will call that "information advantage". Rational investors know that supervision acts based on the best available information.

---

[17]Seniority is a legal term meaning the following: in the case of bankruptcy, senior liabilities are supposed to be paid before the junior ones.

Therefore, the investors will react based on the interpretation of the supervisory actions.

If they believe that the supervision is competent, rational investors will align with their actions. If, on the other hand, they believe that the supervision is slack and reckless, their reactions will be unpredictable, and most likely not aligned with the supervisor's expectations.

For example, let's explore the rational reaction of investors on the supervisory announcement that a bank has a capital shortage and that supervisor took action to strengthen it.

If the investors believe that the supervisor is competent, they would assume that it already recognised the real magnitude of the problem and decided that the preservation of the bank is feasible. Therefore, they would retain their relationship with the bank. By doing so, they would support the supervisory action.

If, on the other hand, investors think that the supervisor is reckless, they would assume that the supervisor only recognised a part of the problem, announcing an action with an uncertain outcome. The investors will be confident that the situation is not better than the supervisor had judged, but they will assume that it could be worse. Maybe a lot worse. Therefore, they are much more likely to sever the relationship with the affected bank, increasing the likelihood of failure of the supervisory attempts.

Basel 2 properly recognised that market discipline is still an important part of the architecture. It will continue to be so. However, in the existent regulatory architecture, it is not and cannot be an alternative to banking supervision. Supervision and the market discipline jointly form financial stability architecture in which the supervision is the dominant construction element. The confidence of the market participants in banking supervision makes market discipline the force supportive to financial stability. Without it, it is just a blind and unpredictive force able to rock a ship quite severely and very untimely.

The financial system is one of the most important pillars for the proper functioning of modern society. Unfortunately, such a position makes it also potentially one of the most dangerous institutional structures.

The challenge for the regulator is to balance demands in such a way which will keep the banking system free enough to be competitive, while sufficiently restrained to prevent it from causing a mishap. The demanding task is rendered more difficult by the fact that regulators must do it successfully in the real world while facing real bankers and politicians.

References

Admati, A., & Hellwig, M. (2014). *The bankers' new clothes*. Princeton University Press.

Bandt, O. D., & Hartmann, P. (1998). What is systemic risk today? In *Conference on Risk Measurement and Systemic Risk* (pp. 37–83). BoJ.

Geert, M. (2012). *Was wenn Europa scheitert*. Pantheon Verlag.

Kay, J. (2015). *Other people's money*. Profile Books, ISBN 978-1781254431.

Kulu, L., Randveer, M., & Uusküla, L. (2011). The impact of private debt on economic growth. EESTI PANK Working Paper Series; ISSN 1406-7161; 10.
Lehmann, A. (2016, 10 27). Private sector debt matters. Retrieved from https://bruegel.org/, https://bruegel.org/2016/10/private-sector-debt-matters-and-better-data-means-better-policy/.
Lin, S. A. (1976). *Theory and measurement of economic externalities*. Academic Press.
Marshall, A. (1890). Principles of economics. palgrave classics in economics series standing order. ISBN: 978–0–230–24927–1.
Mukunda, G. (2018, September 25). The social and political costs of the financial crisis, 10 Years Later. Retrieved from Harvard Business Review https://hbr.org/2018/09/the-social-and-political-costs-of-the-financial-crisis-10-years-later.
Nier, E., & Bauman, U. (2006, June). Market discipline, disclosure and moral hazard in banking. *Journal of Financial Intermediation* (pp 332–361).
Samuelson, P. (1948). *Economics*, McGraw-Hill Education. ISBN: 0070747415.
Stiglitz, J. E. (2010). *Freefall*, W W Norton & Company. ISBN 9780393077070.
Takáts, E., & Upper, C. (2013, July). Credit and growth after financial crises. BIS Working Papers No 416.
www.iasplus.com. (2019). Retrieved from https://www.iasplus.com/en/standards/ias.
www.ifrs.org. (2019). Retrieved from https://www.ifrs.org/issued-standards/list-of-standards/.
www.wikiaccounting.com. (2019). Retrieved from https://www.wikiaccounting.com/meaning-true-fair-view-audit/.

Chapter 2
How that All Come to Be?

Abstract Finance is, always was and always will be a source of instability. By putting volatility into motion and controlling it, finance provides tremendous service. Bankers create money out of thin air—how could that be stable? The fruits of this instability facilitate trade, production and employment for improving people's lives. The emergence of finance in the late thirteenth century facilitates the development of long-distance trade, ending medieval autarchy. The finance converts debt into money, removing limitations for business emerging from a limited amount of specie. Its attraction to law and order turned the rule of law into a competitive advantage. The price for all the benefits we have from finance is instability. Banking supervision has a task to keep it on the check.

People carefully listen to bankers' opinions about all financial and business issues. Experts in finance have almost a magical aura, able to understand and foresee future developments.

Nothing can be further from the truth than this. Bankers and financial experts are as capable of predicting the future as any educated person. Their job, if correctly done, has nothing magical in it. Quite the opposite, it is painstakingly detailed and procedural. So much so, that it keeps them so occupied that it is not very likely that they have time to foresee future much beyond their nose.

On the other hand, the commercial bankers[1] are very far from image od shroud individuals accepting enormous risks to get undeserved bonuses. They are at least as timid and law obeying people as the average citizen is. It also goes with the nature of their job. Not a lot of bold and brave people full of greed and initiative would manage to climb through the ladders of the bank's hierarchy. That requires different qualities.

If that is so, why do they create so much trouble? Why finance periodically breaks apart our economy? Usually, at the moment when we feel most comfortable with it.

---

[1]Different from investment banker. For difference see glossarry: Difference between investment and commercial banks.

D. Odak, *A Political Economy of Banking Supervision*,
https://doi.org/10.1007/978-3-030-48547-4_2

Finance can do it because it is, always was and always will be a source of instability. It is inherently unstable. The instability is the source of its power. By putting this instability into motion, it provides us with tremendous service. Bankers create money out of thin air—how could that be stable? Nonetheless, the fruits of this instability are the funds which facilitate trade, production, employment and all the activities to improving the life of people.

Before banks and finance appeared, everything was stable. Completion of every transaction was payment with specie or equally valuable good. Such operations were so marvellously riskless and so inefficient and expensive that they were millstone hanging around the neck of the medieval economy.

There was always debt as a part of the trade. The debt was bilateral, and its settlement was payment by debtor to the creditor.

The advent of finance opened the possibility to increase the number of transactions and decrease their cost. It did it by taking the debt to entirely a new level. The debt became money—efficient, cheap money having ample supply, but likewise quite dangerous money. Different from gold and silver, this one was able to disappear from your hands and to do even nastier tricks. Despite all that, it soon replaced specie in long-distance commerce. With the support of new money, long-distance trade achieved, after late antique, unprecedented expansion.

To see how it happened, we need to take a step back and try to understand how finance was born as a child of the real economy. Already with its first toddling steps, this child made a huge difference. It enabled people to produce and trade more. Finance was among the major catalysts of the changes transforming the medieval society into the modern one.

The financial world today appears to be functioning in a kind of parallel universe. It spends a lot of resources, apparently without producing anything useful. No one has ever eaten bread baked by a bank or driven a car built by a bank. For any practical purpose, banks appear to be useless. Left radicals even call them parasites.

But the fact is that without a financial system, we would never have been able to produce so much bread and cars, not to mention smartphones. Even communists, when they tried to get rid of banks, quickly understood that it was a bad idea.

The reason why the world of finance looks so strange and unpractical is its sophistication achieved over centuries. This sophistication made it hard to understand not only for non-professionals but also for people involved in finance. It became a reliable supporter and a major disruptor of the economy, shifting suddenly between those two roles on the sheer amazement of even the most farsighted financial experts. So, to see how finance supported the creation of a smartphone, let's go back to the times when its connection with reality was much easier to understand.

Our story begins almost a millennium ago. The first, toddling steps in the creation of financial markets, correspond with the re-invention of trade finance in the thirteenth century. Beyond this revolution was a straightforward but mighty innovation—a promissory note. It enabled debt to become money. If I own someone ten ounces of silver, I give him a promissory note promising that I will pay ten ounces of silver after 60 days to the bearer of the note.

That was a significant innovation. I do not promise to pay creditor but the bearer. Whoever brings this note to me on that date, will get those ten ounces of silver. Therefore, whoever believes that I will honestly pay, will take the note as almost equivalent of ten ounces of silver. "Almost" is called discount and it covers interest and risk.

Then another mighty innovation was an endorsement. If my creditors pay their debt with my promissory note, they endorse it. It means that they promised to pay to the bearer of the note same amount if I don't do it. With adding more endorsements, the promissory note becomes more valuable, as more people guaranteed the payment of the debt.

Trading with promissory notes simplified payments and expanded credit, enabling a boom in commodities trading which ensued from the fourteenth century. Allegedly, it all started with Marco Polo, who brought the concepts of spaghetti and promissory notes from his trip to China.

We are not sure about spaghetti, but for the promissory note, it is not likely. The first known place committed to trading commodities and notes were the city of Bruges in Belgium, as far back as 1285. There was an inn operated by a gentleman called Robert van der Buerse. We can even guess that the gentleman lent his name to all financial markets—the bourse. If that is true, we should rule Marco Polo out. He came back from China only in 1295.

In this inn, local traders met with those from the Italian republics to trade commodities and promissory notes. Soon, the establishment of many similar trading places followed throughout Belgium, the Low Countries and Northern Italy. A century later, the first banks joined the game of finance.

What was so special about that trade? Until then, all payments were made in precious metals or commodities. Payment complicated business a great deal. Carrying around gold was quite an exercise in those difficult times. A love between bandits, pirates and "pieces of eight" is well known to every kid today: the risks and the costs of money transfer almost limited trade to bartering.

On the other hand, in times of limited communication, bartering was quite a tricky business. Transferring a ship of grain with many costs and perils from Genoa to Antwerp, only to learn that it is cheaper there than at home, is not a recipe for success. So, during times preceding the invention of the financial industry, trade, especially long-distance trade, was quite limited, focused only on specific, usually luxury commodities and represented a negligible percentage of the estimated GDP.[2]

The establishment of trade finance made things much easier and cheaper. Let us describe a hypothetical case: In the fifteenth century, a Hanseatic trader from Gotland accepted a promissory note in Genoa as payment for furs he just delivered from Russia. As silk was expensive in Genoa, he jumped on a horse and within a week brought the note to Venetia. There he paid a load of silk with it. The merchant who sold the silk did not know him, but he knew the issuer of the promissory note very well. Without a promissory note, the merchant would have to load the gold in a cart, hire soldiers to protect it, and pay all their expenses for almost a month-long

[2]Wallerstein, Modern World-System I (1974, p. 23).

journey. With the promissory note, he rode alone, carrying just a piece of paper spending only a small fraction of the time and money.

The Venetian trader then gave the bill to a Ragusan merchant for spices. The new owner took a ship to Antwerp to buy a shipload of wheat. The wheat trader from Antwerp then came with the note to der Buerse's inn and offered it for sale. A local merchant bought the note at a discount, closing the seller's debt for a load of timber in his books. Finally, the buyer sent the bill to Genoa, with an instruction to settle with the proceeds the debt of his colleague who bought wine from the issuer, as the colleague already sold him good Swedish iron.

Just a piece of paper moved all that merchandise without any movement of gold. Furs, silk, spices, wheat, timber, wine, and iron found their buyers and went to places where people needed them. All that happened without the cost of gold transfer and the limitations of bartering.

Without this system, such trading activity would not have been possible. It would have required a slow, expensive and risky gold shipment. First from Genoa to Venetia, then to Ragusa, all the way to Bruges, back to Genoa, all the way to Sweden and then back to Genoa. Such transfer, even in the unlikely case that it occurred without an incident, would take a few years and cost a significant part of the gold.

The implementation of "finance" enabled much faster and safer payment, a system that increased trade severalfolds, motivating autarchic fiefdoms to produce more for the market. The production for the market brought about specialisation, lower prices and a relative abundance of goods.

That was a friendly face of the Janus. But there was also the ugly one. That was instability. The system enabled cumulation of debt, and it was sensitive to the performance of all its participants. Whenever someone fails to perform, it makes not only promissory note worthless for his creditor, but also it causes the merchants endorsing the draft to have unexpected cash outflow. That could cause them to fail on their obligations, sending the shock further. If the chain of events expanded enough, it could create a crisis of the confidence and decrease amount of debt acceptable as the money. With less money available, the wheels of commerce could slow down, affecting everyone's welfare.

The importance of debt enforcement did us another big favour. Finance was strongly attracted to law and order. It required an efficient enforcement and protection mechanism. Therefore, financial markets developed mainly in places with reliable legal protection. Chartered cities or republics were the most attractive for merchants.

God endowed lords and princes with the right to strip subjects of assets at will. The right extended even to the life of their subjects. When lords had such powers, it is quite apparent what was their typical reaction on attempted enforcement of debt collection. As they suffered from a chronicle shortage of gold to pay for their more or less permanent wars, they were not shy to use their powers. So, running any lucrative business under their jurisdiction required getting and maintaining the ruler's love. It was expensive and uncertain. After all, lords and princes were mortals, usually enthusiastic about spending a lot of time on battlefields, and their successors were endowed with the original divine right, unattached to the promises of the predecessor.

In the chartered cities and republics rulers were less bold. The primary reason was their limited time in office and a requirement to be re-elected by their peers. Besides, they were mostly members of the trading aristocracy, and they had a different understanding of the world than the old military aristocracy.

They were honestly concerned about the "fair" treatment of traders coming to their cities with thriving businesses. It was a matter of pure self-interest. If those merchants left alive and happy, others would come with their gold and merchandise. Trade would soon bring more gold to the town than one could steal from any of them. To make that happen, they provided efficient physical protection for the merchandise in ports and warehouses, protected the lives and assets of guests and also established courts enforcing contracts predictably. That was, of course, a slow process, but already in the fifteenth century, the relative prosperity of some cities and republics was evident. Some of them grew so rich and powerful that they were able to challenge their nominal masters militarily. Gradually, the lucrative habit of protecting merchants spread and created the foundations of the present-day legal system.

Another key element is the development of financial technology and the legal system. Credibility was undoubtedly important, but credibility without enforcement was not convincing.

During those times, financial flows remained closely connected to merchandise. The financial system was rudimentary, but as such, it provided a steady, even decisive positive influence on the growth of the real economy. It became more dynamic but also more sensitive.

Until that time, money was a rock—firm, stable, reliable, but inert. Then suddenly, something so elusive as the promise became—money. After that magic, the world could not be stable any more. Thus, the dance began.

Banks were a new crucial invention which brought finance to an entirely new level. They removed many obstacles that stood in the way of the development of modern society.

The first problem was the Middle-Ages deflation. Throughout the Middle-Ages prices, including wages, were under a systematic downward pressure. Before the invention of banks (and the discovery of America),[3] there was a permanent shortage of gold and silver. Two reasons caused that all participants in the economy wanted to have some savings. So, they withdraw the coins from circulation as a treasury. As the prices tended to fall, that way of saving also proved lucrative.[4]

A second reason was the trade with the Far East. Europe imported silk and spices from India and China. Europe did not have enough merchandise to offer in exchange. So, it paid mainly with gold and silver.

Coins stored in savings and sent to India and China were no longer available for payments. The European production of precious metals was smaller than its outflow. Technology and the nature of the economic cycle limited the velocity of circulation of the remaining currency. Consequently, there was permanent deflationary pressure.

[3]The invention of banks and discovery of America occurred almost simultaneously. Banks enabled a better use of specie in payments, while specie flowed from America in unpreceded quantities.

[4]www.britannica.com (2019).

After entering the scene, banks created a wonder: if I put my savings in a bank, it remains available for your payments if the bank gives you credit. Also, the technology of money transfer enabled the same quantity of gold to facilitate much more payments. Bank transfers allowed the transmission of gold without an expensive shipment of specie. Payments were made merely by debiting and crediting bank accounts. Now apparently gold becomes as good money as the promise is. Nevertheless, there was a trick. It wasn't gold; it was a promise to get gold. Sometimes, as we will soon see, it was a huge difference.

After the establishment of banks, the availability of metal was not directly dictating the availability of means of payment anymore. On the other hand, it opened different risks: banks could easily make more promises than they could fulfil. Then, they could have no money when people came to take it. People, of course, got angry if they didn't get their money. So, what they usually did was breaking the bank's counter, called "banca" in Italian. The bank ended up with a broken stand. Therefore, the term "banca-rotta"—bankrupted.

Bankers, facing those perils, gradually understood that the art of successful banking consists of keeping a balance between expanding the credit and maintaining sufficient reserves to pay out depositors. So, specie kept the amount of available money in check, but more flexibly than before.

Periods of steady growth caused an expansion of credit. In those times, banks tended to decrease reserves and invest in business opportunities. By doing so, they supported the growth of the economy but also exposed banks and their clients to more risk.

In times of economic hardship, quite the opposite happened. Depositors become restless, forcing banks to keep more reserves. To get those reserves, banks need to cash in their earlier investments. Such a mechanism created the characteristic banking behaviour, popularly known as "taking away the umbrella as soon as the rain starts".

Banks very soon became the major pro-cyclical factor in the economy—strengthening the growth in favourable times while making downturns more severe. They got blamed for that, accused to be the factor of economic instability. Indeed, they were. It was in fact to their credit: the stability they shook away was a medieval millennial recession.

Development of banks and finance joined the wonders that were already happening. Production per capita began growing at a steady pace for the first time in history.

Today history appears to us a steady flow of human development. We tend to forget that GDP per capita, measured in quantities produced, did not show any systematic growth between ancient Egypt and medieval Europe. There were better and worse times, but in the long-run, the capacity of a man to produce remained quite similar. The enormous wealth of Rome was not an indication of its productivity, but the level of deprivation of its slaves. Agriculture was the primary value creator, and agricultural technology applied in ancient Egypt was not much different from the technology utilised in Europe in the eleventh century. Since the introduction of the animal-powered plough, about five thousand years ago, nothing notable happened.

Now it slowly started to change, and this time change persisted. The initial "shock" came from the real sector: deep ploughing, the three-field system, horseshoe and padded horse collar made the first push, creating more commodities eligible for trade. Then the financial system appeared, facilitating the specialisation and expansion of the business. Such development increased production and productivity.

Cities began growing and developing again, but for most of the people, the old order remained stable. Peasants, although producing more, remained equally poor. Cheap labour made a substantial investment in better tools unprofitable. Therefore, the lords and merchants became richer just by exploiting peasants, who had no way of improving their position. Being poor, they were not buyers of city products, limiting the expansion of their industry. Making expensive shoes for a merchant is a good job for a shoe-maker, but nothing compared to making a thousand cheap shoes for peasants. In those times, peasants didn't have the money to buy such shoes, so they made themselves what they could.

Then a new deal came from an unexpected direction—the Plague. In the fourteenth century, the Black Death emptied entire villages. Fields, except the best ones, were returned to the forest, while labour became expensive.

Better use of labour became essential, and for the first time in history, workers had the power to raise their voice. Empty villages allowed them to leave. To attract workers in your villages, you must pay them well. To pay them, they must be productive. All technical inventions were put to work to achieve it. Investments in labour-saving technologies sharply increased, and merchants were eager to support them. The cycle of technological improvements had accelerated.

Now better-paid workers became buyers. First, they bought wine and ale, then shoes and even garments. Industry and trade expanded to satisfy their demand.

As productivity grew, markets grew, prices became more transparent across Europe. It strongly incentivised the best producers to increase production. To do so, they frequently asked their buyers for credit, promising them a higher quantity of cheaper commodities next year. Hopeful for a considerable profit, the buyers took a loan from a bank and forwarded it to the producers. Such credit had to be in the form of specie, gold or silver because they were used to pay squires or peasants, not yet included in the financial system. They required payment in metal.

Let us now make a case of financial shock and the crisis banking and finance made possible.

Oat was the most profitable commodity last year. There was a war between two princes, and they required a lot of oat for their horses, pushing its price up. A lot of credit went into the production of oat, and the production increased notably. Then the war suddenly stopped.

We will call the event a shock. Despite all the happiness it would bring to a lot of people, it would also make some of them quite miserable. Horses now needed less oat. As markets became overflooded with it, its price fell sharply.

Producers paid their debt to the merchants, as they owned a quantity of the oat. However, merchants were unable to repay their liability towards the banks. If many merchants had taken similar credits, most of them would fail. We shall call that the first wave of failing. It includes only merchants who failed because of the fall of the oat price.

When a merchant fails, all promissory notes issued by him bounce on maturity. Then, the owner of the bill can collect the debt from anyone who owned the promissory note before. Therefore, if the issuer is unable to pay, people that endorsed the note should pay instead of the issuer.

Some of them will become insolvent as they have an unexpected cash outflow. There is also a particular case if the bank fails because of the losses it suffered from the loans given to the failed merchants. A similar predicament is faced by those that delivered merchandise on credit to the merchant, who obviously will not pay.

Those failing because of their counterparties failing due to the drop in the oat price, we shall call the second wave.

After the second wave, things are getting complicated. In case of a significant shock, multiple sources of distress arise on the market. People lose money on accounts in a failed bank, become unemployed when firms fail, stores they used to visit lose business. It is hard to trace a single source of shock any more. Tensions are increasing, liquidity and turnover are falling and uncollectible debts are growing. In this phase, the system's robustness is on the test. If there are no further significant failures, especially in the financial sector, then the situation is likely to stabilise gradually.

In that respect, we can recognise alternatives: processes can be self-stabilising or self-destabilising. If every successive wave gets smaller and smaller, without significant failures of companies not directly affected, we may talk about a self-stabilising process. It usually occurs within an industry, leaving no severe traces on the economy as a whole. A lot of people would get hurt, but the following year economy would produce more. Of course, instead of oat, peasants would produce something else, but without any harm to common welfare.

If, on the other hand, each wave gets bigger and bigger, we are probably sailing towards a significant financial crisis. Rule of thumb—the stronger the initial shock is, and the more market participants are affected, the bigger is the chance that the process will be self-destabilising. The watershed between the two is usually a reaction to the financial sector, especially banking. The more banking gets hurt, and the more banks fail, the higher is the likelihood of a significant crisis.

As the self-destabilising process takes shape, the financial sector jumps in. Unfortunately, not to the rescue! The merchants and banks not involved in the initial shock know that the crisis would hurt many people, but they don't know exactly whom. Their natural reaction is to collect loans and stop giving new ones until the situation clarifies. They also hoard liquidity to meet the requests of their depositors and vendors.

As a new production cycle begins, less credit is available. Without credit, producers will plant less. Also, for their subsistence, they will rely more on their production and less on the market. Consequently, the overall demand will fall, prices will fall and less business will remain profitable.

Insufficient credit, falling prices and loss of profitability would decrease economic activity. Produced quantities would drop, and common welfare got worse than the year before. As a consequence, we would all have less work and get poorer.

Such a simplified description, of course, did not take into account all those institutions and instruments we usually connect with financial crises. Those are, for example, the stock exchange, collateralised default swaps, derivatives, insurance, stock, bonds and mutual funds. All of them add layers of complexity and interconnection. They make the reaction more unpredictable and could be instrumental for a significant increase or decrease in the system's stability. In the case of 2008, they were substantial destabilising factors.

We deliberately did not add them to keep a case simple. The connection is here visible and simple: shock, failure of participants, spreading od shock, decreasing credit-impaired liquidity-slower trade—slower production. Therefore, the problem is not "overproduction", but it is "under-demand". The decrease in demand was created by the collapse of credit initiated by loss of confidence. Credit and confidence are the same things. Credere in Latin means trust.

The example we discussed above was a case of "external shock". The event was not a consequence of some distortion in the financial system or structure of the economy. A single isolated incident caused it. If the war had not stopped, the merchants and bankers would have been happy.

Economic activity usually requires time. To earn handsomely, one should have the most profitable merchandise available when people need it the most. Entrepreneur considers the most likely course of events. That kind of thinking is called speculation. Once you determine the expected course of events, you adjust your activities to your expectations, aiming at maximising your income.

Sometimes, there is a negative perception about the speculation. However, it is wrong. We are all substantially speculators. A farmer planting carrot, a student enrolling in the university, a worker taking a job in a factory—they are all speculators. They act based on their rational expectations based on the information they have in an attempt to maximise their future income.

Speculations move markets. They enable people to mobilise resources in meaningful economic activity. Nonetheless, under certain conditions, they can hurt the economy hard.

Rational economic activity is a consequence of rational expectations. People will always produce and acquire merchandise or securities with the best economic outlook—according to their expectations.

The distribution of expectations is vital for financial stability. If the market participants' expectations are randomly distributed,[5] the financial system is stable. Any course of events will make some people earn, and some lose, but it will end up more or less as a zero-sum game. However, if everyone places their bets on the same side, then financial stability is under threat.

We will discuss the consequences of such distorted, "biased" expectations latter. For the time being, we need to recognise them as a source of the problem. It means

[5]Glossary, Efficient-market hypothesis.

that the market consensus is frequently a source of a problem. When everyone agrees that something is a good idea, it could easily mean that we look at the origin of a future crisis. That occurred with stock in 1929 and with flats in 2008 and with tulip bulbs in 1637. It also happened, as we will see, with many other assets in the course of history.

It is important to remember—when everyone agrees, it is not a good sign.

In our story, the merchants knew the princes involved and remembered how much they hated each other. They knew that there was no chance for peace until one of them is dead. As both were young and strong, everyone bet on a long war and took credit to plant oat.

During the winter campaign, one of the princes contracted pneumonia and died invalidating the assumptions of the speculation. His brother was a good friend with his relative on the opposite side. So, the war stopped, but only after the signature of all contracts and planting of the fields. As everyone bet on the same side, everyone got hurt. It would be much better if the princess were old and sick, then stakes would be divided and damage smaller.

To sum it up, improvements in productivity from the eleventh century gradually increased production. Surpluses began to trade. Trade and innovation created finance and then in turn finance boost trade. They both were the foundation for the establishment of the first banks. Through a magical transformation, credit became money. That allowed much faster and cheaper payments, making trade flourish and encouraging long-distance trade and specialisation. However, this system of trade generated instability. An earlier unthinkable mountain of debt introduced new, until then unbeknown risks. The game of finance began, for better or worse.

Finally, even though finance made a lot of mischiefs in its history, when you sit in your car and use a smartphone to order delivery from the local supermarket, you must remember that none of those things would exist without finance.

We should not blame finance for being mischievous. As we have seen, it is a price for huge benefits humankind got from it. After all, life is not risk avoidance; life is risk management. Finance gives us a lot of incentive to do it, as it rewards those doing it well, and mercilessly penalise recklessness. Most of all, it is instability breeding instability.

As increased instability increases rewards, it is challenging to harness it. That is bad news for banking supervision, as harnessing finance is its task. Many people expect a reward from increased instability and do not like the one who tries to prevent it.

References

Wallerstein, I. (1974). *Modern world-system I*, Academic Press.

www.britannica.com. (2019, November). Retrieved from https://www.britannica.com/topic/history-of-Europe/Prices-and-inflation.

Chapter 3
Big Depression—Events Forcing the Regulator's Hand

Abstract The consequence of relying on market discipline to guide finance is the worst global economic crisis ever. President Roosevelt decides to intervene radically. He stabilises heavily distressed banking by the introduction of deposit guarantee, strong supervision and structural separation. This scheme makes the banks' liabilities more stable and cheaper.

Though we said in the beginning that the market is the best regulator of economic activity, it does not apply to the banking sector. In that area, the market failed almost a century ago, during the worst depression the world has ever seen—the Great depression.

US president in the mid-twenties of the twentieth century, Coolidge, was a man in love with the market. The market returned his passion. It gave him a fast-growing US economy. Everything went up fast: salaries, real estate prices, stock. It appeared that there was no boundary for growth.

His Secretary of Commerce and eventual successor, Hoover, said in early 1929: "Given the chance to go forward with the policies of the last eight years, we shall soon with the help of God, be in sight of the day when poverty will be banished from this nation." Hoover had his doubts,[1] but when he came into office in March 1929, he decided to pray to the gods of the free market to avoid, and later to clear the mess. Nevertheless, he proved severely wrong. Much different from the assumptions of neoclassical economic theory, the way those gods behaved in the financial crisis did not help anyone. Quite the opposite, that made things lousy and then made them even worse.

When the crisis struck, he tried to intervene, but he did not have the institutional means to do it properly. With his background in "small government" ideology, he was not willing to create institutions and the means needed for an efficient reaction.

[1]"But in 1925 and 1926, with Hoover and Miller pushing to tighten credit policy, Strong was able to hide behind the Fed's charter and do nothing." Kindle, location 4383.

"In the fall of 1925, Hoover decided to launch a campaign against the pervasive atmosphere of speculation that he claimed was infecting the whole country." Kindle, location 4339 (Liaquat, 2009).

D. Odak, *A Political Economy of Banking Supervision*,
https://doi.org/10.1007/978-3-030-48547-4_3

During the period of his presidency, more than 3000 banks failed, and the stock exchange index went down by 80%. Overall losses on the stock exchange alone were estimated to be about 30 billion in 1930 dollars. It would be about 450 billion in 2019 dollars.

The losses arising from the banking crisis cannot be accurately estimated, but they were also horrendous. We should keep in mind that 3000 banks failed and that no deposit insurance had existed yet. So, depositors got their money through the regular bankruptcy procedure. Even if the bankruptcy recovered part of the funds for the depositors, the funds would be unavailable to them for an extended period, sometimes for years.

During his presidency, the unemployment rate reached 22%. A vast number of workers and middle-class people lost their jobs and homes and moved to the so-called Hoovervilles—slums of makeshift houses built everywhere, even in Central Park in New York. The American GDP sunk by 25%,[2] while global output declined by an astonishing 15%. The worst phase of the depression lasted for almost 4 years. In comparison, the worldwide recession of 2009 lasted just a year, and the global GDP dropped by 1%.

The consequence of the concept relying on market and market discipline to guide and restrain finance was the worst global economic crisis ever.

The Great Depression ruined the US banking system so much that it finally created enough political will to impose strict rules on banking. Those rules worked well until the period of chaos was forgotten, and naturally, the fear of finance subsided, resulting in the abolishment of the Glass-Steagall Act.

When we talk about those developments, we should notice how reluctant US politics was to intervene in the banking system. An intervention came only in 1933, 4 years after the beginning of the Depression. It happened when the only realistic alternative was the collapse of the banking system with thousands of banks failing simultaneously, after more than 3000 had already failed since 1929.

In 1933, president Roosevelt replaced Hoover. He understood that market forces during the last 4 years only increased the chaos in the economy and finance. So, he decided to try something else—to intervene radically, trying to turn things around. He did so successfully, at least temporarily.

The most acute crisis he inherited from his predecessor when he came into office was in the field of banking. The banking system had already been beyond the brink of collapse—it was in a state of utter, uncontained panic. All 48 states declared state bank holidays in February; some state banks had already been closed for two weeks without setting reopening dates. Roosevelt came into office on 4 March 1933, declared the national banking holiday on 6 March, and pushed through Congress the Emergency Banking Act introducing 100% deposit guarantees. That did the trick—after the institutions reopened on 13 March, depositors stood in line again. This time to return cash to the bank.

[2]"Production in almost every country has collapsed—in the two worst hit, the United States and Germany, it had fallen 40%." (Liaquat, 2009).

We can see that the deposit guarantee, and the subsequent strict banking supervision, was not introduced to constrain or hamper the development of the banking and financial sectors. It was introduced for precisely the opposite intention, to save the industry from inevitable and immediate collapse. Therefore, the political options were limited. Not giving the guarantee would immediately cause increased risks in the financial system, while a guarantee without effective supervision would increase the likelihood of a moral hazard. The only feasible solution was the present structure: a deposit guarantee with effective supervision.

There are two reasons why it took politics so long to intervene in banking. The first reason was that earlier it was not necessary. During the stock exchange crash in 1929, the paradox was that banks covered their risks associated with the stock exchange relatively well. The most critical exposures were associated with the so-called "margin loans". Those loans financed the stock exchange speculation of the banks' clients. The collaterals for those loans were securities more valuable than a loan. Therefore, the customer bears the first risk of loss, usually 25%. Although several banks had failed already at the beginning of the crisis, they did not make a notable systematic impact.

The second reason was political. President Hoover ideologically opposed the systematic government intervention in the economy, believing that the market is the best and the most efficient guide for the allocation of resources.

Just by chance, developments invalidated both reasons in the early spring of 1933. Almost all banks were closed and unable to re-open when the new president took office in March that year. So, the new president dealt with the issue the best way he could, establishing deposit insurance and strict banking regulation. The regulation was not a consequence of some ideologic concept. It was just a pragmatic response to the situation.

Banking had become too important, too complex and too interconnected to be efficiently guided by the market. During almost the century following the event, it did not become less so.

Concerning the period leading to the Great Depression, it is more important what banks did to their customers than what they did to themselves. They marketed margin loans aggressively to the general public, advising clients to invest their savings in hazardous schemes. Credit was abundant and readily available.

Later, when things went south, banks were able to close margin loans mostly without critical losses, but billions of savings disappeared into thin air. Most of the people suffering the losses were members of the newly formed middle class—qualified and white-collar workers. The middle class provided the principal markets for the recently booming industries, such as cars, electronics and household appliances.

Integrated activities of commercial and investment banks caused market volatility by providing finance for asset purchase, therefore, pushing prices ever higher and faster. During 18 months, from the beginning of 1928 until summer 1929, the DJIA almost doubled. The economy was fundamentally sound, no doubt about it, but not so much better than a year before. The only notable difference was the volume of margin loans and the intensity of their sales by brokers and banks. That overheated the market, separating prices widely from the so-called fundaments.

Interestingly, no one knows what caused the initial stock price fall on September 4. We do not know where the crash came from, but we know what it did. When the prices finally turned around, the mechanism acted in the opposite direction and did so even harder. It is called the "escalator up, elevator down" chart. As soon as prices went down, the bank contacted all borrowers having margin loans to replenish their down payment. Some of them did not respond, and their stock went on sale, pushing the prices further down. The bank then required a new down payment, and the downward spiral went on.

The sheer volumes of the margin loans provided a massive sale push, making an increasing number of borrowers insolvent and unable to cover their margins. The process became too forceful to overcome it with any attempted intervention. The margin debt cliff, built through the decade, collapsed within a few months and nothing could be done to prevent it. It was simply too big.

Preventing such things from happening again was maybe the most crucial reason for the Glass-Steagall separation. Today we would call it—consumer protection.

The doubling of the stock price in 18 months was associated with the mild increase in economic growth, while returning the stock prices to the level they had only 3 years ago wreaked havoc in the real economy, plummeting industrial production in the US by 45%. In that example, we can notice the asymmetry, an exciting phenomenon we will try to describe and understand. It is frequently present in the interaction between the real economy and finance. In good times financial growth barely increases GDP growth, while in bad times, it hits really severely.

Just a change of some accounting figures in the books stops real machines all over the world. It seems incomprehensible. If those machines produce things people need, why don't they continue producing?

The reason is the "propensity to spend". Production makes sense only if someone buys those products. If people stop buying, factories will stop producing. When they stop producing, their workers and owners lose income. They also decrease spending, increasing the problem further.

In an optimistic atmosphere, people are willing to spend their entire income, and even to borrow for spending.

In the late 1920s, the increase in stock prices increased the income and assets of a significant part of the population. Although those people were also heavily indebted, they reacted to the rise in the net value of their assets by increased spending.

When they just looked at the numbers, they thought that they were savers. They consumed only a small part of their earnings, and the net value of their assets momentously increased. The economy reacted favourably to the higher demand. It responded partly by increasing the supply, and partly by raising prices. As the industry and agriculture were able to increase the supply, there was no noticeable inflation of consumer prices. But boom went the other way—housing, investment goods and stocks increased their prices significantly. That drove higher employment and investments.

When the stock prices fell back, these people lost their savings. Their willingness and ability to spend, and especially to spend on expensive things such as houses, cars, radios, household appliances, gravely decreased. The sale of vehicles immediately dropped so much that, within 2 years, Ford laid off two-thirds of its workers. Unemployed people, a lot of them already without any savings, stopped spending and moved to shelters or some Hooverville. The lack of demand added to the predicament, running things further down.

All in all, at the peak in 1933, about a quarter of the available working force was unemployed. Then banks also got severely hit. The shock did not come from the stock exchange but the banks' traditional business. Agriculture hit them hard.[3] As people became unemployed while a notable part of their savings disappeared in the stock exchange crash, they did not have enough money to buy as much food as they used to.

Consequently, farmers stopped buying industrial products, pushing the industry further down and in the process, decreasing, even more, the demand for their products.

Then another external shock added to the pain—the so-called "Dust Bowl". That was a period of droughts destroying crops in the Midwest during the 1930s. Farmers lost twice: due to the drought which lasted until 1940, and due to the falling prices of their products. Just in the period from 1930 to 1933, overall prices fell by 26%, and agricultural prices even more. Some products were priced so low that farmers could not pay for the gas to deliver them to the market. In those circumstances, naturally, a lot of farmers failed to repay their debts.

The consequence was the foreclosure of ruined farms. After they were foreclosed, there was no market. No one wanted to offer anything for most of the farms. Finally, debtors overflooded the banks with illiquid assets of uncertain value. Most of those banks were very regional and not diversified, so they were unable to cover their losses by other activities. They finally lost the trust of their clients and peers and failed.

It all went spectacularly wrong. The public opinion was astonished by shocking developments: firms and banks got closed one after another. Even the most cautious and hardworking people first lost their income, then their savings. Only a few kilometres further, in the countryside, there was mass destruction of perfectly good food, while in the towns queues of starving people waited for hours to get a loaf of bread.

People wondered whether what they saw really was "the most efficient economic system" and "permanent progress"? Depression ceased to be an economic issue. The situation in the economy and finance had become highly political. Communists were taking over the unions, thus becoming major coordinators of the workers' industrial actions. The radical right also had its organisations, focused on beating those they do not like. There was a strong disillusion directed towards "freedom" and "democracy", since a significant and growing number of people would have chosen to eat every day instead to vote every fourth year—if someone would have offered them such a choice.

Only after things got politically so radical, while an increasing number of banks were failing or temporarily closing, the inauguration of the new president finally

[3]"Most of the banks that failed during the 1920s and 1930s were located in agricultural areas and evidence indicates that the primary contributor to bank distress during the 1920s and 1930s was declines in agricultural income and land values…" (Calomiris & Haber, 2014).

enabled US politics to move towards stricter rules in banking and finance. It is worth noting that bankers were not opposing the action. Quite the opposite—it appeared as salvation for most of the state banks. Banks received tremendous benefits from the regulation, the most important of them being FDIC, the first nation-wide deposit insurance scheme. By introducing this scheme, the banks' liabilities became more stable and cheaper.

References

Calomiris, C. W., & Haber, S. H. (2014). *Fragile by design*, Princeton University Press. ISBN 9780691168357.

Liaquat, A. (2009). *Lords of finance*, Penguin Books. ISBN1440697965.

Chapter 4
Great Recession—The Ugly Daughter of Deregulation

Abstract The banking system in the Western world is stable during the Glass-Steagall period, from 1935 until the beginning of the "great recession". Until the implementation of the Act, there are periodic banking crises in the US, followed by depressions. After 1935 there is no major banking crisis or depression until 2008. In the late twentieth century, investment bankers are itching to lay their hands on the liquidity in boring commercial banks. They convince the economists and politicians that liberalisation will create benefits for the economy. Economists get convinced despite lacking theoretical ground for such an expectation. Facing consensus of "industry and academy", politicians then took a deep breath and jump. Later it is easy to blame supervisors for the consequences.

When we deliberate financial regulation, we should keep eyes on empirical evidence. The essential question is: "Is long-term financial stability possible at all? Was there any long-term period in recent history in which the financial system was not caught up in periodic turmoil?" Let us look into some evidence concerning that.

The answer is clear: concerning banks yes, in fact, there was! The banking system in the US, and generally in the Western world, was quite stable in the period after the implementation of the so-called Glass-Steagall Act in 1935 until the beginning of the "great recession" in 2008.[1] That was quite a long period—73 years without a major international banking crisis in developed economies.[2]

---

[1]"It was just that the United States had been spared such bubbles for decades after the Great Depression because of the regulation the government had put in place after that trauma. Once deregulation had taken hold, it was only a matter of time before these horrors of the past would return. The so-called financial innovation had just enabled the bubble to become bigger before it burst..." (Stiglitz, 2010, p. 27).

[2]"It (the US) had major banking crises in 1837, 1839, 1867, 1861, 1873, 1884, 1890, 1893, 1896, 1907, 1920, 1930–33, the 1980s, and 2007–09." (Calomiris & Haber, 2014, p. 5). Comment: The 1980 crisis was a savings and loan crisis. Those institutions were not "banks" but were regulated by special law: the Federal Home Loan Bank Act.

D. Odak, *A Political Economy of Banking Supervision*,
https://doi.org/10.1007/978-3-030-48547-4_4

The Act resolved two essential things: firstly, it strictly separated commercial from investment banking. Secondly, it empowered institutions to closely and assertively supervise commercial banks.

There is a logic in dividing those businesses into two categories, limiting their interconnectedness. Investment and commercial banks have different risk profiles and business models. The Glass-Steagall Act separated investment and commercial banking, preventing the transfer of risks between them. Even their business volume was limited. A significant shareholder of a commercial bank was not allowed to, directly or indirectly, own a substantial shareholding in an investment bank and vice versa.

During the period regulated by the Act, the global financial system was relatively stable. It lasted for the best part of the century.

That does not mean that there was no market crisis. Indeed, investment banks and speculators explore borders constantly. This is their job. By doing so, they generate ups and downs. Some of those oscillations were quite steep. Some of the "downs" caused mild recessions. Still, until 2008 nothing resembling 1929 occurred.

The Glass-Steagall Act was diluted and softened during the 1980s and replaced by the Dodd-Frank Act in 1999.

During the period when the law was in force, there was only one financial crisis with an almost systematic impact on the US financial system. That crisis affected savings and loan banks, a form of building societies. The stabilisation of those banks cost about 150 billion in 1990 dollars of real, un-refunded tax-payers' money. That would be about 300 billion in 2019 dollars or almost half of the TARP—the package approved for the stabilisation of the US banking system in 2009. Unlike TARP money that was repaid with hefty interest, savings and loan banks repaid nothing.

That crisis and its costs only highlighted the benefits of the Act. Different regulations governed savings and loan associations.

Until the implementation of the Glass-Steagall Act, there were periodic major banking crises in the US, almost each followed by several years of depression. During the nineteenth century, depressions arose every 20 years, almost punctual as a clock: 1819, 1837, 1857, 1873, 1893. Then at the turn of the centuries, things became somewhat disorderly: 1896, 1901, 1907 and then again about 20 years until 1929. After 1935 there was no major banking crisis or depression before 2008.

All those facts did not disturb the advocates of deregulation to push for the removal of the Act.[3] Quite the opposite, the lack of any recent financial crisis emboldened them.[4] When a crisis would finally come, they said that the Act would not prevent it.

---

[3]"Greenspan joined deregulatory forces with …Robert Rubin, Rubin's deputy Lawrence Summers, and this Third-Wayish trio cheer-led the frenzy of financial innovation now exploding across US trading rooms.

In November 1999 this new breed of American anti-regulators brought down their biggest trophy kill, the repeal of the Glass-Steagall Act…" (Shaxson, 2019, p. 159).

[4]The regulatory approach at the turn of the millennium nicely illustrates a quote by William McDonough, President of the New York Federal Reserve: "Every firm does, and on my view should, take a certain amount of calculated risk in allowing new creativity to take place and requiring the internal control apparatus to be a little breathless running behind it" (Engler & Essinger, 2000, p. 200).

Still, we should not live under the impression that returning to the same rules would surely prevent future financial crises. Such a conclusion would be overly optimistic. Nothing can provide such a guarantee. The best you can hope for is to minimise the likelihood of an undesired outcome. Structural separation would undoubtedly help in that respect.

Towards the beginning of the twenty-first century, it was consensus between mainstream economists—the strict regulation of banking and finance is the factor decreasing economic growth. Despite being general, that consensus was not a consequence of some fundamental theoretical breakthrough proving or indicating that financial growth would significantly increase real economic growth. Concerning financial products that finally backfired in 2008–2009, derivatives, there was no significant theoretical work explaining why and how would their uncontrolled expansion supports the real economy.

Dr. Milton Friedman, frequently perceived as a most eloquent advocate of deregulation, in fact, in his theoretical works, did not point out any benefits from the excessive credit or monetary growth. Quite the opposite, he warned that any such growth exceeding the capacity of the real economy to grow would only produce inflation.

Despite such lack of theoretical ground for their belief, the mentioned pragmatical consensus of economists took over politics. Deregulation became a keyword of the day. Not only laws were changed to enable faster growth of the financial sector, but also budgets of regulatory agencies were under scrutiny and rationalisation measures.

It is easy to see whether the deregulation of banking in the late twentieth century strengthened the growth of the US economy. If we observe the GDP growth rate in the period, we can see that the growth rate achieved in 1999, the year of replacing the Glass-Steagall Act, has not been attained ever since. Already in 2001, when all frantic activities on the financial markets took place with blazing speed, the growth rate of the US economy was below 1%. The average growth rate of the US economy in the period from 1994 to 1999 was 4.03%, compared to 2.5% from 2001 to 2007. The liberalisation of finance didn't do anything to support growth. It is not a surprise, as there was no reason to expect it to do it. Nevertheless, it contributed significantly to the cumulation of risks. Those risks subsequently caused the contraction of the real economy, wiping out a significant part of already weak growth of the period.

Regardless of whether the regulation can harm the growth, one must have a strong stomach to say that economic and human consequences of events such as in 1929 or 2008 did not significantly exceed the positive impact of the deregulation. But the evidence points in the other direction—deregulation did cumulative damage. It did not increase growth and caused contraction, market distortion, the collapse of confidence in financial instruments and most of all, unneeded human suffering.

Nevertheless, we cannot deny that the people claiming that the causes of 2008 have nothing to do with the change of the banking regulation also presented strong arguments. It is impossible to firmly insist that Glass-Steagall would have prevented the events leading up to 2008 had it remained in force. It had worked well for 64 years, but the law was written to avoid the events leading to the 1929 crisis, not the 2008 crisis. The sources of the new turmoil were predominantly traditional banking operations allowed by the law and the derivatives created based on them, not regulated by the law. Portfolio sale and securitisation were entirely in line with the law, and they were widespread during the Glass-Steagall era.[5]

Paradoxically, regulators supported securitisation as a risk management strategy during the Glass-Steagall period. It enabled diversification, preventing the accumulation of regional risk characteristic for local banks in the 1930s. So, from a regulatory perspective, we could claim that what brought us to 2008 was sort of "too much of a good thing". A change of the law did not materially change the regulatory approach to securitisation. As securitisation was unquestionably the primary source of the risks causing 2008, the conclusion that a change of the law has nothing to do with the runup towards the crisis is not necessarily wrong.

However, it only appears so. If we dig deeper, we will see that "too much" was brought forward by the impact and influence of the investment bankers. Their actions turned traditional risk management tools into risk-generating tools. By adding so many bells and whistles to the securitisation, the process of financial innovation changed it beyond recognition.[6] Their activity created so much demand for asset-based securities that banks lost any causality between the accepted risks and the cost of risks. They created loans, sold them to investment bankers and got fees for that. So, they did not have any motive to be selective when giving loans. Consequently, the predatory lending practice became the primary risk generator in the system. No one was aware of that, and even worse, no one was supposed to be aware.

When all the pieces got together, the train was rolling down a slope under full steam. Two bankers were putting as much coal as possible into the firebox. There was no driver; the champions of deregulation had fired him. Investment bankers also removed the brakes. Just in case: to prevent any attempt at slowing down the economic growth. What could go wrong?

Blaming only bankers and supervisors[7] for the ensuing accident appears as an oversimplification. None of them had the power to change the rules.

Immediately after introducing Dodd-Franck, the securitisation market grew fast with a notable change in its nature.[8] It could also be a spurious correlation, as the old law did not prevent any of those things occurring before. But despite being allowed by the law, such things did not happen during the period governed by Glass-Steagall.[9]

---

[5]Estrella (2002).

[6]"...purpose and effect was not to spread risk more effectively by passing it to those better equipped to handle it, but to dump it on those who understand less about it." (Kay, 2015, p. 73).

[7]"None of this is meant to excuse them -in my view, the regulatory failure is inexcusable- but only to explain their astonishing passivity.

Another part of the reason may have been actual or perceived political pressures." (Blinder, 2013, p. 59).

[8]According to FRED data (Sant Luis FED) the total value of real estate loans securitised by financial companies was 53 bn US$ in 1990, 191 bn US$ in 1999, growing to 600 bn US$ in 2008 (FRED, 2019).

[9]According to (Estrella, 2002), in 2000 the private sector MBS was about 10% of the total mortgage market.

The real source of the problem appears to be a change in the structure of bank governances. The change of the law brought forward fast ownership and consequently, a management integration of investment and commercial banks. In that integration, more aggressive investment bankers had the upper hand, and their culture became dominant. Such culture enabled the change in the securitisation process described earlier. That integration was possible only without the Glass-Steagall Act.

Let us try to summarise the story about the deregulation. In the late twentieth century, investment bankers were itching to lay their hands on the vast idling liquidity in those boring commercial banks and do some magic with it. They convinced the economists and politicians that financial liberalisation would create immense benefits for the economy. Economists get convinced despite not having any model which would justify such an expectation. Facing consensus of "industry and academy", politicians then looked back and saw no notable difficulties with the financial system during the last two generations. They took a deep breath and jumped. Later it was easy to blame bankers and supervisors for the consequences.

Again, we notice asymmetry in action: just by looking at the statistics, we quickly see that financial liberalisation did not have a visible positive impact on the real economy. Some silent voices claim that growth would have been even slower without it, but they aren't convincing.

The point is that deregulation increased risks and casually, or maybe as a cause, corresponded with financial calamity, without bringing any visible benefit for the real economy before doing damage. From such a perspective, it is hard to reach any conclusion except that it was a wrong move.

Nonetheless, there is also good news about regulatory efforts. In discussions about the Great recession, people tend to overlook it. If we compare the level of damage done to the global economy by the "great recession" in 2008 and by the "great depression" which started in 1929, we will notice that it was incomparably less costly this time.

That was certainly not a consequence of lower cumulated risks. Quite the opposite. In the runup towards 1929, risks cumulated in a relatively isolated population of capital markets investors. The financial system was well protected against it by a wall of liquid collateral, while it had no immediate impact on the real economy. Comparing those initial risks with the risks that triggered a simultaneous collapse of the housing market and significant financial institutions in 2008 is like comparing a firework to a ballistic rocket. As we earlier said, the stronger initial shock is, more likely major financial crisis become. The initial impact of the Great recession was a proper foundation for a perfect storm.

Despite such a spectacular initial strike, the development of the national and global regulatory and institutional framework made the difference. Improvements in medication significantly decreased the potential damage caused by a lightheaded and careless approach towards the prevention. This time institutions and offset programs, able to prevent and intervene, were much better prepared. The institutional structure and knowledge enabled much faster and bolder reactions than it was possible in 1929. Those institutions provided buffers for the market dynamics and avoided repeating the market collapse of the 30 s. Banking supervision was a very important part of the structure, and its contribution to the productive reaction to the crisis was significant.

Still, we cannot say that the crisis of 2008 was cheap. In the US alone, the ex-post intervention in the 2008 crisis proved to be bearable from the government debt perspective. All other consequences on people and society were terrible, sometimes disastrous. Entire neighbourhoods were wiped out, the lives of families crushed, families left homeless, mothers and fathers thrown into a quagmire of unemployment.

We should be aware that there is no guarantee that crisis containment would always be so successful. Some countries, such as Ireland and Bulgaria, paid dearly for the imaginative banking of their bankers.

The ability to efficiently deal with the crisis should not breed contempt and encourage the assumption that we can now readily accept the risks. In each crisis, the consequences and risks are enormous, and the situation can easily get out of control. All those risks, as well as the human sufferings caused by it, created urgency for measures aimed at avoiding a crisis or at least decreasing its impact on people.

It is important to note that one of the primary reasons why the US did relatively well in 2008 is the cautious stance of its banking supervision. Quite the opposite from public perception, US supervision was not head-on supporting reckless practices.[10] The resistance of its banking regulators delayed the implementation of the Basel II Accord in the US. Although there were weakly capitalised institutions in the US, they were on average nowhere nearly as weak as their counterparts enjoying all the benefits of the newly established regulatory framework. That made a huge difference in crisis management in the US and Europe. As we will see, it also caused the main difference between the actual shape of the US and Eurozone financial sectors today.

Some people still claim that Glass-Steagall was unnecessarily restrictive and that it hampered the development of the financial industry in the USA. Now we know that while reliable old GS was around, the financial world was a safer place.[11] Three-quarters of a century without an international banking crisis in developed economies overlapped with 64 years of the law, while the first global financial crisis in almost a century closely followed its demise. Are those only spurious correlations? Would it have happened if the law had remained in force? We cannot know for sure.

For example, Canada, which adheres to a type of rules based on Glass-Steagall, did not have trouble with its banking system after 2008, although its economy got hit.

Avoiding crises altogether is not possible. The cyclic nature of economic growth is an embedded characteristic of the market economy. Nonetheless, learning how to prevent and cushion their effects is a realistic proposal. As the comparison between

[10]"One [precondition for accepting Basel II advanced approach] was a three-year transition period that capped the amount of capital reduction for any individual bank at 5% per year, though the caps would come off after the third year. Another was permanent 10% cap on the amount of total capital that could decline among all banks using advanced approaches." (Bair, 2012, p. 33).

[11]In the aftermath of the Great Depression, the government addressed the questions, what had caused the depression and how can it prevent a recurrence? The regulatory structure that it adopted served the country and the world well, presiding over an unprecedented period of stability and growth. The Glass-Steagall Act of 1933 was the cornerstone of that regulatory edifice (Stiglitz, 2010, p. 162).

1929 and 2008 indicates, we already learned a lot. Still, there is yet a lot to be discovered. Unfortunately, we will have to do most of the learning the hard way—by handling the crises.

Handling of the crisis will take place in an uncertain and always unique environment. Every crisis, just as every car crash is unique. To make passengers safer, the producer improves car handling, but also adds some redundant passive safety to the car. They add a more robust frame, better airbags and safer harnesses. They would increase the probability of survival if the driver made a mistake despite improved handling.

That is what banking regulators also should do. Improve our ability to handle the crisis, but also add some passive safety in the form of more resilient balance sheet.

References

Bair, S. (2012). Bull by the Horns. Simon and Schuster paperback. ISBN 9781451672503.

Blinder, A. S. (2013). *After the music stopped*, Penguin Books. ISBN 014312448X.

Calomiris, C. W., & Haber, S. H. (2014). *Fragile by design*, Princeton University Press. ISBN 9780691168357.

Engler, H., & Essinger, J. (2000). *The future of banking*. Reuters Limited.

Estrella, A. (2002, May). Securitization and the efficacy of monetary policy. *Economic Policy Review*, 13.

FRED. (2019). https://fred.stlouisfed.org. Retrieved from (https://fred.stlouisfed.org/series/DTRTNM).

Kay, J. (2015). *Other people's money*, Profile Books. ISBN 978-1781254431.

Shaxson, N. (2019). *The finance curse*, Vintage Digital. ISBN 1847925383.

Stiglitz, J. E. (2010). *Freefall*, W W Norton & Company. ISBN 9780393077070.

Chapter 5
The Asymmetry

Abstract The growth of the financial system modestly influences the growth of the economy, while sharply increases the instability of the system. We do not live much better if the water supply pumps more water, but a failed water supply ruins our lives. During the Glass-Steagall period, structural separation keeps the asymmetry at bay. Innovative investment banking makes waves in capital markets freely, while protected by a legal wall, the dull commercial banking is what it is supposed to be, dull. The financial industry's most devastating social impact emerges from the impact financial crises have on political stability. The failure of a large bank creates such a disruption that regulators reached a consensus that such banks should not "fail disorderly".

As we said in the beginning, this is a book about asymmetry. We have already several times seen it in action. It is an essential feature of the financial system—it is more capable of doing damage then accelerating economic growth. Consequently, if someone tries to push the growth of the economy by stimulating the growth of the financial system, that would typically modestly influence growth. At the same time, it would sharply increase risks in the system. If those risks materialise, the consequent economic decline would be much steeper than earlier growth was.

Before we go further with the subject, there is something we must always keep in our mind. The fact that banking and finance could be dangerous does not make them less critical. Quite the opposite, they are dangerous because they are essential, even critical activities.

We will begin by asking: "What causes asymmetry, and why does only finance have such influence?"

Asymmetry is undoubtedly not only a peculiarity of finance. It is an attribute of all industries whose dysfunction can severely diminish the GDP, while its improvement can hardly contribute to economic growth. Several sectors could have a very similar impact on the economy. They cannot help a lot, but they can do real damage. Those are the industries which improved our life the most. Those are, for example, water supply, electricity, railways and telecommunications.

D. Odak, *A Political Economy of Banking Supervision*,
https://doi.org/10.1007/978-3-030-48547-4_5

Each of them, when introduced, was a game-changer. They significantly increased the productivity of labour. Today they contribute to the economy, employ people, build constructions, create innovations, but their contribution to economic growth is much smaller than the damage their major dysfunction could cause.

Let us give an example. If someone told you that we would live much better if the water supply pumps more water, you would be amazed, even amused. On the other hand, if the same person said that a failed water supply would ruin our lives, you would immediately agree.

Asymmetry emerges from the fact that the smooth operation of those utilities creates the fundament for all social and economic activities. Most of the other businesses, if stopped, would decrease the GDP by their output and the multiplier attached. Those activities, if dysfunctional, obstruct the functioning of the economy as a whole. Additionally, such events quickly and significantly decrease the quality of life and influence political stability.

Fortunately for us, today we learned how to avoid and manage a "water crisis" or an "electricity crisis". But we have not yet overcome financial crises. The reason is simple: water and electricity producers clearly understand their role and place in the world. Therefore, they do their job, keeping their heads down and carefully watching the costs and risks. No one expects them to do some magic in the process.

However, finance is something altogether different. It is so magical that it consistently attracts innovation and imagination.[1] It is pushed over and over again to the forefront of social development. While its contribution is limited, the risks emerging from imaginative finance always represent a threat to the aorta of our economy—the payment system.

Finance is sexy and attractive. It deals with money, and money has a magical appeal. Outside of a desert, no one struggles to acquire a big barrel of water, while almost everyone dreams about taking home a few million.

Young, ambitious, and talented people join the game of finance to achieve that. They know that success is possible only by changing rules, by doing something unexpected. Those unexpected things are just that—unexpected, for better and worse. So, a side effect of taking a few million homes is usually the creation of some innovative risks.

Those risks could be recognised and managed, but it takes time to learn how. As the processes are innovative, the risks are also creative.[2] They frequently hide and multiply in the dark until they enter with force. Then the world begins to tremble.

To decrease those risks, the framework of the good old Glass-Steagall Act could be helpful. That was precisely the reason it was successful in its time. The law separated innovative investment banking from infrastructural, dull commercial banking. The separation worked.

The asymmetry was kept at bay. Dynamic and innovative investment banking was allowed to splash and make waves in relatively isolated capital markets freely.

[1]Engler and Essinger (2000).

[2]Litan (2019).

Protected by a legal wall, the dull commercial banking was what it is supposed to be—dull.

However, let us go back to the question of how should banking regulation be designed. We earlier compared two approaches—one dealing with dangerous, but not disastrous consequences, and the other applicable to the activities threatening us with unrepairable damage. We compared aviation and nuclear power as examples. We also proposed that approach towards finance should be more in line with the approach towards nuclear power.

Some could regard it as an exaggeration. It appears that no financial meltdown can cause damage anywhere near the damage caused if, let us assume, New York became permanently uninhabitable. So, it is easy to disagree that the financial industry is more threatening than nuclear power.

But the financial industry's most prominent social impact is not mainly reflected in the, recognised or unrecognised, costs of the financial crisis. Those costs are enormous, and we will never know how big they are. Still, they are not of such magnitude to be among the worst risks humanity is facing. Danger lurks much deeper and below the surface.

Take, for example, Albania, a picturesque Mediterranean country. Just 7 years after getting peacefully rid of one of the most stringent communist regimes in the world, the impoverished European country exploded in anarchy.[3] It peacefully crushed communism, but the unregulated financial industry caused a civil war.

People, unfamiliar with the free market, believed that deposit takers offering exorbitant rates have a sustainable business model. Of course, that was not the case. They just followed old Ponzi's scheme, trying to attract more money into deposits before running away. Attracted by the promised earnings, people brought them the hard currency they had hidden from the communists for years. They believed that capitalism would consist of endless financial magic. Instead of magic, they saw a trick. Their savings disappeared in front of their eyes.

They got angry and loud, requesting the government to offset their losses. The government had no ground to do so, and they refused. Then ex-communists spotted the weakness of the new regime and got the army on their side. A civil war broke out between the military backing communists and the police defending the government. The battles lasted for 6 months claiming more than 2000 lives. Surprisingly enough, its consequence was the return to power of ex-communists, which was quite unthinkable just a year earlier.

The Albanian case is just a small one. The consequences of financial distress could be much broader. For example, the last financial crisis in 2008 was a global threat. The deliberate and robust support provided for the financial system helped to mitigate it. Nevertheless, there was a potential global threat to our way of life. That is far from an exaggeration.

We should never underestimate the emotional attachment of people to their money. It is a strong bond worth respect. Money offers proof of success, a prosperous future, an illusion of safety and the hope of joy. Being suddenly deprived of it is one of the

[3] Jusufi (2017).

major setbacks that could occur to any human being. An immediate natural reaction is an attempt to win it back. That impulse is so strong that it would disregard all other values, including public safety, general welfare and common sense.

Another problem is the loss of income. If, due to crisis, people find themselves unable to support their families, they are desperate and ready for anything.

When a large number of people experience substantial loss, simultaneously and as a consequence of the same financial abuse, they usually demand protection from the government. They claim that the damage they suffered was not a consequence of their poor judgment, but the government's mistake. Having no legal ground, they tend to resort to violence. Marginal political groups, ultra-left or right, immediately blend in, trying to turn protesters into their "infantry". Depending on the number of people involved and the stability of the political system, they can become quite a serious threat to the existing "way of life".

Countries with a long history of democracy and market economy are more immune to such developments and generally better able to weather them. Countries, where either element is fragile or missing, could suffer long-term adverse consequences affecting their whole population. For example, the banking crisis in Argentina at the beginning of 2000 created a situation where 7 out of 10 children were poor in a country whose GDP dropped by an astonishing 30%. No nuclear reactor failure could have such consequences.

Of course, such a radical conclusion could be debatable, so let's offer a compromise. The reasonable conclusion is that both risks are grave enough to treat them with the utmost caution. Which threat is more prominent? Let us hope we will never learn.

In conclusion, we will bring up another story connecting the financial industry to a historical event. After WWI, enormous war reparations burdened Germany. A consequence was runaway inflation[4] and loss of social cohesion in the country. Those difficulties decreased in the late 20s, due to international trade and credit flow from the USA and the UK. The financial crisis beginning in 1929 reversed both: international orders for the German industry plummeted, and creditors called back their loans. The economy sank. The NSDAP party, winning only 2.6% of the votes in the 1928 elections, scored 19% in the 1930 elections. That was a political shock setting in motion chain of events leading the world to the biggest human-made disaster ever.

When we compare the risks emerging from finance and nuclear power, we should not forget that those events also included two atomic bombs and that if a war on that scale happens again, it could be many more nuclear bombs involved.

Technically, when we talk about the 1929 crisis, we talk about capital markets, not about bankers. Still, bankers had a prominent role in the events leading to Black Tuesday.

With a disclaimer that I am not a historian, we should be careful in making conclusions here. In the examples from Albania and Argentina, the cause of their

[4]The task of keeping Germany adequately supplied with currency notes became a major logistic operation involving "133 printing works with 1783 machines ... and more than 30 paper mills" (Liaquat, 2009) Kindle loc 1868.

peril was a single relatively isolated financial event. In the case of Germany in the early 1930s, things were much more complicated. The adverse economic events caused by Great depression were unquestionably a significant supporting factor in those developments. Still, it could be wrong to single them out as the cause of political events.

Those events had the whole host of other causes accumulated in the period between 1918 and 1930. The financial shock was "only" a triggering event. However, it hit already weary Germany so hard that a significant number of its citizens lost faith in its infant democracy.

The 1928 election results indicate that, if the economic situation remained stable, 2.8% of votes would hardly be a ground for NSDAP to form or even participate in a government.[5] Therefore, we cannot say that the financial industry directly caused the biggest human-made disaster of all time, but unfortunately, it contributed to its making.

This story confirms what we earlier noticed. Politics and finance are firmly connected, even intermingled. That is always a source of risk, but especially in sharp downturns. Then irresponsible people get firm arguments proving in the eyes of a lot of people mismanagement and incapacity of democratic government. If those people are able politicians, they can use those arguments as a basis for gaining power. Once getting power, they will continue to be what they were before—irresponsible. That is the most significant single risk emerging from the banking and finance—potentially the most prominent source of the asymmetry in the case of finance. This risk alone makes worth spending significant resources on banking supervision.

It is crucial to prevent or manage the failure of banks, especially significant ones. That significantly decreases risks for financial stability. Increased resilience of the institutions gives supervisors more elbow room. More capital the banks have, they are more resilient, and the asymmetry is less dangerous.

Everyone knows that. Despite that, a fancy game always plays around banking supervision. It is a consequence of the mentioned intermingling of finance and politics. For example, to get more resilient banking, if there is no market for shares, it is enough to withhold some dividends and maybe bonuses. Retaining earning would resolve or at least significantly decrease the problem of weak capital in the majority of the institutions.

Nevertheless, there is a conventional narrative that dividends and bonuses are not the only sacrifices needed. The sacrifice of some economic growth is allegedly the consequence of such a policy. As banks would be required to increase capital, they would give fewer loans to the economy, decreasing GDP growth rate.[6]

Before discussing it further, let us reiterate that no one has yet proved that the growth of bank credit causes the growth of the economy. We have seen convincing proofs for two entirely different outcomes: when the economy grows, the growth of

---

[5] Voth, Peydró, and Doerr (2019).

[6] "For example, practically all of the studies that have been provided in support of Basel III assume that there is a cost to society when banks issue new equity, but these studies do not provide a satisfactory explanation of this assumption." (Admati & Hellwig, 2014, p. 180).

credit follows; but when credit, especially housing loans, grows fast, the likelihood of a recession looms overhead.[7] Therefore, even if the banks would restrain credit growth, that should not significantly affect the growth of the economy. Nevertheless, they would not do it.

Acting rationally, they should devise a strategy maximising shareholders' return. In the attached model,[8] we demonstrated that the capital requirement should not change the optimal pace of credit growth. The same portfolio would maximise returns on capital despite the size of the capital. The significant determinants of credit growth are required profitability of the portfolio, funding price, interest on loans, but most of all, risk expectations and the bank's prevailing share price.

For existing shareholders, it is better to accept a dilution of their shareholding than to waste the growth opportunity as long as the last unit of the underwritten shares enables the bank to generate more than average profit. So, rational shareholders would request management to adjust the bank's growth to this level, deciding on optimal pricing and appropriate risk acceptance to achieve it.

Banks are, of course, unable to do such fine-tuning in daily business. They set their targets based on the starting point, market evaluation and available resources. But implicitly, the optimisation mechanism in the background should nevertheless be the same.

The most important reason why the fast growth of the portfolio decreases the profitability of the bank is the riskiness of loans given in haste. The more ambitious your growth target is, the more risk you must accept.

On the other hand, if the desired loan growth would be slower, banks would be more cautious. Therefore, they would proportionally suffer fewer losses. There is an optimal growth path where banks accept the optimal expected credit risk and maximise expected profit. So, competent management would propose such growth dynamics despite the capital requirement.

Such a strategy would well serve the social responsibilities of banks. Faster growth un-proportionally increases the number of clients subsequently experiencing difficulties with loan repayment. Thus, with a bank's slower portfolio growth, fewer clients would find themselves in harm's way.

There is a difference between optimal loan growth in the situation of capital surplus and scarce capital. A bank with a capital surplus would be ready to accept more risk than a bank with scarce capital. Instead of requiring average profitability from marginal investments, it would expand credit as long as it expects positive returns. That difference should not visibly affect economic growth, but it would increase the share of non-performing loans in the portfolio.

The only situation in which the model does not enable the bank to achieve optimal portfolio is when there is no demand for shares at an acceptable price. In such a situation, the bank would not be able to grant loans. If that occurs in a single bank, it is a clear indication of its weakness and a signal for shareholders that they must do something decisively and quickly. However, if it occurs on a systemic level,

---

[7]Borio, Drehmann, and Xia (2018).

[8]Glossary—Model of optimisation of a bank's profitability.

threatening credit flow to the economy, it must be an alarm bell for supervisors. That is the signal that something went very wrong, and that it went wrong on the systemic level.

No one serious would claim today that capital is too expensive. On an efficient market, such as the EU capital market, if you reasonably ask for money, you will get it. The expected return depends on the financial results, the quality of the business plan and the issuer's credibility.

Throughout history, banks were typically traded above the book value. Prices fall below the book value only in times of crises. For example, in the US during the last 70 years, P/B was below one during the period of stagflation and immediately after 2009. Why are European banks so low priced after 7 years of uninterrupted economic growth? This question invites another, even more chilling question: what would be their value once a crisis would strike?

The issue of "the price of capital", when present on the systematic level, directly challenges the credibility of banking regulation and supervision. It questions the purposefulness of the present European regulatory environment. Finding the answer to this question is, as we will see, something that must be done unless we want to face the nasty nature of the asymmetry.

Besides its ability to supply the economy with credit, there is another source of potential distress banking could create. People usually perceive the generation of credit as the most significant influence of banking on the real economy. That is another misapprehension.

Loans are not the most critical product of banking. The most vital contribution of banking to the economy is in the area of payments. Despite its obvious importance, the payments go below the radar. They are taken for granted.

When you open a tap, you expect fresh and clean water to pour out of it. You also expect to pay your debt when you push plastic over the counter. That is not something worth wondering about or praise as long as it works. However, if it stops, it could be a nasty event. Fortunately, it is improbable to happen—at least in the entire economy. But partially it happens all the time.

Payments are supposed to function smoothly and flawlessly, and no one except a few specialists considers them as something important. We have forgotten how magical is the payment by merely pushing plastic or generating payment orders on the Internet. How cheap and convenient that is. Apart from being convenient, it is also the precondition for reaching and maintaining the present level of overall wealth. Without it, we would be much poorer.

So, any large-scale disruption in the functioning of payments is potentially disastrous. Getting back to non-banking means of payments: cash, gold or silver, or the worst of all, Bitcoin, would steeply decrease the maximally possible number of transactions. Those transactions create the GDP. Fewer payments would mean a smaller GDP. If the number of transactions was to drop significantly, the GDP would be much lower.

Every bank failure causes a notable disruption in the payment system. If the disruption reaches such intensity to hamper its function on the systematic level, as we already said, the consequences could be severe.

Payments are the most vital function of banks. The stability of banks is a precondition for the stability of the payment system. There is no alternative structure able to replace the payment system run by banks. The settlement of all stock exchange transactions goes through banks. The performance of all securities and derivatives depends on being cleared through banks. Insurance, mutual and pension funds heavily depend on banking. The banks are in charge of safekeeping and, last but not least, provide cash when needed.

Although some of the financial activities could be competition for banks in the ordinary course of business, their performance entirely depends on banks. Without operational banks, insurers, the stock exchange and investment funds cannot work.

The system of payments has a similar influence on the economy as, for example, an electric utility. If it stops, the flows in the economy will undoubtedly slow down, eventually even grind to halt. The sensitivity of the payment system is somewhat lower than the sensitivity of other functions of a bank. The reason for that is the critical importance of a functioning payment system for the economy, and the inability to create any workable alternative within a reasonable time. Therefore, it is hard to imagine the situation in which would a payment system of some systematically important bank stop and remain halted. The pressure on politics would be too high to withstand it, and they would find some solution soon. Nevertheless, even temporary stoppage could create serious problems.

Besides payment, banks have other essential functions in the financial system. When we say "provision of loans", we should not think only of large "one-off" loans such as investments or housing loans. Any disruption in providing such loans would be detrimental, but will not create a critical problem in the short term. Nonetheless, there are loans with the potential to deliver a vital blow quickly.

Today, modern life functions "on daily credit". Using facilities such as credit cards and overdrafts, families buy their daily provisions. Similar facilities enable companies to pay their obligations timely. Being deprived of such daily credit could create not only a severe problem for companies but also render a lot of people unable to buy food.

Bank failure stops or severely hampers all those activities. If we talk about large banks, such disruption is so massive and so unsettling that regulators reached a consensus that, to keep the asymmetry at bay, strategically important banks should not "fail disorderly". If they should fail, they are supposed to "fail orderly".

References

Admati, A., & Hellwig, M. (2014). *The bankers' new clothes*, Princeton University Press.

Borio, C., Drehmann, M., & Xia, D. (2018, December). The financial cycle and recession risk. *BIS Quarterly Review*.

Engler, H., & Essinger, J. (2000). *The future of banking*, Reuters Limited.

Jusufi, I. (2017, April). Albania's Transformation since 1997: Successes and failures. *Croatian International Relations Review*, *23*, 81–115.

Liaquat, A. (2009). *Lords of finance*, Penguin Books. ISBN1440697965.

Litan, R. E. (2019, November). https://www.bbvaopenmind.com. Retrieved from https://www.bbvaopenmind.com/en/articles/financial-innovation-a-balanced-look/.

Voth, H.-J., Peydró, J.-L., & Doerr, S. (2019, April 16). https://www.weforum.org. Retrieved from https://www.weforum.org/agenda/2019/04/how-failing-banks-paved-hitlers-path-to-power-financial-crisis-and-right-wing-extremism-in-germany-1931–33/.

Chapter 6
How Can Supervision Prevent Financial Crises?

Abstract Supervision cannot prevent market disturbances, potentially causing a crisis. It retains its impact through long-term measures making the banking system more resilient to externals shocks. This process consists of five steps: setting standards, licencing, oversight, rectifying action and firefighting. The supervision is the application of those five steps in a coordinated manner. Performed in the correct order, they enable banks to withstand shocks without causing them. However, the regulatory requirement should be so balanced that investment in bank shares remains attractive. Otherwise, banks cannot raise the capital and meet the requirements.

Now, let go back to our fairytale about oat and princes. Disregarding the fact that in those dark times there was no banking supervision, let us bring up the question: what banking supervision could do in this case to prevent a crisis?

In the described timeframe, there is only one correct answer—nothing. The emphasis is on the phrase: "in the described timeframe". All had happened between autumn and summer. During 9 months, the supervision could not become aware of the process, especially as the most critical part of the process was happening between merchants and producers. The merchants created an open position in their books big enough to produce a systematic impact, but no one oversaw the merchants.

Properly overseeing a single bank, including the production of all required reports, takes about 6 months. The oversight process reviews an earlier reporting date. So, supervisors would ideally have the reports from the first semester of the preceding year reviewed in few banks when the crisis would hit. In those reports, there would be no loans given for planting oat.

The fact that we asked the wrong question does not mean that the supervision cannot help in such cases. Its major task is not to fight present crises, but to decrease the likelihood of future ones, or at least to diminish their severity. In the short term, responsibility lay on bankers, their knowledge and common sense. Supervision does not run banks.

To fulfil its task, first and foremost, the regulator should always assume that there will be a future severe crisis. That is a one-sided bet: if the assumption is right, banks will be ready. If it is false, the supervisors will be successful.

D. Odak, *A Political Economy of Banking Supervision*,
https://doi.org/10.1007/978-3-030-48547-4_6

When we plan how to maintain financial stability, we should be aware that any strategy based on the assumption that a group of wise people would be able to recognise risks, warn and prevent a crisis each time, is naïve.[1]

As in our example, the mess starts when a particular shock invalidates important assumptions driving the actions of market participants. A shock always causes a sudden change in prices. The shock could be caused by objective reasons, such as supply shock or demand shock, as in the case we discussed.

Alternatively, we can perceive as a shock the correction of an earlier blunder, as it was the case with tulips, 1929, dot.coms or 2008.

Whatever the source of the shock, one-sided expectations of market participants could significantly elevate risks. That means if the majority of the participants on the market share the same outlook about future developments, and bet their money on it, the risk would be higher than in the case of independent, randomly distributed expectations of the participants. If expectations are independent and unbiased, the impact of any shock could be significantly cancelled, causing no systematic problems on the market and to the financial system.

The situation is quite different when there are correlated and biased expectations. People invest their money in line with their expectations. If they all invest in the same way, when a shock arrives, they all lose and very few people win. Then that build-up has the potential to explode into a crisis. A systematic crisis is more likely if both coincide: the shock and biased expectations.

We can define a shock as being "objective" if there was a rational reason to believe that events would go the other way, but those expectations nevertheless proved wrong. In our case, it was highly probable that the war would last for an extended period, and people invested accordingly. Then a sudden change occurred and created a shock. As things always change, some changes will inevitably be adverse to some people. Changes gain systematic importance only if they are harmful to many. Therefore, objective shocks are unavoidable, but they become a severe threat only if, before they occur, a significant part of the market participants shared a similar outlook.

Unfortunately, investors tend to share a similar outlook. This phenomenon has a fancy name—"herd instinct". When seeing others doing something and earning, people tend to imitate them. That is now even formalised and encouraged by "copy-cat" trading platforms such as eToro.[2] Therefore, significantly correlated expectations are also unavoidable. Knowing that, we can safely say that objective shocks will inevitably periodically hit correlated and biased markets. It is essential to prepare the system to deal with such situations once they appear.

Different from sudden and unannounced objective shocks, in the case of "market bubbles", it appears as they can be recognised and deflated before they burst. Wishful thinking! In reality, it seldom happens. Bubbles are correlated and biased expectations on steroids—a kind of mass psychologic phenomenon. In the ex-post researches, the creation of bubbles usually appears to be avoidable, only if everyone wouldn't

[1] "…predicting important discrete events may be a form of charlatanism. In perhaps 99 out of 100 cases, we are likely to be wrong." (Milanović, 2016).

[2] eToro (2019).

become so enthusiastic about the same thing at the same time. Nevertheless, they usually do.

The creation of a bubble started when a strange idea acquired widespread acceptance. As healthy, educated and decent people are involved, we could anticipate that it would be enough to say "People, that is stupid!" and clearly explain why, and the risk would disappear.

Life has taught us that that would not happen.[3] The misperception is usually so firmly embedded and has so strong a methodological and mathematical explanation that no one can convincingly argue otherwise. The outcome achieved by the best and brightest leaders in the economy ex-post sometimes appears as the work of someone mad as a hatter.

The distorted perception that initiated the inflation of the bubble is usually an expectation that the price of some assets will permanently grow. The recent price increase reinforced by a theory explaining why it is rational to expect future price growth supports such anticipation. For example, a shortage of oil will push its price up as civilisation will inevitably need more and more, and the reserves are limited. Monetary instability will motivate more and more people to invest in gold. The limited supply of bitcoin will increase its value when quantitative easing increases monetary supply. The price of tulip bulbs will permanently grow because... here we even miss an idea why.

Such a perception spreads supported by convincing historical records and apparently reasonable narrative. Finally, most of the people got convinced by it, and so much so that they were ready to bet everything on it.

It is just unbelievable what became an object of such delusions in the past. The most famous are tulip bulbs, but we should not forget the Louisiana marches, gold, websites, flats, shares, random bytes scattered in computers, spices, oil, shopping malls—a detailed list would be too long. We should not forget that each and every one of them had their convincing narrative sounding reasonable to contemporaries.

When the majority decides that the price of exactly that thing will grow, they would undoubtedly be right. People will start buying it, and the price must go up. The realised expectations convince the reluctant ones to join in, pushing the price towards the equilibrium price based on those assumptions.

Now comes the trick making the entire clutter appear entirely rational. If the asset is durable, and its assumed permanent rate of price growth is higher than the discount rate the investor uses, the equilibrium price is plus infinite.

Such calculation creates a firm mathematical foundation for lunacy. A commodity with such a marvellous outlook attracts much money and its price skyrockets. Doubt arises when within 3 months it achieves the price forecasted by the theory for the year 3206. Then someone notices that it occurred one thousand one hundred eighty-six years earlier than expected. Even if initial assumptions are all correct, the achieved price level is now supposed to stagnate for a millennium. When you take a calculator in your hands, delusion pops up, and suddenly the price from 3206 comes back to 2020.

[3]Posen (2006).

A piece of new information can cause such reversals, for example, snow melting in February 1637 and revealing fields in Holland planted with tulips instead of wheat and sunflower. Alternatively, a reversal could emerge out of the blue, as on 4 September 1929. But in the case of the bubble, we do not need a shock to burst it. Quite the opposite, we just need to come to our senses.[4] In a downturn, prices usually return to the level prevailing just a year or two earlier. Nothing happened, but short-term confusion. It would be just a joke when asymmetry would not jump in.

While prices grow, the economy experiences certain benefits, but not much. However, when prices fall, under certain conditions, it could trigger the dreaded "domino effect". The appearance of such effect is unpredictable and depends on a lot of factors. Significant is the size of the market affected by the prevalence of biased expectation and the interconnectedness of that market with the financial industry. It also depends on the exposure of the banks and financial firms to the affected commodity, directly or by financing others. For example, bitcoin was too small and too isolated from the financial industry to be any threat. Dot coms were large enough to activate a decent shockwave and bring the US economy below 1% of the growth rate.

When such misperceptions appear on the broad front on the stock market or housing market, we can be confident that we have a big hitter just waiting for a trigger. The trigger always comes, sooner or later. People eventually always come to their senses.

It is exceptionally challenging to stop such a process. To achieve that, you must remain convinced that you are right while everyone else is wrong. It requires incredible vanity to stay that confident!

Remaining convinced is difficult, but it is just the beginning. To stop the risk build-up effectively, you must find enough influential people thinking like you and willing to support you. As the perception is widespread, it is quite a demanding task.

Finally, as we will soon learn, if you manage to achieve your objective, that will be on your peril. You will only suffer insults and damage for doing it. Therefore, it is improbable to find so stubborn, smart and selfless people. For all those reasons, market bubbles cannot be timely recognised and deflated.[5]

Despite the repeating pattern, over and over again, it seems that the learning curve of the human race is quite flat in this respect. The forces inflating the bubble are so dominant in the run-up phase that, whoever stands in their way, would merely be shovelled aside. Politics, business, the press and the general public are working together in that phase, piling up dirt for the future landslide, so coordinated, eager and focused that no institution has the power and wisdom to stop them.

For example, president Hoover knew that the stock-exchange was overheated. If he had reacted when he came into office in March 1929, there could have been two

---

[4]The dynamic of the market would usually follow two laws declared by King (2017, p. 34):

"First law of financial crises: an unsustainable position can continue for far longer than you would believe possible."

"Second law of financial crises: when an unsustainable position ends it happens faster than you could imagine.".

[5]See glossary—Bubble.

possible outcomes: either the public would have ridiculed him, or if taken seriously, he would have caused a crisis 6 months earlier. Then everyone would blame him for the reckless behaviour, which had caused the crisis, and he would be politically dead. Therefore, the only reasonable thing for him to do was what he did—nothing.

An earlier crisis would indeed have been less violent than the one that happened 6 months later. The DJIA would have been about 20% lower, so the fall would have been gentler, with much fewer side effects. Maybe the process would have even become self-stabilising.

However, that is not the point. The point is that there would have been no crisis in September, and history would remember only the one in March caused by Hoover's recklessness. People would not know what they avoided. Hoover's award for saving the nation and the world from evil would be endless ridicule and expulsion from decent society.

People take public office to be respected, admired and, if possible, get rich. Preventing crisis in the late run-up phase would not serve well any of those purposes. The only thing you could reasonably do, if you thought you saw it coming, is to prepare an excuse. That means prepare documents proving that you were aware of the situation and gave a timely warning. But if doing so, you must be very cautious: the smallest possible number of people should see it, and it is better if no one understands it until the crisis hits.

Reluctance to intervene in perceived market distortions also has a fancy name—"inactivity bias". The inactivity is entirely in line with the dominant theory. According to the efficient market hypothesis, market bubbles are not possible. Price changes represent a reflection of rational expectations. The problem is that those expectations change. Relatively mild change in expectations, in case of a durable asset, especially in a low-interest environment, could cause a dramatic change in prices.

There is an additional problem. A formal one, but with severe consequences for our ability to understand reality. Theoretical distribution of random events, named Gauss curve, has 99.7% of all events within three standard deviations from the average. Observed economic distributions usually have about 99% od all observations within three standard deviations from average. Though distributions look very similar and the difference isn't significant for the majority of events, they become indeed different in so-called "tails" of the distributions, area of almost impossible events. The paradox is—further from the average we go, more significant the difference between theory and observed distributions is.[6] We found ourselves in the reality where events with calculated probability one in a hundred thousand years occur once in a hundred years or even more frequently. Impossible becomes unlikely but possible. As the methodology systematically underestimates the likelihood of an extreme event, theoretically rational expectations can easily prove practically irrational.

[6]"The LCTM risk model told them that the loss they incurred on one day at the end of August 1998 should have occurred once every 80 trillion years. It happened again the following week." (Engler & Essinger, 2000, p. 127).

In the end, a pathetic 0.7% difference makes such a mass. It made it almost impossible to distinguish between bubbles—i.e. irrational behaviour and unlikely but fundamentally sound change of the price.

We always distinguish them at the end. Only we cannot do it ex-ante.

Therefore, sophisticated fancy footwork of "macro-prudential supervision", the banking supervision activity tasked with the prevention of crises by recognising timely market distortions, would unavoidably face "inactivity bias". Furthermore, rare occasions when they will overcome the bias and intervene on the market will earn them a bad name and reputation. As we have seen in the Hoover example, saving the world is not a good policy when people see only the damage you did, not the one that could have been if you did not act. On the other hand, not saving the world, though it was your job to do it, will not make you look any better.

So, "This time is different" will continue to rule. Despite its undeserved notoriety, the phrase is factually correct. Every time is different, while impossible is only unlikely. Such an environment makes preemptive actions extremely difficult and risky. The inactivity bias is a perfectly rational reaction.

Now back to the question: If it cannot prevent crises, how can banking supervision be used to decrease the likelihood and possible impact of a crisis?

We started from the assumption that there will be a future crisis, and that it would be severe. Since it will come, it is essential to decrease its impact. The reaction of the financial sector frequently distinguishes a shock from a crisis. The more the banks get hurt by the shock, the more likely it will cause a significant crisis. Therefore, preparing banks to act as a shock absorber, not as an amplifier, is key for decreasing the probability of a major disaster.

To effectively absorb losses caused by a shock, banks need their own funds. So, we should make them have it, and have enough of it. If banks absorb the shock and continue their regular activity, there will be no subsequent banking crisis, and the crisis in the real sector would most likely be relatively mild.

To prepare banks for such events, regulators and banks maintain continuous communication processes. We will break down the processes in five steps:

The first step is setting standards. Regulators design the so-called "regulatory requirements". They are compulsory for all banks under their jurisdiction. Banking regulation, based on the banking law, sets those requirements. The design of the regulation should achieve two primary objectives: the requirements should keep banks firm in the face of undesirable developments; however, they should be reasonable enough to motivate shareholders to invest in the banks' shares. The reason is simple: if the shareholders do not buy the shares, the banks cannot acquire capital and meet the requirements.

Based on the requirements, the supervision prepares a report about each bank. The report customises regulatory requirements for the situation in each institution. Such a document is complex, but for practical purposes, it boils down to the amount of required capital. The required amount cover recognised risks the bank has already accepted, depending on its risk profile. The risk profile depends on the bank's portfolio structure and business model, but also on the quality of management and internal controls.

Risk weights are an essential part of the process. They are multiples that multiply the assets of each bank. The sum of all such multiples is called risk-weighted assets. Each risk weight indicates the regulator's opinion about the risk associated with a particular asset.[7]

We know from experience that each asset does not bear the same risk. Therefore, regulators reasoned, different assets do not require the same amount of capital. For example, cash or money in the central bank carries no risk. It is not likely that such receivables will decrease its nominal value.

On the other hand, we all know that debtors are likely to fail when repaying loans. They frequently pay less or later than contracted. Transforming this knowledge into risk weights, the weight of credit without collateral is 100%, while the risk of cash is 0%.

Based on the structure of a bank's portfolio, and its risk profile, the regulator determines the amount of own funds the bank should exceed at all times. The adjustment of the bank's risk profile evaluates the quality of its internal controls, i.e. the bank's ability to recognise and manage risks.

The second step is licencing: the regulator should authorise every bank, every principal shareholder, and every key manager. Getting a license means that the government trusts that person enough to accept an unlimited financial liability by guaranteeing her or his business operation. So, although it appears as a routine, it is, in fact, a great honour to be licenced to do banking.

The third step is an oversight. By strict oversight, the regulator checks whether a bank's reports are accurate and realistic. Overseers check if the bank reported capital correctly, i.e. whether the bank's assets and liabilities have been adequately valued. That requires checking both: accounting policies and accounting practices. Furthermore, overseers review risk management rules and practices, their adequacy and implementation. Based on that review, the bank's risk profile is determined.

The bank accepts risks. It daily accepts credit, market, operational and concentration risk.[8] Though credit risk is the usual suspect for a failed bank, market and concentration risk also took a heavy toll. Sometimes they act directly, hurting the bank's balance sheet, and sometimes indirectly, harming clients and therefore increasing credit risk. In terms of operational risk, hardly any bank has ever collapsed just because of it, but it could be a critical contributing factor for difficulties with other risks. An excellent example of such a case was Barings. It failed due to market risk, but only because of inadequate operational procedures enabling its uncontrolled accumulation.

The fourth step is taking rectifying action. Whenever overseers observe that a bank deviates from regulation or good practices, the regulator gives orders or guidelines to the bank, and the bank should adhere to them. By adhering to the orders, the bank maintains compliance with the regulation.

The fifth step is firefighting. Once it becomes evident that the bank cannot or will not establish compliance, the regulator applies firefighting strategies, either to

---

[7]Glossary—Risk weights.

[8]Glossary—Concentration risk.

reorganise the bank in a way to achieve full compliance or to remove it from the market. To accomplish that, a broad spectrum of tools is available. If need be, the supervisor is allowed to take full control over the bank by replacing management and supervisory boards. The assembly is the bank's only decision-making body supervisors cannot displace. The law protects private property. Therefore, owners should keep their prerogatives as long as they are owners.

Another means of firefighting is dealing with systemic risks when they become apparent. The systemic risk could present itself in several forms, from a fluctuation of the exchange rate or the interest rates on the market, accumulation of bad loans, credit crunch, to an outflow of deposits from an individual bank or the system as a whole.

Supervision is the application of all those five steps together in a coordinated manner. People sometimes focus too much on oversight, perceiving it as the key part of the supervision. Oversight is just a segment; not even the most important one. It is more important to make reasonable rules.

Therefore, regulation is the key to efficient supervision. Supervision has a broad range of tools available for establishing the compliance of a bank. But those tools are ineffective if the bank is compliant. Therefore, if the rules allow something the supervision does not like, the same rules cannot offer the tools to prevent it.

That is the reason why creating rules is more important than monitoring them. In each act of licencing, overseeing, taking rectifying action or firefighting, a bank has a legal remedy available. So, if rules are unclear or improper, the supervisory action could be cancelled or changed by a court. If the regulation allows excessive risks, supervisors have no tool to address those risks.

While looking at those rules and procedures, one can get a feeling that there is a conflict between banks and supervisors. Nevertheless, banks belong to shareholders, and there is certainly no conflict between diligent shareholders and supervisors. Supervisors are necessarily and naturally on the shareholders' side.

The logic is simple: as long as the shareholders' investment is safe, and they earn well, supervisors are calm. On the other hand, shareholders should be happy to have one more pair of eyes looking at the management, just in case.

Despite that symmetry of interest, shareholders feel uneasy about the supervision. Some shareholders are worried about regulatory overhang with a potentially strong impact on the value of their assets. Simplifying and fixing rules for an extended period should make shareholders happy. Shareholders must give something in return—in this case, some more capital.

Other shareholders are aggressive towards regulators suspecting that their banks will prove to be worthless if evaluated using the "gone concern" methodology. In those cases, we cannot talk about conflict, but we can only speak about the mission of supervision. Its purpose is to prevent moral hazard. Therefore, supervision should resolve the conflict either by convincing those shareholders that they are wrong or by proving them right. Either solution is a good one.

When we mentioned more capital, such a request should not be excessive. The regulator should require a bank to provide enough capital to protect itself against "manageable losses". That means against any development causing significant but bearable losses. In chaotic situations, such as wars, revolutions or comet strike, equity alone cannot protect the functioning of a bank. No amount of money would help in those circumstances, so it makes no sense requiring banks to prepare for them.

Now we move out of the realm of empirical evidence. The reason is that we are not any more dealing with risk, but with uncertainty or better said ambiguity. It means that the proper approach is a guess instead of analysis. We will later, during the discussion about the applicability of the econometric models (Chap. 9), go deeper into the subject. For the time being, we will just say that ambiguity is ambiguous. Therefore, we need to calibrate requirements in such a way that they make a bank robust enough to withstand manageable losses and go on with regular business or to be saved at a reasonable cost. It means to remain solvent at the peak of the loss.

A guess is that the upper limit for a percentage of loss of the credit portfolio representing "manageable losses" is about 15%. That is not a percentage of non-performing loans, but write-off at the end of the collection process as a percentage of total loans. If we assume loss given default (LGD) of 33%, then it means we talk about the NPL ratio of 45%. Preparing for worse than that is probably too much.[9]

Therefore, by requiring risk-weighted capital adequacy of 20%,[10] we are reasonably sure that the bank would withstand such losses. Not only withstand, but also remain solvent. That should be enough for most of the banks to survive any shock, or to get an affordable bailout. Such amount of the capital would not be enough for a bank to survive what happened to regional US banks during "dust bowl" years. Still, it would enable them to comfortably weather losses that occurred to US banks in 2008–9, or European banks in the period 2012–2015.

Besides the capital adequacy requirement, regulation should have the leverage requirement. The new version of the Basel Accord recognised that. It also defined the minimum leverage at 3%. Such resilience is not very impressive![11]

Leverage is the measure of the percentage of capital in total assets of the bank. For example, a 10% leverage means that the bank finances 10% of all its assets with capital. A 100% leverage means that the bank has no liabilities, only equity. The other extreme is 0%. It means that the bank has no capital at all. The rule of thumb is: the lower the capital, the higher the rate of return.

In the Basel framework, leverage is only a supportive measure, not a major one. The risk-sensitive rules are the main line of protection, and leverage is only an alternative in the case that a bank operates at extremely low risk. This measure is needed as a bank can pursue the strategy to invest its assets in government bonds and similar items with low or zero risk weight. Such an approach could cumulate market risks and concentration risk while risk-weighted assets, and consequently, the capital requirement could remain very low. We can even think of portfolio with 0

[9]Glossary: The resilience of the alternative regulatory structure.

[10]Standardised approach.

[11]"There is no legitimate reason for the proposed Basel III requirements to be so outrageously low. These requirements reflect the political impact that the banks have had on the policy debate" (Admati & Hellwig, 2014, p. 179).

risk weight. Without leverage, the bank would be allowed to operate a vast balance sheet while retaining only legally minimal capital.

Such balance sheets nevertheless contain market risks. If the bank accounts for the portfolio "mark to market", then it is exposed to the market price of bonds, while with the accounting based on "historic costs", it is exposed to interest rate risk. Those market risks would usually be volatile during a crisis, and they can quickly deplete the bank's capital.

Furthermore, leverage provides confidence. While clients of the bank need analysis to understand the full meaning of the capital adequacy ratio, the meaning and comparability of leverage are straightforward. Therefore, if one wants to compare jurisdictions, the easiest way to judge their resilience is by comparing average leverage. According to the World Bank, the average for the world is somewhat over 10%. Being close to that figure signalise that the banking in the jurisdiction is reasonably safe.

References

Admati, A., & Hellwig, M. (2014). *The bankers' new clothes*, Princeton University Press.

Engler, H., & Essinger, J. (2000). *The future of banking*, Reuters Limited.

eToro. (2019). www.etoro.com. Retrieved from https://www.etoro.com.

King, M. (2017). *The end of alchemy: Money, banking and the future of the global economy*, W W Norton & Company. ISBN 0393353575.

Milanović, B. (2016). *Global inequality*, Belknap Press, An Imprint of Harvard University Press. ISBN 978-0674984035.

Posen, A. S. (2006, March). Why Central Banks should not burst bubbles. *International Finance*, 109–124.

Chapter 7
What Should Supervision Do?

Abstract The supervision decides how much capital each bank needs. If new capital does not bring pro-rata new income, the return on the existing shares will decrease. Their value will fall. That is the reason why an increase in the capital never happens without compulsive regulation. A short trip through the accounting mirror presents a wonderland where the meaning of the word real is unreal, supervisors are white knights, and mighty accounting magic keeps zombie banks wandering around alive. The answer to the question: "What should supervision do?" is "Whatever it takes to make sure that the bank has required capital (and some more on top of it) and enough liquidity to timely meet all its obligations."

The supervision decides how much capital each bank needs. The amount of required capital determines how profitable the investment in a bank's shares would be. The more capital the bank has, the lower the return per unit would be. Banks mostly earn on other peoples' money.

In the case of 0% leverage, if the bank is profitable, the yield on each invested euro is infinitely high. So, everyone would gladly invest 0 EURO in its shares. A bank with 0% leverage is fun while it lasts, but it is susceptible to losses. The slightest loss will make it fail.

Quite the opposite, the higher the leverage, the more robust the bank. If, for example, a bank operates only with its own money with 100% leverage—it won't be very profitable, but it just can't fail. The bank has no obligations it could fail to meet.

Of course, it is just a theoretical example. A bank cannot perform its major tasks if it does not take deposits. Therefore, the ratio should be lower than 100%. Judging how much is high enough to retain robustness, but small enough to make an investment in the bank's shares attractive—this is the fine art of rulemaking in banking.

The reason why regulation insists that banks should have a certain amount of capital is the fact that banks are limited liability corporations. Therefore, from the shareholders' perspective, investment is never negative. If the real value of a bank is negative, from the shareholders perspective, it is zero. Only the government and

D. Odak, *A Political Economy of Banking Supervision*,
https://doi.org/10.1007/978-3-030-48547-4_7

uninsured creditors are worried by negative figures, as we said while discussing the moral hazard.

Of course, zero investment means that shareholders face no risks, and the rate of return on investment is infinitely high. Therefore, they would not care about risks if there is any profit in sight. The risks nevertheless exist, and they burden the bank's creditors and government instead of the shareholders. Under those circumstances, risk-taking becomes a typical example of an externality—a hidden one.

Preventing such a situation on behalf of the government, supervision takes the precaution. It requires banks to have a certain amount of capital.

When the supervision requires a bank to obtain additional funds, shareholders must decide how to do that. They should either invest more own money or ask others to invest their money. An alternative course of action could also be decreasing the required capital by reducing risk-weighted assets.[1]

Shareholders do not like giving more money or letting others do so. The reason is called dilution. Investors in new capital buy new shares. Consequently, if new capital does not bring in new income, the return on the existing shares will decrease. Their value will fall.

Shareholders also do not like it if a bank implements the policy of decreasing capital requirements. It could be harmful to a bank.

Whenever possible, shareholders will opt for an alternative solution—issuing so-called convertible or subordinated bonds. These bonds are, in the case of bankruptcy, paid before capital but after other creditors of the bank. Therefore, they can be recognised as equity by the regulator, provided that they meet certain preconditions.

Subordinated and convertible debt eligible to be included in equity is more expensive than senior or guaranteed debt. Still, shareholders would opt for that solution as long as the interest on that loan is lower than the expected profit before tax.

Profit is taxable while the interest paid is tax-deductible. So, if the profit tax rate is 20% and there is no dividend tax, the cash outflow for a bank when paying an 80 EUR dividend is equal to paying 100 EUR interest. That creates a situation where shareholders can be quite generous with providers of subordinated debt and still earn handsomely.

An additional benefit is that providers of the additional or "tier 2" capital have no voting rights and they do not participate in the decision-making. Therefore, too much reliance on tier 2 again opens the moral hazard risk. If shareholders' or tier one capital is too small, then they could take risks on behalf of the providers of tier 2 capital. To prevent that, the regulator also decides on the minimal amount of tier 1 capital the bank must have in its liabilities.

As stated before, if a bank doubles its equity, it will cut the shareholders' return on existing shares almost by half. If the return on investment is 10%, then equity is increased by issuing the same number of new shares, the yield will drop to slightly above 5%. For the shareholder, it is better to take that amount as a loan approved as tier 2 capital having an interest of 5%. As it is tax-deductible, shareholders will still

[1]Glossary: Delaveraging.

earn over 6%. Nevertheless, for the shareholders, the best would be to do nothing. Then, they would make 10%.

That is the reason why an increase in capital would never happen without compulsive regulatory action. Even when it materialises, it is usually optimised for existent portfolio and planned growth with minimal buffers. As explained earlier, in the existing environment, there is not enough market pressure on a bank to justify a capital increase above the minimum. Therefore, minimal regulatory requirements should make sure that the bank fulfilling them is tough enough to survive prospective shocks. To weather the storm, the bank needs the real capital, not only declared one.

Request to have "the real capital" could sound like an apparent and reasonable requirement for anyone not familiar with banking. We all know that real money means the money you can show, either as cash, as a number on the account, or a liquid asset worth such amount. Well, we think we know it.

Beware! We are now passing through the accounting looking glass. The meaning of the word "real" is somewhat vague, even rude on this side. Rituals of mistic and magic hereby blur the reality. Those rituals take place, not beyond the mirror, but flickering computer screens. In such a dangerous world where dark sorcery freely runs amok, the safety of ordinary people lays in the hands of the bold knights. The knights are standing on the last stand—desperately trying to defend the meaning of the reality.

Let us start the description of that noble fight with a speech their leader made on the eve of the battle. He said in a thundering voice.

"Here we stand, and we shall here rise or fall, but we should not yield. We would need all of our bravery and strength, our heart and mind to defend the reality till our last breath. The truth of financial reporting. The dark forces of misrepresentation are swarming toward us, while our wavering allies, accountants and auditors, silently change sides. If our line breaks and we run away, dark forces will take the whole world from this side of the mirror, and will wait for the first crack in it to surge to the other side and overwhelm it.

Therefore, prepare your non-performance searching arrows, value adjusting slicing swords and procedural spears, shine legal armour and get ready for the battle. We will find non-performance, slice its value to real and make sure that procedures are straight and sharp!

We will carry in front of us holly grail of realistic valuation to protect and inspire us in the most daring moments."

Then one of the knights standing in the first row shouted: "Why are we standing here alone? Where are shareholders whose ass we try to cover? Where is public whose money we try to save? Where are the politicians promising to the people that our fight will be successful?"

The leader replied in stout, while somewhat quieter voice: "The leaders of the dark side enchant the shareholders. Shareholders even hired brave samurais, auditors, to protect them from the dark side. Unfortunately, they changed side. Now shareholders hate us, believing that we are their enemies. The public does not understand what are we doing. They do not care until it is too late. They are also disappointed in us as we do not protect bank customers well! Politicians inspire us with their speeches, but every time they end the speech warning that no violence should occur, dark wizards should not be hurt and no value adjusted!".

Then he thundered again: "Nevertheless, whatever comes our way, we will stand and fight! Others will later understand!".

"Easy, boss, easy", said small knight standing in the last row, in somewhat shabby and rusty armour. "There is no question we should find a way to defend reality. It is important, indeed. We all know that. You also know that we do not have a faint heart and are not afraid of danger and effort. But what good will we make if we all fall here? Let us recognise the reality of our fight for reality—everyone is against us, or they do not care. If we stay here, we can win a battle or two. However, even if we prevail, the new will always come. Politicians will then change side. They will see us spreading the violence! Jointly, they will eventually surround and subdue us. We will be helpless and powerless to do anything. It is better if we pretend that we joined them as a reliable ally. Then we can change them from inside, bringing them gradually back to the side of reality. No one knows better than us how surreal the reality can be. Our enemies have no chance against us in that game if we are flexible. Politicians are right. No violence is needed!".

The leader stood there in his shining white armour. The shadow of ambiguity went across his face as he opened his mouth and took a breath to speak, but no sound left his mouth. He stood motionless with open mouth for a few seconds, while murmur between knights grew.

We will end this story here. We will never learn how it ended. Maybe it is better that way. Most important moral of the story is that the holy grail of banking supervision is its ability to impose realistic valuation. Impose means to enforce, if needed. Without such capability, supervision is weak.

Banking is all about accounting. In a bank, there is nothing but accounts. There are accounts and transactions between accounts. Nothing else matters. Even the shiny building with those stereotype pillars in front is rented. The bank leases branches and computers—nothing tangible matters in banking. Banking is a pure accounting idealism. One who cannot deal with accounts, cannot deal with banks.

A bank is a virtual world of interconnected accounts. Those accounts stand firm on the bedrock of a bank's net value. Capital guarantees that all numbers registered on the accounts can be paid timely and in full. If the capital disappeared, those accounts became some kind of ghosts: they seemed to be there, but there was nothing inside. You still have money on your account, but the bank cannot pay you unless someone else gives it credit.

The nature of the banking business makes it very unlikely that all deposits will be repaid on maturity. That feature enables a bank to exist forever in such a state; let us call it a zombie. A zombie bank with ghost accounts is not something that can be seen only in horror movies; we occasionally have them around us.[2] Only we don't recognise them until it's too late.

---

[2]Onaran (2017).

We already learned that, as long as other banks believe that the bank is OK, it is OK. Keeping the trust of other banks requires retaining the idea of capital. To continue its existence, the zombie bank must do it. The idea of capital is money declared, although the bank cannot show it if required to do so. That capital is not "real" if we apply earlier mentioned standards. However, the term "real" is questionable in banking. As payment of all deposits is never required, the existence of the capital is always a speculative assumption. Luckily, we are still on the other side of the mirror. Therefore, let us use some magic to solve the problem.

As any powerful magic, this one requires certain rituals. Whenever people perform those rituals properly, the bank will always have enough other peoples' money for all practical purposes. No one will notice that the bank has no own cash. As always with zombies, performing magic the right way is critical for the zombie to walk safely in broad daylight.

To be successful, magic must be so powerful that even people in the bank believe in it. Where could such a powerful spell be cast?

International Accounting Standards sometimes appear like magic. For example, there are different ways to account for assets and liabilities. Each of them gives a different result. For example, let us compare the historical cost and the mark-to-market method.

In mark-to-market, accounting uses an item's prevailing market price as its accounting value: the amount we can reasonably expect to get for it if we decide to sell it here and now.

Quite differently, when using the historical cost method, the bank accounts for all items as if they were worth as much as the firm has invested in them. The accounting value of the investment is independent of its present market price.

The portfolio in a bank's treasury is predominantly "mark-to-market", while in commercial divisions, mainly "historical cost" is used.

Sometimes, the consequences are quite strange. For example, if the Treasury has 100 million EUR of 10-year government bonds, and a market interest rate increase of 1%, the portfolio's accounting value decreases by almost 10 million EUR. The bank's net worth will drop by that amount. On the other hand, if the bank classified the same portfolio as held to maturity in the commercial banking division of the same bank, i.e. by applying historical-cost-based accounting, nothing would happen. So, with everything being equal, at the year-end, depending on whether the same assets hold the treasury or the corporate division of the same bank, the bank's net value would differ by 10 million EUR.

But there is no magic yet! Those accounting rules, though they could appear illogical to someone not trained in accounting, do not allow any magic. You must place your bets and hold firm. So, in the "historical cost" portfolio, you will recognise neither loses nor wins as the asset's market price changes. They will gradually materialise through profit and loss accounts until maturity.

The reasoning behind it is clear: if you are not willing to sell those assets now or before maturity, their present market price is irrelevant to you—only the expected cash flow of the instrument matters. If you intend to sell it, then the situation is quite the opposite, only the market value matters. The cash flow attached is irrelevant.

Still, there is a place in the balance sheet offering ample space for interpretation of the rules. The accounts of the assets whose counterparties do not pay timely. We will call those assets non-performing assets, usually loans.

The ability to do magic with those assets is very convenient. Space for the magic appears timely. Most frequently, banks experience losses when their debtors become unable to pay. In those times, non-performing assets suddenly increase. If there is a way to ignore those insolvent debtors, the bank would retain its equity and would not have problems even though its debtors obviously have them.

We even have a convenient measure of the intensity of magic—it is called "Texas ratio". The ratio measures the share of the net value of non-performing loans in the equity of a bank. The higher it is, the bank invests more equity in non-performing assets.

Now, let's go back to the technology behind the magic. If before the establishment of the non-performance, the non-performing assets were accounted based on historical cost, the accounting rules for their valuation are now defined by IFRS 9. The substance of the standard is that the value of the non-performing asset is no more recognised based on historical costs. The item's accounting value should become the net present value of its expected cash flow. Net present value means that expected future cash flows must be discounted with the applicable interest rate—the later it comes, the less it is worth.

Finally, the word "expected" carries a mighty magic wand! The future is always murky. Guess how much someone will pay in the future, although he does not pay now! The true answer to that question hides in the deepest shadows of the murky water. Whatever you say, no one can prove you wrong.

The accounting standard requires management to guess. Auditors cannot prove such guess wrong. If supervisors are not allowed to intervene, it becomes a beautiful and safe place for doing magic.

Here collateral comes into play. Future cash flow equals the market value of the collateral reduced by the expected cost of its liquidation. The bank can now create a hall of smoke and mirrors. The amount of the future cash flow is equal to the assumed price they will sell the collateral for, sometime in the future. To evaluate it you need two guesses: how much and when.

So, let's propose two answers: "For the evaluated amount" and "After two years". Then next year the bank again says: we will sell it in 2 years, then a year later again after 2 years. Each year the cash flow forecast runs away another year into the future. When the supervisor asks the bank how many mortgaged flats it sold this year, and the answer is: "None. We cannot sell those flats. People live in them. What do you take us for?"

OK, and how many non-performing mortgages do you have?

About 5.000.

And what is your average planned collection period?

Two years.

The assets were evaluated based on the estimated cash flow. The management makes the estimation. Auditors only confirm that, assuming the estimation is correct, the accounting value calculation is accurate. Supervisors were not supposed to interfere—and magic was born!

Besides non-performing loans, there are other possible places to do magic—for example, the valuation of derivatives, primarily illiquid ones. Then, the valuation of software or infamous goodwill. Though those are potential places for magic, they are much more visible and demanding than NPL-s. Therefore, non-performing loans are the best place to search for magic in a bank.

In banking, it is crucial to make the numbers fit. Here they do not. Without the power of supervisors to challenge the accounts, they will continue to defy the rules of mathematics as we learned them in primary school. The first indicator of the presence of a zombie bank are numbers that do not fit.

Now, it is time to leave accounting wonderland behind and come back to our usual side of the mirror.

Formally fulfilling regulatory requirements is one side of the story, while the quality of the fulfilment is quite another. If supervisors wish to ensure a quality fulfilment of its demand, it must make oversight and then convince the bank to accept reality as the supervisor sees it.

That is not an easy task. A resolution requesting adjustment of assets value is a legal act. Therefore, it must withstand a legal challenge. To do it, the supervisor first must prove that the accounting valuation is not accurate. Until now, we all understand that it is a tricky task. What is the realistic value of non-existent cash flow that could possibly begin sometimes in the future? I can claim "a lot", while you disagree. Only time will prove who is right.

However, we must determine its value today. Otherwise, we do not know how much capital the bank has. Here we cannot think about any sophisticated method. We talk about guessing, and most of all, we talk about who is in charge to imagine. If guesses are different, whose opinion will prevail?

There are two possible answers, and only one can be the right one:

- In case of doubt, the management should determine the value of the assets, as it has the mandate given by shareholders to do so; or
- In case of doubt, the supervisors should evaluate the assets, as they got such mandate from the parliament to protect the public interest.

Those are two possible approaches. In the EU first answer prevails, while in the rest of the world second. The first answer requires the supervisor to undertake more work and legal risk to impose value adjustment to a bank.

Giving the supervisor authority to guess is necessary, but not enough to ensure financial stability. Systematic approach and standardisation of the supervisory methodology are also required. Sometimes supervisors are afraid to press banks hard to rectify the situation. They appear more afraid of the banks' possible failure than the bankers are. Bankers see it and use it to their advantage. To their advantage does not mean the shareholders' benefit.

Avoidance of such a situation requires a highly standardised methodology of supervision. Also, the people in charge of certain banking groups should periodically rotate. It is not good if they feel responsible for the findings from the past oversights. It is also useful if they know that someone else will be in charge of the next control. If they are responsible for the same bank for an extended period, supervisors could be afraid to press the bank hard. The bank, if it fails, would collapse right on their head.

In such a situation, supervisors face the following dilemma: "If I don't look, I can't see, and I don't know what to do. Things can develop in a very wrong way, and someone will come and ask me why I did not look. If, on the other hand, I look, I can see it. If I see and do not act, I am responsible even more then in the first case. If I move, my action can bring me into big trouble. To look or not to look, that is the question!".

In such a situation, a kind of peeking strategy is probably the best fit. To apply it properly, supervisors needed a new approach and new tools supporting such an approach.

For example, supervisors will be less afraid to look if the supervisors would not be allowed to order an adjustment of the bank's accounts. It would be very convenient. Without requesting a value adjustment, supervisors cannot say that the bank does not have enough capital.

Checking whether the accounts are realistic was their main job for decades. However, with a new concept, things should be different. Instead of such a particularistic and obsolete approach, the regulator should promote a new holistic and forward-looking methodology. Management and auditors are in charge of such technical matter as evaluation and accounts, while supervisors are responsible for getting the holistic picture of a bank. That means they should focus on the whole bank and group, instead of its dissected parts, for example, individual accounts. Such a holistic approach enables the supervisor to understand the bank as a living organism, not as a mere sum of its parts. That brings supervision to an entirely new level.

Having this formula in place, now they can look, they can even see, but sorry, they aren't supposed to act. Oh, pardon! They are. They can state supervisory expectations that the management will change specific procedures and ensure its application within a given timeframe. If management does it, supervisors will be happy. If management does not do it, supervisors will be unhappy. Then they will write another expectation.

However, it is not so important, as it is hard to order a change of procedure for guessing. Guessing is in the core of the process, and obviously cannot be procedurally solved.

There are alternative remedies for dealing with too brave banks. For example, if supervisors find that a bank overvalues its assets, then supervisors should increase the bank's capital requirement. That is theoretically an excellent remedy. Practically, when a bank values its assets at will, and it already uses that freedom with impunity, it has any regulatory requirement within easy reach. Besides, the supervisory judgment in the SREP process is constrained, while the bankers' imagination is famous for the lack of any constraints.

Such an approach solves the issue of potential bank failure. If the supervisor is not allowed to decrease the bank's capital, the bank can't fail. But still, without the ability to fail a bank and to issue the order to change valuation, how can supervisors influence bankers?

They found a convenient tool for that purpose! Its name is the stress test. The stress test finds an excellent way around the most demanding point in the oversight process—identification of non-compliance and technical insolvency. It recognizes instead possible future non-compliance. So, instead of failing a bank, a supervisor establishes a "potential future shortage of own funds in case of stress," the recommendation is to "precautionarily re-capitalize." That is called "capital guidance." If the findings of the stress test are accurate, and if the bank follows the guidance, it will not fail. So, the supervision will fulfil its purpose.

However, there are some loose ends. First is the methodology of the test. It investigates what will happen in a specific case. If GDP will fall by 2%, causing an increase in unemployment of 5%, what would happen to the bank? The analysed scenarios describe events in details to ensure uniform conduct of banks during the test.

If the bank will not become insolvent in this scenario, are there maybe some other scenarios which would render bank insolvent? The scenario usually does not explore what will happen in an unlikely case as it is an outbreak of a new virus in China. It would be more accurate to say that the bank will not fail in the case of the stress described in the stress test, providing that the bank did proper calculations in the stress test. In the case of different stress or wrong calculations, who could say?

That brings us to the fact that the banks themselves perform the stress test. It means that the banks get stress scenarios, and then they run their portfolio through such a situation, calculating the consequences. Supervisor supervises what they do. We can only wonder how the bank will recognise that it can be in problems in 2 years if its corporate governances do not realise it is in difficulties today.

Furthermore, there is an issue of disclosure of the results of individual banks. The stress test is a speculative exercise checking "what could be if would be". If supervisors run the stress test, its aggregate results can undoubtedly be published. The disclosure of individual results is methodologically questionable.

Accounting disclosure could be misleading without very detailed methodological explanation. Stress test disclosure is potentially misleading despite all detailed methodological explanation.

Also, enforcement of the capital guidances can be a problem. Sometimes it could be impractical or even impossible for the bank to comply with it. So, what could be done in such situations? The bank is, after all, for the time being compliant.

Stress tests are excellent and useful exercises. They should be performed by banks frequently, and their results incorporated in plans and risk management documents of the bank. Nevertheless, they are primary bank management, not a supervisory tool. Banks should adapt them to their situation, and instead of a single specific case, they should cover a wide range of circumstances.

The supervision can also use the stress test to check if some specific risk represents an excessive threat to the system. Nonetheless, it would be reckless to turn it into the principal supervisory tool. It is even more doubtful whether granular disclosure of individual bank's performance on the stress test respects request for the level playfield. Such disclosure is perceived as supplement and reinforcement for disclosure of the capital. It is not! It only demonstrates how the bank alone evaluates how will the bank's balance sheet react in the one specific case, and under the unrealistic assumption of a static balance sheet.[3] The publishing could induce the unjustified decrease or increase of the pressure of the market discipline on individual banks.

Stress test checks what would happen in a single specific case, while capital is available in any case. Even in the most frequently the most dangerous one—the unforeseen. For example, in this unlikely virus case.

The stress test is a useful and legitimate supervisory tool, and the assumption of the static balance sheet is sound methodology. It, as a tool, has its limitations, and it can only supplement classic oversight.

When the supervisor publishes individual results of the stress test and capital guidances, it appears almost if the supervisor intends to use the market as a mean of pressure on the banks. The law gives supervisors their information advantage by authorising them to access any document in the bank. The purpose of the advantage is recognition and rectification of weaknesses in individual banks without the involvement of market discipline.

In the case of a stress test, the communication strategy made a kind of half turn. Instead of using the information advantage to intervene, supervisors would deliver stress test results to the public. The public will then exercise the market discipline on banks, hopefully achieving what the supervision desires.

It is a possible approach, still much riskier and more complicated than a direct approach. It faces a question of all questions: what will happen to such transparency if supervision stumbles over something big? Everybody guesses the answer to that question, and the guess influences the impact of the publication.

Whichever tools supervisor use, it should keep in mind that the entire process of checking and increasing capital, besides obviously growing the bank's resilience, creates one crucial precondition for the efficient bank's corporate governances. The firm beliefs of shareholders in the value of their bank is one of the cornerstones of the bank's stability. Firm belief means they are convinced that the bank is worth more then its accounts say. Besides, they should be confident that the significant amount remains even in the case of the bank's liquidation. We call such valuation "gone concern"—the value of a firm without the benefit of its business.

If the shareholders and potential investors in the shares believe so, the supervisor's job is more comfortable. Knowing that they have a lot of money to lose, they will do everything to keep it. The only real supervisory concern is making sure that they believe it and to check whether they behave accordingly.

The situation is much trickier when a bank is valuable to its shareholders only in the "going concern" valuation. This means that shareholders consider the business, but not the assets of the bank as relevant. If they believe that the value in the "gone

---

[3]The assumption that the management will do nothing to offset adverse developement.

concern" is—gone, it is from their perspective the same as if the bank has no capital. They will have a strong tendency towards the moral hazard.

To be consistently successful, the supervisor should convince the shareholders about the value of their institution. The easiest way to do that is making them believe that the bank's financial statements are conservative. Conservative means that they can reasonably expect more money from the assets held by the bank than their accounting value is today. The easiest way to achieve that is by ensuring conservative accounting—in the case of doubt, always account for fewer assets and more liability. Long story short—shareholders believe that the accounts are conservative if and only if they consider standards imposed by superiors as unreasonable.

Auditors will not agree with such approach—they say that shareholders do not invest for their children's or grandchildren's benefit, but themselves. Therefore, they should be able to recognise and collect their earnings when they occur based on the accounting standards.

Such logic emerges from accounting standards, and it fully applies to any industry without a comprehensive government guarantee. Banks get a lot of benefits from the deposit guarantee, so it is reasonable to expect a simple quid pro quo. Therefore, they should be more conservative. An institution earning money from borrowed government credibility should protect its guarantor—it is a fair deal.

If the bank exploits the received guarantees to get cheaper and more stable deposits than its credibility would otherwise provide, it should not use brave and innovative accounting to create excessive cash flow from dividends. That way, some risk is transferred to taxpayers.

Besides, the beauty of conservative accounting is that it creates no costs for a bank and shareholders. The real value of assets remains the same, and it will emerge once assets are collected or liquidated. After the bank cashes those assets in, it will account for the received value, not more and not less. At that moment, its accounting value before the liquidation is irrelevant. Therefore, being conservative is the only means of delaying the recognition of these assets' value. Depending on the applicable discount rate, in the long term, the shareholders of a conservative bank will have roughly the same net present worth of cash flow as the shareholders of a similar bank using a less conservative approach to accounting.

Later paid dividends would be partially offset by later paid profit tax. Besides, rational investors would prefer a lower risk for the same present value of the cash flow. The safer cash flow is the one coming from a conservative bank.

That brings us to another reason in favour of the conservative disclosure. It will typically result in a higher valuation of shares—especially higher price/book and price/earnings ratios. It is a kind of virtuous circle—collecting additional capital is simple and beneficial for the shareholders if the bank keeps those ratios high. Then the bank can facilitate its growth and maintain the firm market position.

Some people challenge the claim that shareholders' feeling about the bank influence corporate governances. They claim that typically management took full control over the bank and the only thing shareholders could do is sell their shares if they are unhappy. If it were so, it would not mean that shareholders do not influence corporate governances. If people sell cheap, consolidators buy. It indeed affects corporate governances. However, it is not the only influence shareholders have.

There are bodies representing shareholders of the bank. One of them is the General assembly, while other is Supervisory board or non-executive part of the board of directors.

Let us peek what one of the ladies in the Supervisory board thinks while receiving a report from the management. In the report, she noticed a significant overvaluation of an asset she knows well.

In the first case, she has doubts about the quality of the bank's balance sheet. She would deliberate: "Ok, the report is false. But I am not responsible for the report, management is. They can get away with it. Auditors already both it. This way, the bank would avoid losses. Declaring losses is dangerous, especially as I am not sure that this exaggeration is the only one. Things could play out the wrong way. This way, we will receive a dividend next year. Maybe I even manage to get rid of those shares for a good price."

Of course, she will remain silent and support the report.

Now, let us do the same with a member of a board convinced that the balance sheet is significantly undervalued: "What? Why are they doing it? Do they want us to pay taxes we need not pay? Maybe my impression was wrong; maybe the bank is not in such good shape I assumed. Anyway, we should see what is going on."

She will raise a question and require management explanation.

So, in the first case, there will be no official comment and the report will be approved, bringing the bank deeper into moral hazard situation and motivating management to do it again. In the second case, a question and answer will enter minutes, causing an explanation or modification of the report. Management would learn a lesson and avoid similar actions in the future.

Such small events cumulate in something we call "culture" of the bank. It is surprising how, once established, the culture is firm and how it stubbornly determines the destiny of the institution. The best fundament for the conservative culture is a firm balance sheet.

Therefore, that is the main thing supervisors should do. Make sure that the culture in the bank is conservative. There is an easy way to achieve it—penalise different behaviours and make sure that all banks have required capital in a conservative balance sheet. Management will then make sure that shareholders know that, while shareholders will watch over management to protect their money.

Naturally, it would not mean that the supervisors' job ends here. Balance sheets of banks are complicated patchworks. They permanently boil and produce geysers of surprises. Even in the most conservative and well-run banks, some events could be large enough to overcome corporate culture and create strong incentives to put them under the carpet. Supervisors should always be around and look carefully.

If we boil down tasks of the supervisor, the answer to the question: "What should supervision do?" is "Whatever it takes to make sure that the bank has required capital (and some more on top of it) and enough liquidity to timely meet all its obligations."

Reference

Onaran, Y. (2017, July 11). https://www.bloomberg.com/. Retrieved from https://www.bloomberg.com/quicktake/zombie-banks.

Chapter 8
What Supervisors Should Not Do?

Abstract Supervisors should not receive other tasks besides improving the resilience of the banking system. There are at least three reasons why it is not a good idea: distracting focus, public pressure on supervisor not related to supervision and the conflict of interest. A broader scope of supervisory responsibility potentially infringes the equality of banks before the law. Their rights can be significantly diminished compared with other persons, natural and legal. Should supervision consider the effects its measures have on the banks' clients and should it use available tools and authority to achieve other political objectives besides the resilience of the banking system?

It would be easy to reach regulatory consensus around the proposed answer to the question: "What should supervisors do?". Though not everyone would agree with all methodological comments in the last chapter, they will all agree that the supervision should focus on capital, liquidity and resilience of banks and banking system.

However, let us ask inverse, yet almost as important issue—"What supervisors should not do?". Here, the proposed answer is also simple, although possibly more controversial: "Anything else".

We already said that prudential supervision conducts a crucial task. The quality of its performance has significant consequences for stability, not only of the financial system but also for other fields of our society. The job is important enough to require full and undivided focus. Whatever is banking supervision requested to do besides its primary task increases the probability of mistake or omission in the major field of the activity.

Also, when one can choose between activities, it opens the possibility to avoid the most unpleasant task at hand. Dealing with a bank that is already deep into moral hazard is always singularly, the most unpleasant task supervisor could have. Therefore, inspecting bank for money laundering instead is much less painful.

The scope and tasks of agencies conducting banking supervision frequently extend beyond prudential supervision. The supervision also oversees anti-money laundering, consumer protection and some other fields of banking operations. There are at least three reasons why it is not a good idea.

D. Odak, *A Political Economy of Banking Supervision*,
https://doi.org/10.1007/978-3-030-48547-4_8

The first one is the possibility to distract focus. Consumer protection and anti-money laundering activities periodically draw very intensive and unpleasant public attention. Under such pressure, the supervisory authority might decide to redirect resources to those fields weakening the prudential arm.

The second reason is the possibility of orchestrated pressure on supervisor not related to supervision. Interested parties can arrange public pressure on the supervisors exactly to achieve this effect—to draw supervisory focus and resources away from prudential activities, towards other responsibilities given to the supervisory agency.

The third reason is the conflict of interest. The supervision is in charge of stability of the banking, while properly conducting and protecting other laws could require imposing substantial limitations and fines to the banks, potentially harming their business.

The banking supervision is frequently the most competent agency for conducting oversight in the credit institutions. It appears rational to use this capacity and put some more burden on it. However, such an approach can backfire for all the reasons mentioned earlier.

The rationality of the concentration is only apparent. Unless the resources to fulfil other tasks are taken away from the prudential supervision, staffing the supervision to do those tasks requires at least the same cost and full-time equivalent as the establishment of the new agency.

The banking supervision is the activity under permanent scrutiny from banking, politics and public. Broader the scope of its responsibility is, there are more points the agency must communicate with the public and the industry. That offers more points for coordinated PR pressure on the supervisor. The public communication, especially about such slippery subjects as customer protection, could seriously compromise the credibility of the supervisor, worsening its reputation. In the time of the crisis, feeble prestige would not help the supervisor to do its real job well.

The mentioned conflict could go both ways. For example, the agency could be hesitant to initiate a procedure for money laundering against a weak bank, as that could create severe difficulties for the bank. When the bank has problems, then prudential supervision has them too.

Also, conflict of interest could appear in the opposite direction—supervisor can apply pressure using tools of prudential supervision to achieve objectives of, for example, customer protection. Though it could be tempting to use, even implicitly, prudential tools to protect customers, that is not the intention of the law. Using the prudential tools for other purposes could compromise them in the long run.

The logic of the law regulating banking supervision is that the bank has no secrets before supervisors. All bank's documents and personnel are permanently available to the supervisor on demand. The logic of such a lack of legal protection is clear—the importance of financial stability removes bank from protection any citizen has—the right to lie, or at least remain silent in own protection and hide proofs against self. Nevertheless, the use of such tools for identification of possible criminal activities, such as money laundering, with potential misdeed done by the bank, could raise a question concerning unconditional openness.

A similar situation exists concerning customer protection. Bank's documents assessed for prudential purposes could prove wrongdoing and significantly damage the material position of the bank. Damage could emerge from administrative fine, but also potentially as indemnification to customers ruled by the court.

Such an arrangement potentially infringes equality of banks before the law, as their rights would be significantly different compared with other persons, natural and legal.

One could ask: "So what? They already have the obligation of full disclosure, and no one is making a problem about it. Why would it now become a problem? Supervision also can do nasty things to the bank. Besides, if supervision sees some criminal activity during the control, it will report it. What is the problem?"

There are differences. Proceedings against bank concerning supervisory measures do not harm the material rights of the bank. They could influence the position of the shareholders, but not of the bank unless the bank failed. Supervisors do not order the bank to give away any money. They request a change of the accounting values or increase of the capital.

Those orders can influence the position of the shareholders, but only if they are not willing to provide requested capital. Otherwise, the value of their assets stays the same. We already said that the bank has what it has, not what it accounts. Therefore, the change in the accounting value will not influence anyone's material rights.

The bank and its managers can be fined, but again only for the breach of the banking law. Though those penalties are sometimes significant, they are all part of the banking law, and all are determined in the administrative, not in the criminal or civil court procedure.

The supervisor should report any criminal wrongdoing upon which it stumbles. The wording is deliberate—supervisors are not supposed to look for criminal activities. That is the job of other government agencies. Nevertheless, when they become aware of a crime, like any citizen, they should report it.

There is a risk that systematic use of supervisory rights to achieve material gains for the third parties or criminal law enforcement objectives could create a constitutional ground to challenge unlimited openness to the supervisors. It would be very wrong if it occurs.

Those activities were allocated to the banking supervision by politicians as they perceive that supervision supervises the banks. If someone supervises banks, it is logical that the same agency will monitor if there is any money laundering or the breach of consumer rights there.

Nevertheless, if we follow the same logic, then the banking supervision should also be responsible for checking electrical installations in the bank, not to mention whether the bank's drivers drive according to the speed limit. If those two examples appear out of place, why doesn't anti-money-laundering (AMLTF) and consumer protection?

No doubt that both AMLTF and customer protection must be strictly overseen. Still, there is a doubt whether a present arrangement, giving them as an additional task to the banking supervisor, helps to achieve it. Methodology, laws and the standard operational procedures for those activities have nothing familiar with banking supervision. Consequently, the skills bank supervisors acquired during their education and work experience can contribute very little to the success of those activities. Why would knowledge of experienced certified financial analyst with an auditor exam be of any value for the preparation of a case against the bank abusing customer's trust?

The extended responsibility could overstretch and defocus supervisors. The public attacks are possible because of reasons associated with consumer protection or AMLTF. At the same time, it also makes AMLTF and consumer protection weaker as they must squeeze in an organisational and procedural straitjacket that does not necessarily suit them. Also, it potentially makes legal cases emerging from both procedures more sensitive, as they always can be contaminated by material acquired for prudential purposes. If such an arrangement fits someone's interest, it exactly benefits the banks willing to do bad things.

Consequently, there is no reason to make supervisory agencies responsible for the supervision of anything else besides banking law and bylaws. Its activity should focus exclusively on improving the resilience of banks and the banking system. Giving them other tasks only make them weaker in their real job.

Though it could appear contrary to what is earlier said, it does not mean that other agencies cannot use the resources of banking supervision in the investigations beyond the scope of the banking law. People employed in supervision have potentially useful skills and knowledge for such investigations. However, those activities should be organised and supervised by people skilful in such tasks. For example, people from the public attorney office or anti-money-laundering office. People from supervision should join for specific time and mission.

While on such task, they should not correspond with the bank as supervisors or invoke authorities of the prudential supervision. Finally, the outcome and success of those activities should not be the task or responsibility of the supervisor.

There could also be some doubts concerning the supervision of information technology in banks as a stand-alone activity. Though it methodologically significantly differs from classical banking supervision, it is today certainly an integral part of banking supervision. Quality and especially robustness of the banking informational system could become a significant threat to the stability of the individual bank. It did not yet happen, but it is worth developing capacity within supervision capable of judging technological risks the banks undertake. Understanding technical robustness and risks usefully supplement the understanding of capital resilience.

Last but not least, let us discuss significant side effects of some of the supervisory activities. For example, a consistent effort to recognise losses hidden in non-performing loans could have social consequences. Under more pressure from supervisors, banks would be more aggressive in the collection of bad loans.

The supervisory objective is to recognise the real value of loans, not to force banks to repossess and sell mortgaged houses. Supervisors only want to be sure that banks have enough capital. Nonetheless, such enforcement has material consequences. If the supervision pushes banks hard to recognise losses, the banks will do everything to avoid it. They will initiate aggressive collection and then sell mortgaged flats, hoping to demonstrate that their losses are smaller than the supervisor assumes.

Also, they would make very loud and clear that they are doing it because supervisors compelled them to do it. They will say it, hoping that it would cause public pressure on supervisors.

The outcome could make more people homeless! How could it be a desirable outcome of banking supervision?

An alternative approach could be a relaxed one. Real estates are mortgaged, and they will be collected one day. So, who cares? People will find jobs and continue their repayments. What is wrong if the bank waits for a few years? No one will get hurt if those loans retain a high value in the bank's books.

However, if the bank pays dividends and bonuses, instead of covering its losses, its capital could be significantly diminished. Then the capital could easily prove inadequate in the event of stress.

When deciding about regulation, we should be aware that a too optimistic bank accounting, if practised by several important banks, increases the risks for financial stability. If those risks materialise to a significant degree, they could represent a severe threat to political stability and the functioning of the legal system. In those circumstances, political risks could become unpredictable and unmanageable. Therefore, more conservative accounting is a vital contributing factor for political stability. As we demonstrated earlier, it could become a severe threat.

One can say that the process of repossessing mortgages would not precisely help political stability and gain popular support for the functioning legal system. However, that is not a responsibility of banking supervision. The problems of too many overindebted people are political, and politics should deal with it. Elected representatives are responsible for the allocation of tax money and laws protecting property or debtors. Supervision, as the unelected technocratic authority, should not interfere in those relationships beyond accounting treatment.

Every debt is someone's asset. The modern legal system protects debtors. The process of debt collection lasts for years, eliminating the possibility of abuse. Supervisors should rely on judiciary and politics to do their work and focus on the task at hand. That means making sure that banks have enough capital and conservative accounting.

There is another temptation facing supervisors. They could deliberately try to induce side effects. By use of risk weights to channel banking credit for the purpose they deem proper. For example, how could someone be against motivating banks to finance green energy or startups? To encourage them, supervisors could decrease risk weights for such loans.

Here we again face a political issue. Giving market advantages and subsidies to specific activities is the political issue and responsibility of elected representatives. Banking supervision should not interfere. Though one could claim that decreasing risk weights for particular purposes is not precisely a subsidy, that would be wrong. It is both—support and a subsidy. It provides support by tilting a level playfield. Activities with lower risk weights receive more favourable financing, improving their competitiveness.

The subsidy is given by decreasing capital requirements, weakening the bank and increasing the risk for taxpayers.

Concerning the case of lenient approach towards bad housing loans in challenging times, though it is a professional no-no, one can have sympathy. It is a hard decision to do something that could hurt another human being. There is a ground for understanding for the one whose hand could tremble. Quite the contrary, abusing calibration of supervisory tools to achieve side effects is not acceptable. Especially not as a mean to achieve things that are not part of supervisory responsibility. Supervisor's job is to make sure that banks have enough capital, not to decide which industries should have competitive advantages. If politics want it, it has other tools to achieve it.

Chapter 9
Basel 1, 2, 3, 3&1/2

Abstract The Basel Accord is an international standard in banking supervision. It is an agreement between supervisors. Based on it, jurisdictions create regulation. BiS checks compliance of authorities with the standard. Basel I—first international standard in banking supervision appears in 1988, 14 years after Basel committee begins its work. That is a bold step in the right direction, enabling global standardisation of the banking industry. Basel II—announced in 2004. Introducing the three-pillar approach and dealing with the risks Basel I neglected. Besides, it introduced IRB, probably the most devastating idea in the banking regulation. Basel III—2014 and 2017—nicknamed three and a half, an attempt to undo worst part of the Basel II. Unfortunately halfhearted, as reluctance to recognise mistake remains.

Before we describe the development of the Basel accord, let us first explain what it is, and even more importantly, what it is not. There is some misunderstanding, as people permanently ask "How will Basel IV influence banking."

The Basel accord is not a regulation, and it does not directly influence anything. It is an agreement between supervisors. Based on it, different jurisdictions create their regulation. They do it by adjusting the framework of the agreement to best suit their needs. Therefore, on the regulatory treatment of any specific position in any bank, decisive say will have national competent authority (NCA). While writing the regulation, NCA has no obligation to apply all the methodologies proposed in the accord. The compliance to the Basel accord is established based on the principle "comply or explain". Any explainable deviation that does not impair safety is acceptable.

Therefore, when and how will a particular definition from Basel III be applied on specific bank decides NCA. BiS checks compliance of jurisdictions, not compliance of banks. Periodically BiS confirms that authorities are compliant, partially compliant or non-compliant.

As a consequence, it is not possible to recognise the influence of the original text of the accord on the specific bank. To understand it, one should read the regulation developed and implemented by NCA.

D. Odak, *A Political Economy of Banking Supervision*,
https://doi.org/10.1007/978-3-030-48547-4_9

The reason for the introduction of the Basel accord is the supervision of internationally active banks. Such an agreement enables the supervisor in the EU to understand how is a bank in the US supervised. Having that knowledge, it can adequately judge risks the EU bank undertakes in the relationship with US bank.

The accord regulates only the biggest banks. Other bank supervisors can supervise according to the national rules, without impediment to compliance with Basel. Nonetheless, some jurisdictions, EU among them, decided to apply the accord on all banks. Such an approach creates a sometimes excessive administrative burden for smaller banks, as the agreement was not written for them.

The Basel Accords are the most famous and only globally applied international standards in banking supervision. The creation of the first one began when the banking supervisors from the most important countries got together in 1974 motivated by a strange incident where several banks lost much money in transactions nominally bearing no risk. So, they deliberated how to deal with such situations. The accord had long birth throes—it took them 14 years to produce their first accord in 1988.

That was the Basel accord. Today we call it Basel I—first international standard in banking supervision. Until then, every country made its independent rules for the banking industry without any universal standards. The implementation of the accord means that every state continued to act independently, but compliance with the agreement is checked and declared. The Basel Accord was the first to set the essential standards. Every bank must have 8% capital on its risk-weighted assets to be solvent. Banks calculate risk-weighted assets by multiplying balance sheet positions with risk weights. Cash, deposits with central and domestic government debt bears no risk, and a bank can have an unlimited amount of those assets.

Though we could notice that governments also get bust from time to time, creators of the accord had the G 10 in mind. Those people do not get bankrupt.

The accord did not cover all risks. The most significant uncovered risk was a market risk, represented, for example, by interest rate risk. If the long-term rate increase by 1%, the price of bonds with ten-year maturity would drop by 10%. The accord lives balance sheet unprotected from such risk, as it allows extreme exposure to government bonds. The bank does not hold any capital against that risk. Authors of the accord were aware of that.

That was not an omission. The committee set only minimal standards, while they substantially relied on the bankers and the supervisors to also follow common sense while designing and applying the rules. There is nothing in the accord preventing regulators from covering this and other risks. Even without any regulation, a diligent supervisor would not neglect a fact that a bank with a few millions of equity amassed billions of long-term bonds financed from money-market deposits.

Except for the 0% risk weight, there were 20, 50 and 100% brackets. Most of the commercial banks' "bread and butter" business was in the 100% section, while mortgages were in 50%.

That was a bold step in the right direction, enabling global standardisation of the banking industry. Still, not everyone was happy with such a solution. People said "Listen, it is not OK that a loan to an excellent company requires the same capital as a loan to an almost bankrupted one. We must take care of that!".

This question did the trick. Regulators considered the dilemma legitimate. They agreed to address the issue, and the committee diligently sat down to resolve it. Fortunately, it was settled only in 2004, with the announcement of Basel II. Though it did some damage, cumbersome implementation procedure prevented it from developing its full effect before 2008, while after 2008 everybody received a wake-up call. Therefore, the Basel Accord did not significantly contribute to the crisis. We cannot say that it wouldn't have if the regulation only had some more time to "sink in".

In some aspects, the new accord was a step in the wrong direction. Although now almost everyone understands it, some are reluctant to admit such a massive blunder. This reluctance is one of the crucial factors in the creation of the present uncomfortable situation in EU banking and the supervisory community.

At first sight, there were no essential changes between Basel I and II. The new accord did not change the earlier prescribed risk weights in the standardised approach. It addressed other risks, such as market risk, neglected in the first accord. It implemented the "three-pillar" approach, declaring more reliance on public disclosure and market discipline. So, it looked promising at first sight.

The devil, as always, was in the details. The accord authorised the use of two alternative approaches to credit risk: the standardised and the "internal ratings-based"—we described the standardised approach earlier. The internal ratings-based approach, the so-called IRB approach, was a new kid on the block.

The authorisation of the IRB approach solved the puzzle we mentioned earlier. Regulators wanted "risk sensitivity". As usual, they got what they wanted.

The idea behind IRB was to use the massive data warehouses banks gather about client behaviour for the definition of capital requirement. They already used those data in the loan approval process. The econometric models predicted the likelihood of future defaults. The experience with those models was extensive and convincing—their introduction improved the quality of retail credit portfolios.

Having such convincing experience, regulators said, why wouldn't each client have a risk weight associated with her or his peer group? The risk weight reflects the client's historical behaviour, and it would be determined by two major characteristics of earlier defaulted clients with similar behaviour: the probability of default (PD) and the loss given default (LGD).

The probability of default was the historical percentage of clients with similar characteristics as the observed one that defaulted on their contract. There is an option whether to use annual or "lifetime" PD. Lifetime means the contracted period. PD was an individual parameter—each client gets her or his PD based on "internal rating". Internal rating is a strange idea. Its meaning is: if rating agencies would do the rating of this client, how would they rate her?

Loss given default is not an individual parameter. LGD is calculated for each portfolio (product). There is LGD for a mortgage loan, for a consumer loan, for car loan etc. It is the percentage of the loan historically lost in the event of default. All defaulted loans do not represent a loss for a bank. The bank initiates collection after each default, collecting a part of the defaulted loans, while a part would be permanently lost. The latter component, compared to the defaulted amount, equals LGD.

The expected loss (EL) of each client is the multiple of PD attributed to the particular client, LGD calculated for a specific loan and ED—exposure on default. Basel II concluded that if a bank has enough capital to cover EL of all its clients, then it is solid as a rock.

The methodology applied in calculating PD is econometrics. It uses regression analysis based on historical data to identify potential parameters in functions describing the behaviour of observed phenomenon. Using that methodology, we could create models that quite comprehensively explain past behaviour. Some people, trying to look into the future, decided that those explanations can also provide insight into future developments. If the model explained the past using historical data, they reasoned, it can even predict the future based on present data. Unfortunately, those predictions did not prove very reliable![1]

One should be meticulous before using such models for prediction.[2] Banks successfully applied the models to automate the approval process. They enabled banks to process retail credit faster, safer and cheaper. The development of those models began long before Basel II, and their good results were a very influential factor in creating the new accord.

Fundamentally, banks made applications checking the same things as credit officers did earlier. The applications analysed client data available to them: the regularity of salaries, the frequency of credit card payments made in casinos or bars, information on whether the client is freshly divorced, frequent large cash withdrawals and so on.

The approval system then compares the client's past behaviour to recognised segments of clients exhibiting similar behaviour. The final result is the recognition of PD for the client. Then, based on the PD, the system makes a proposition. If the PD is lower than the earlier determined "cut-off" line, the client obtains approval for the required loan. If the PD is higher, the system rejects the request.

Those proposals provided by the model proved to be, due to a more systematic nature of data review and unbiased approach, on average better than the credit officer's recommendations. Also, they were indeed cheaper. Such use of the models improves the safety and operational costs of banks.

Those models were relatively simple in terms of statistics and IT development. They didn't require "top brass" in mathematics. However, after Basel II, when the models became a measure of required capital and therefore legally challengeable by supervision, banks became interested in mathematics. They paid high salaries to brilliant students and mathematicians to work for them.

There was intense pressure of shareholders on management to implement the IRB approach. The fast expansion of banking assets urgently demanded new capital. In the US, total assets in the period from 2000–2008 almost doubled. In the UK during the same period, total assets went up two and a half times. In continental Europe,

[1] "correlation does not imply a cause". It is notoriously easy to slip from correlations to false conclusions about causes (Blackmore, 2017).

[2] Because drawing a sample from the future is not possible, economists taking this approach assume that the future is drawn from the same distribution as the past (Bookstaber, 2017, p. 84).

growth was more moderate. In Germany, banking assets grew by 31%, but in Eastern Europe, growth was notably faster. Overall, to retain compliance, shareholders were required to reinvest most of the banks' profits. We already said that shareholders are unhappy if they should do that.

Then brilliant people, with PhDs in physics and mathematics, made persuasive presentations about the characteristics of their models. Those models will make sure that the capital in a bank is just right, enabling banks to grow without retaining profit or diluting their shareholders. Delighted by such an outlook, the shareholders missed the doctors' warning that those models more explain than predict, especially if we talk about required capital in a dynamic environment.

The main feature of the "dynamic environment" are irregular and discrete changes in peoples' economic behaviour. Given enough time, econometrics would recognise them as changes in known functional relationships. However, it happens long after the changes occurred. Econometrics is unable to predict them. It was never even intended to.

How can we claim that, although those models were a successful part of the loan approval process for a long time? They, without a doubt, demonstrated excellent historical performance.

The models demonstrated the ability to distinguish clients more or less likely to repay their loan in a stable environment. Such recognition, though very useful for decision-making, tells us nothing about the amount of capital a bank would need in the event of a significant crisis.

Furthermore, in the evaluation of the models, banks used data collected during a long period of relatively stable economic growth. In the period when the IRB implementation started, more or less, almost everybody paid back. Based on that, the expected finding of the models was predictable—banks need no equity.

Somehow everyone forgot that equity is here precisely to protect banks when things critically change and when earlier evaluated functions do not hold any more. That created preconditions for this victory of science over common sense.

Such a regulatory opportunity created a strong temptation for shareholders and managers. After a long period on a calm sea, the captain was allowed to load his ship at will. Greed sometimes got stronger than caution.[3] When the storm finally came, some vessels were hopelessly overloaded.

After the accord was agreed, most of the significant banks started implementing the new internal rating-based risk weights. Unsurprisingly, they all indicated lower risk weights than the standardised approach. The magic is that IRB after a long calm period decreases the risk weights. The consequence is a simultaneous increase in capital adequacy and a decrease in leverage.

But back then, no one observed leverage. The focus was on capital adequacy. As risk density, the average capital requirement per unit of assets, decreased, adequacy looked quite sufficient. Everything seemed fine.

[3]"Yet these clever people managed things less well—much less well—than their less intellectually distinguished predecessors. Although clever, they were rarely as clever as they thought…" (Kay, 2015, p. 15).

In some countries, supervisors were generally uncomfortable with those developments. In others, they were enthusiastic. After all, it was a declaration of the Basel Committee. You cannot expect people to take you seriously if you say that you know better.

Those that did not show enthusiasm to move quickly in the new direction were encouraged by a cry of "public opinion". "A too stringent approach makes our banks internationally uncompetitive", "Less income, fewer jobs", "Unreasonable requirements destroy entrepreneurship", "We are falling behind".

People shouting at regulators somehow forgot to say that banks do most of their international business with counterparties having a credit rating. Also, except maybe in London, Frankfurt and Amsterdam, most of the income and jobs in European banks come from domestic markets. EU banks perform international retail and corporate operations predominantly through subsidiaries, which again means on the local market. Each domestic market is, by definition, a level playfield, and the situation in the owner's home country has minimal impact on the subsidiary's competitiveness. It seems like a fair guess that the intention was not to increase competitiveness, but rather to push up dividends.

A stereotype about bankers is that they are always in numbers, calculating and evaluating. It is wrong! When it comes to decision-making in banking, it seems it is all about feelings and hunches. No one bothers with figures. For example, the benefits the economy should experience from decreased capital in banks were never convincingly explained in a theoretical model.

Without a model, there can be no proof. It was just a consensus based on—feelings and hunches—that there would be some damage for the countries delaying the implementation of Basel II. No one knew exactly what kind of damage, but most of the regulators began pushing the implementation of IRB among banks. Fortunately, in most countries, it came too late to do real damage.

Nonetheless, it did some. In some countries banks reacted with so-called front-loading: they moved in the direction of the changes. The banks were, of course, compliant, but they decreased buffers. Banks always operate with own funds above the minimum, so that they could grow and withstand sudden losses. As they expected the requirements to decline, they now narrowed buffers and worked hard on the implementation of IRB.

The prerequisite for using the IRB approach are models approved by the supervisors. Before Basel II banking supervisors generally did not have much staff with a formal education in mathematics. Chartered financial analysts were much more needed. Now they hired mathematicians. Banks having bigger budgets hired more mathematicians.

The mathematicians lacked experience and training in banking and accounting, but they were strong in mathematics. So, mathematicians working for banks created cute models and proved their validity. Mathematicians working for supervisors admired their brilliant colleagues from the banks, the elegance of their models and the quality of their proofs. They have written formal papers for their councils. In the councils, typically, there were no mathematicians. So, the models were approved.

Once the application of the models started churning out results, some supervisors received wake-up calls. Nevertheless, it was too late. They crossed Rubicon. *Alea iacta est.*

Examining the models became a complicated and demanding business. One can oversee the procedures through which banks realised their results. There is no problem to replicate those procedures, but the verification of the accuracy of data in the data warehouse is virtually impossible.

Nevertheless, most likely, all banks used accurate data. The methodology offered, without any manipulation, small, even extremely low risk weights. It was applied over a long period of low credit risk.

After all, it was the intention, not an abuse of regulation to decrease risk weights. Why would then someone take risks by manipulating data?

The only way to prevent the erosion of the risk weights was to prevent the implementation of IRB models. After approving them, all supervisors can do is swim downstream. When the next bank requests approval of its models, the supervisors had no option but to approve them once the bank meets the formal requirements.

To make a long story short, a group of the most educated and experienced people in the financial industry decided to put the industry's destiny in the hands of mathematicians. The mathematicians gladly accepted this role, though they knew that the task was wrong. They knew that the models only answer the question: "What caused our losses in the past?". None of the models was designed to answer the question: "What will cause our future losses?".

Probably such misunderstanding was created in small steps in the communication between financial experts not too strong in mathematics and mathematicians not educated in finance.

As we already learned, initially someone created an issue by raising an apparently logical question why clients obviously creating different risks for a bank have the same risk weights attached. The question appeared logical, and the search for a tool to resolve it started.

But in reality, that was not the problem at all. The setting of risk weights and capital requirements is an art, not a science. Own funds should withstand unknown future developments. Unless you have a trustworthy crystal ball, you can only guess what kind of future punches the bank's capital should endure.

The most important part of the methodology is: once you guess how much capital a bank needs, you should, just in case, increase it by 50%.[4] The Basel Accord introduced risk weights as certain guessing guidelines, to make sure regulators would not substantially overstate or understate the required capital.

Initiated by the earlier mentioned question, an unclear mental process convinced regulators that each client has its own risk weight which is an exact parameter. After accepting such assumption, it is logical to look for a proper scientifically approved methodology enabling you to recognise those risk weights.

---

[4]"When analysed more properly from society's perspective, the long-term benefits of much higher equity requirements are large, and the costs are hard to find." (Admati & Hellwig, 2014, p. 180).

Once such a search started, econometrics was the only logical answer. The applied methodology was time tested, and the results were excellent. Someone made a convincing presentation about its explanatory powers and ability to recognise risk factors.

In the loan approval process, banks mainly focused on the model using many variables related to individual behaviour. Such models proved to be excellent in recognising risky clients. For example, regular credit card payments at night clubs and casinos sharply increase the probability of loan default. Oh, how wise, how scientific!

It is considered the wisdom of the models, not as a formalisation of common sense. Seeing those tremendous results, the regulators probably agreed that they discovered "the methodology".

Recognising the merits of the methodology, regulators faced a new hurdle. Although the method was promising, the logical problem was that only banks have the data needed for its application. Therefore, only banks can evaluate risk weights, while supervisors should trust them. It felt slightly awkward.

But then someone was struck by a moment of epiphany: "No one cares more about the stability of a bank than bankers do". The Basel Committee agreed and concluded that bankers would undoubtedly do their best to evaluate the proper risk weights.

Therefore, we've got the methodology, and we will allow banks to use it. Still, we will stay very vigilant inspecting them and making sure they act decently. Several bold and smart decisions solved a non-existing problem by giving banks free hands to decide alone how much capital they needed. Again, what could go wrong?

Then banks hired mathematicians. They did not ask them whether the question made sense but paid them handsomely and asked them to forecast their expected losses using a methodology acceptable for supervisors.

Despite all demonstrated shortcomings, the idea still persists. The primary reason for the slow finalisation of Basel III was the request to retain a "risk-sensitive approach". After a lengthy discussion, the Committee agreed to continue using IRB, but with newly introduced limits, so-called floors. It is now limited to, basically, a somewhat decreased standardised approach. Some EU members were among the most feverish IRB supporters.

The stubbornness of the defence is visible from the fact that rest of the Basle III was completed in 2014, while discussion about the risk weights, the main reason for initiation of the new accord, lasted for another 3 years, finished only in December 2017. The period between those two decisions was so long that initially, the agreement was called Basel IV. Now, it has a nickname Basel III and a half.

A concern caused such a lengthy discussion. The fear that, if the models would become obsolete, then all the knowledge they accumulated would be lost. Besides, mathematicians would also become redundant in the banks. They would go back to doing what mathematicians are supposed to do: wear jeans, write software or teach students and write books about theorems, rather than developing end evaluating financial models.

We should not be sorry if that happens. Mathematicians are among the brightest people around, and their present job is, after all, a waste of their talents. Those models are, from the mathematical point of view, quite trivial.

As we discussed earlier, the problem with IRB models was never methodological. It was fundamental. The models are not able to answer the question: "How likely is the shock and how hard a shock could a bank survive?".

Enabling a bank to weather such a shock is the reason why capital is there. The IRB approach pretends that the answer to that question would emerge from the answer to the question "How likely will this particular client repay that particular loan?". Those are two very different questions, so answering the latter correctly gives us no insight into the former.

Theoretically, we can divide the threat to a bank's balance sheet into risks and ambiguity or uncertainty.

A risk is something we can make an educated guess about; we have data to evaluate it and estimate the likelihoods of the outcomes and the financial consequences of those outcomes. On the other hand, ambiguity is ambiguous.

The question about the likelihood of the loan repayment evaluates risks. The trick is that, if a bank accurately evaluates risk, it does not require any capital to cover risks. When it decides about the price of the loan, the bank includes in the price all recognised risks calculated based on historical performances. It set prices and cut-off lines so that, if the circumstances stay the same as in the past, the resulting portfolio has a positive net cash flow. With positive cash flow, you have all the money you may need. If one observes the historical performance of a risky portfolio in any adequately run bank, such observation will only confirm that the bank needs no own funds.

When evaluating risk, you would consider an employed engineer with a family, doing sports and not going to bars as a much better risk than a small street dealer, addict, drunk or gambler.

However, when ambiguity jumps in—for example after 50 years of operation, the local factory was closed, suddenly the engineer lost his job, and his house became worthless, while the dealer improves his business. Everything the model did in the past is wrong. The bank then covers its losses from its prime clients, while the risky ones get along quite well.

Therefore, as ambiguity is ambiguous, the Basel I Approach is much closer to reality. We can go further and say that if ambiguity is ambiguous, why wouldn't all assets in the portfolio require the same amount of capital? We can answer the question correctly in two ways:

We could either convincingly claim that there are reliable experiences distinguishing assets more robust to ambiguities from those whose value is more likely to be affected with future developments. Alternatively, we can accept the argument and devise the approach relying only on leverage.

Abandoning risk weights could be a step too far. For example, cash or short-term deposits in domestic currency with a central bank—they are incredibly robust on losses and having them in the balance sheet does not represent a risk for a bank.

Quite the opposite, having them in balance sheet significantly decrease risks. So, there is no need to keep any capital aside to cover its risks.

The situation is similar with short-term deposits in the best banks and short-term government debt. Longer term government debt and bank deposits would require some capital, as protection from market risk, not credit risk.

Governments and central banks proved historically able to retain nominal solvency no matter what. That means solvency in domestic currency. In extreme circumstances, the government can meet its debt by printing money. Then the money would be worthless, but that is market risk, not credit risk.

On the other hand, all commercial loans should have the same risk weight. A bank holds equity against ambiguity, and there is no way to assume who will be a bad client after ambiguity jumps in.

Alternatively, similar results are achievable using an even further simplified methodology. Leverage could be the only methodological tool, without capital adequacy. Then it should be about 50% higher then if used in combination with risk-weighted capital adequacy. However, this leverage should exclude all the assets bearing no material risks. The excluded assets are, if hold without any further commitment or lien, cash, money on the account in the central bank and short term receivables from domestic government, prime foreign governments and banks.

Still, such an approach would open a significant problem. Long term receivables should be a part of leverage, as they generate material market risk despite creditworthiness of the debtor. Therefore, such a methodology would create a sudden capital requirement threshold for longer-term prime assets.

After the Basel Committee decided to implement Basel II, the floodgate for a decrease of leverage was not wide open in all jurisdictions. Nevertheless, in some jurisdictions, the results were spectacular. Just for example, according to World Bank data, in the UK, leverage went from 7% in 2004 to 4.4% in 2008. In Ireland and France from 5.1 to 3.7%, and the Netherlands from 4.8 to 3.2%. Still, in the Eurozone, dynamics was moderate. Leverage fell by 0.4%. That was a consequence of increased leverage in some jurisdictions. Exemplary in swimming against the current was, for example, Austria, increasing leverage from 4.9 to 6.3%. The increase was also visible in Belgium and Germany but on a low level. Belgium had a leverage of 3.3% after a rise between 2004 and 2008.

Indicators in the US show that leverage not only stayed the same but at 9.3% in 2008 dwarfed all EU jurisdictions. Furthermore, the US made an effective move after the initial shock. The US government force-fed banks with equity, to get even higher leverage. They increased leverage to 12.4% in 2009, peaking at 12.7% in the following year.

On the other hand, the Eurozone increased leverage to 6.8%, which is barely half of the leverage realised in the US, dropping after that again to 5.6%.

This difference determined different approaches towards banking regulation in the US and the EU. The much stronger initial position provided some breathing space to the Americans, and they were reluctant to make any move which could potentially jeopardise it. In the EU, the situation was very different. Banks had very thin, and in some cases, questionable equity.

Strengthening of the regulation while investors are reluctant to invest in the banks' equity could create a shortage of equity. It appeared that the shortfall would be severe. Investors were quite cautious when investing in banks, while governments were afraid to propose an American style re-capitalisation. Both had good reasons.

Besides the issue of potentially insufficient capital, the IRB is by its very nature exceptionally pro-cyclical. After things get bad, IRB would only make them worse. Once the number of defaults increases and losses from those defaults mount up, the models will start to indicate higher risk weights. For feeble risk weights, those below 25%, such an increase could be high enough to make bank non-compliant even though it did not experience any significant losses. Therefore, everybody today knows that IRB regulation would not be applied consistently in a downturn.

That is, in fact, good news. It would be insane to keep it consistent. Nevertheless, being inconsistent also bears risks. It brings us close to a moral hazard situation. Owners could believe that they are insolvent, but regulators would claim otherwise—we already discussed the consequences of such case.

If regulators would insist on consistently applying the models, that would only make things worse for the real economy. A change in risk parameters will be the consequence of materially elevated risks. In such a situation, the market could easily be reluctant to provide fresh equity under conditions acceptable to existing shareholders. Banks would then react by decreasing the loan supply to "risk-weight-heavy" portfolios, corporate and retail alike, and transfer assets to government bonds and similar items. That would impact the economy and hamper its recovery.

Of course, the government could react in the "American style", increasing the equity of banks and enabling them to continue their normal operations. Such a move would most likely be the wisest, but only from an economic perspective. Politically, it would be seen as another bailout of banks with "our money", causing a powerful and negative public and populistic reaction.

We should also keep in mind that financially, such an operation could become doubtful because the losses in some cases could easily prove to be higher than the present, fragile, capital. So, the government could find itself owning nationalised, but still insolvent, banks. Then it would have no choice but to do "whatever it takes" to recover them. This "whatever" could be extremely expensive.

Both political and economic impact, alone or combined, could easily cause a political shake-up. We should always keep in mind how financial turmoil changed the political climate in Germany between 1928 and 1930. Fortunately, such a change appears impossible today. Nonetheless, mentioning Janis Varoufakis as a candidate for minister of finance would make every Greek politician laugh less than a year before he was appointed.

A feasible alternative to government intervention is—triggering the bank's resolution to recapitalise the bank. We will discuss the details of the resolution process later. Still, it is evident that the resolution of a bank only because its models now indicate higher risk weights would send massive shockwaves throughout the financial system.

The firmness of committee decision to keep the IRB approach despite its so apparent adverse impact on both preparation for the crisis and post-crisis recovery is not a reassuring sign.

References

Admati, A., & Hellwig, M. (2014). *The bankers' new clothes*, Princeton University Press.
Blackmore, S. (2017). *Consciousness: A very short introduction*, Oxford University Press. ISBN 0198794738.
Bookstaber, R. (2017). *The end of theory: Financial crises, the failure of economics and the sweep of human interaction*, Princeton University Press. ISBN 9780691169019.
Kay, J. (2015). *Other people's money*, Profile Books. ISBN 978-1781254431.

Chapter 10
Bank Failure and Resolution

Abstract The perfect banking system would be too expensive. Therefore, the failure of banks is imminent, and we should be ready for it. Failing of individual weak banks is acceptable. However, only if the failure is correctly managed. The failed bank goes through resolution. It is a deliberately vague word with a lot of meanings. EU resolution framework assumes "open bank" resolution for strategic banks. It means that the bank would fail and resolve without any discontinuity in operations. Only shareholders and junior creditors of the bank are involved in the resolution. However, a lot of work needs to be done to achieve all preconditions for such a resolution. Most importantly, it would require improvement of the banks' reputation.

> A run on a solvent, liquid, well capitalised and well-managed bank ...is a theoretical possibility; but in practice it is as rare as a milk panic. (Kay, 2015)

The financial system should be the main shock absorber of the economy. The role of the financial system in a crisis is to quickly absorb losses, relieve the economy of its past mistakes and enable it to regain growth momentum. Healthy banking can manage risks, which, if faced by weak banks, create a very uncomfortable situation.

But how do we know that the banks are healthy? Are banks healthy if they meet the regulatory requirement? Are those criteriums correctly "calibrated". If the bank uses all benefits of Basel II, it can be fully compliant and still very fragile.

Can we regard as healthy the bank whose owners do not trust in its health? If the bank is compliant, but its market capitalisation is below required capital, is it healthy? Will we judge the capital by accounts or market capitalisation? What could motivate shareholders to approve accounts, and then sell shares below the book? After all, the shareholders are the most interested and informed about their bank's business. When they think that the bank is not healthy, it is not a matter anyone should take lightly. Either they are irrational, or their decisions are based on something nor declared in the reports.

All those talks and dilemmas culminate in the moment of truth. The moment when the bank declared that it could not meet its obligations as contracted. Then it became clear—it was not resilient enough. The bank did fail.

D. Odak, *A Political Economy of Banking Supervision*,
https://doi.org/10.1007/978-3-030-48547-4_10

Whether we like it or not, failures of banks are unavoidable. It is not possible to design regulatory requirements and an oversight system which could prevent them. Knowing that future bank failures are imminent, we should be ready for them.

It is perfectly OK to have a failed bank here and there if everything is ready for it. The banking system need not be perfect. The perfect banking system would be too expensive. Therefore, the failing of a small number of the weakest banks is acceptable, even welcome. There is always the worst bank. Its removal from the market makes banking better. However, only if the failure is correctly managed.

Though it is unavoidable, we should also keep in mind that the bank's failure, especially during a crisis, is a tricky business. If things get out of hand, the situation could quickly become messy. Regulatory reaction on failure and after failure decides between smooth and exciting outcomes. We will call that process bank resolution. The resolution is the process of "resolving" failed bank.

"Resolving" is a deliberately vague word. In this case, it could have several distinct meanings. It could mean "bankrupt", "wind-down", "take over", "save" and several other things. The overall shape of the failed institution and the means available dictate the way of resolution.

The Resolution authority is an agency in charge of banking resolution. It is not a part of supervision. Nonetheless, supervision and resolution should coordinate their efforts. Orderly failure of the bank significantly helps resolution authority to keep control over the resolution process. To achieve it, the supervisor should decide to close a bank before developments force its hand.

Banks can fail in two ways. One is a "disorderly failure", and the other is an "orderly failure". As opposed to the disorderly failure, the "orderly failure" creates much less commotion on the market.

An orderly failure may sound like an oxymoron to people unaccustomed to banking. The word "orderly" is usually not associated with failure. However, in banking, it is, in fact, the most usual way for banks to go. For example, during some periods, the Federal Deposit Insurance Corporation, the FDIC, closed down almost a bank a week.[1] Those bank failures are very orderly. The bank works until Friday afternoon as usual. Then the FDIC moves in, closing the bank.

Insured depositors get their money the next working day. Quick replacement of credit card is organised, while clients get new accounts at the closest bank. They hardly notice any discontinuity at all, while shareholders and large creditors of the bank experience a problem. They will wait for the end of the bankruptcy procedure to see if something left for them.

The precondition for the orderly failure is that the supervisor uses its information advantage, failing bank before the market makes it fail. The bank enters the process of orderly failure though it did not yet fail to meet any obligation, except regulatory requirements.

However, only intrusive and firm oversight enables banks to fail orderly. When supervisors are hesitant or, from a regulatory aspect, too confined, there will be no orderly failures. Without periodic removal of the weakest banks, problems would

[1] FDIC (2019).

cumulate and come to bear in the worst possible moment. If weak banks are not timely removed from the market, they likely will go alone—untimely. Such a situation frequently creates a moment when the government has no choice but to bail out banks not asking for the price. Therefore, it is a reassuring sign if the supervisor periodically closes a bank. Besides weeding of the financial system, the process keeps resolution authority in good shape and ready for fast reaction.

There is a general misconception that the famous "bank runs" cause bank failures and financial crises. That could have been true in the times of the Florentine Republic and the Wild West, but even then, it was a very uncommon case. Even then, the vast majority of bankrupt banks was insolvent, most of them deeply. The cause of such failure, therefore, was not a bank run, but insolvency. Rumours about impending bankruptcy, in most cases well-founded, caused a bank run which brought the bank down.

Today a bank fails only if the central bank and other banks lose confidence in it. As long as peers consider the bank creditworthy, a bank run is just a nuisance. A bank can even profit from it nicely, as the run is an opportunity to convince depositors to pay a fee and waive accrued interest, only to get their deposits out earlier.

If other banks believe that the bank is solvent, meaning that its receivables are more valuable than its liabilities, they will support it with funds.

Overall, a bank run as such is not a major risk for the banking system, but the reasons triggering it could be. A bank run usually starts when information about the bank's insolvency becomes public. If this information is credible and other banks believe it, the affected bank is doomed. If other banks dismiss it as a rumour, nothing will happen.

The bank fails due to deficiencies in the balance sheet. Therefore, if the balance sheet is weak, the worst possible option is to let the market recognise it. It would mean waiting for a bank run to seal the bank's destiny. The regulators' job is to understand it, instead and before the market. After the recognition, the supervisor should either strengthen or close the bank before the market does it.

To achieve it, supervisors have an information advantage over the market. They are allowed to review all the bank's documentation, and they have ample time to do so. They also have education and experience needed to understand the meaning of each document.

During the oversight, they should recognise non-compliance. Once the supervision learns that a bank is vulnerable, it should quickly decide about the course of action. Without a convincing plan for recovery, the bank should be removed from the market as soon as practical.

Different from other companies, a bank need not be insolvent to fail. If it just has lower equity than required, it is non-compliant. From that position, it could be either failed or recovered, depending on shareholders willingness to support it and the regulator's judgement.

When supervisors find that the bank is not Ok, they should act before other banks recognise it. If the supervisors do not do that, they waste the information advantage given to them precisely for that purpose. Then, the information will reach the market, rumours will spread and the bank could become illiquid and fail disorderly.

If shareholders or the government are willing to support the bank, it is possible to strengthen it instead of closing it. The simplest way is by issuing new shares and collecting new capital. A firm conviction that the regulators' action will be swift and decisive will motivate shareholders to recapitalise bank timely and adequately.

Shareholders usually have an ample opportunity to avoid a bank's failure. The oversight process takes quite sometime, and the bank becomes timely aware of the supervisors' concerns. Therefore, the bank and its shareholders have enough time to cover losses and issue new shares. If shareholders do not stabilise the bank during the process, then, after the formal establishment of non-compliance, the supervision has two options.

The first is to close the bank. If it is a small regional bank without systemic importance, this solution is the simplest and therefore the most likely. If it is a bank of systemic importance, meaning one whose closing could seriously influence the functioning of the system, then, of course, the action should be more cautious. In any case, the response should be decisive. Allowing a technically insolvent bank to operate continuously is very risky. Its insolvency can trigger rumours and a bank run in a situation when the central bank will not be able to support it when applying Bagehot's rule.[2]

Therefore, if the bank is unable to establish compliance, then resolution authority can activate a resolution plan—basically a plan to ensure continuity of the bank's essential functions despite its failure and extinguish non-essential. If all functions are non-essential for the economy, the bank is simply closed and bankrupted. Alternatively, the bank can be re-capitalised using the so-called "bail-in" or "bail-out" techniques. If the bank is re-capitalised, it will continue working as if nothing had happened. In that case, we are facing a dilemma whether the bank failed, or it was saved.

It depends on a prospective. From the shareholders' perspective, the bank failed. They covered its losses from the capital and nothing or little left to them. Therefore, they lost a part or the entire ownership. From the management perspective, the bank also failed, as they were all fired and replaced by resolution management. But from the clients' perspective, the bank was saved. They do not suffer any problems and costs that are usually associated with a bank's failure.

As the sustainability of a bank depends on the trust of other banks, the critical question is: how do the other banks know whether a bank is solvent? Banks look at each other accounts with a grain of salt. They have bad experiences in that respect. Therefore, they all together, always look at the supervisor. If the supervisor indicates concern about a bank, then the other banks will follow suit.

If the supervisor imposes measures on the bank, then other banks hold their breath waiting to see the future course of supervisory action. Only clear and deliberate action can send an unambiguous message. For example, if the supervisor announces the strengthening of the bank, and later let it fail, it would be detrimental to the supervisor's reputation. Next time, the lack of credibility could make any supervisory action more difficult.

[2]"Lend without limit, to solvent firms, against good collateral, at high rates.".

The supervisory credibility is essential, even critical for supervisors' ability to intervene. The banking is the business of turning credibility into income. When recovering the bank in difficulties, supervisor lends its credibility to the institution, which just lost its own. Same occurs in case of the resolution, only this time the resolution authority is the one who provides reputation.

The reputation of the resolution authority becomes especially critical in the case of bail-in. The bail-in appears to be a new kid on the block. It sounds as something opposite to a bail-out. However, bail-in and bail-out are the same things financed by different people. A bail-out is usually funded by the government, while the bank's creditors finance a bail-in.

Of course, not all creditors. For example, your money on your current account is perfectly safe in the process. The resolution authority would only take the money of those investors who invested in riskier financial instruments, and their money would be, after covering the losses with existent equity, bailed-in as capital.

The resolution process would force the owners of instruments eligible for conversion to convert them into the bank's shares. The conversion should first encompass the so-called CoCos—contingent convertible instruments. These are bonds issued by the bank and contracted in such a way to convert into capital if certain pre-agreed conditions ensue. Usually, it means if a bank cannot meet the regulatory requirements.

In the process, unless the bank had extremely high losses, the bailed-in investors would not lose their money. They would, by converting their receivables, cease to be creditors and become the bank's shareholders. Then, it is up to them to establish corporate governances, select management and protect their investment. If they run the bank well, they can even earn something.

The idea that one could earn by becoming a shareholder of a bankrupt bank may appear strange. It is certainly not. At the end of the process, they would become shareholders of a fully compliant and stable bank. All losses would be covered, and portfolio moped up.

That is the point where the credibility of the resolution authority comes into play. The original shareholders would cover the losses. The value of their shares decreases, or it is wiped out. Clients will be confused, and a lot of unhappy people will talk bad about the bank. Someone should then convincingly tell them that the bank is now OK. It is not easy.

The bail-in instrument is something new. In the case of the bailout, clients of the bank perceive that the government or the other bank performing bail-out stands behind the bank. Therefore, they continue business with the bank, relying on the new owner knowing that it now cannot let the bank go.

In the case of bail-in, there is no one behind the bank. The market is not familiar with such an operation. Bank's new shareholders are unhappy, and they will probably make it public. Bank has the management gathered in haste and not familiar with a bank. Neither of them can provide credibility. Therefore, only the resolution authority can do it. The successful resolution through bail-in requires deliberate and brave, yet wise resolution authority—a daunting task.

After covering all the losses, the resolution authority converts eligible financial instruments issued by the bank into new capital. If that would not be enough to replenish the capital fully, the resolution can dig further. It can choose new instruments with the least seniority and bail them in until the bank meets the conditions for authorisation.[3] Alternatively, after bail-in, they can decide to perform bail-out.

Once they reinforced the balance sheet with fresh capital, the new owners are supposed to establish corporate governances as a cornerstone for the bank's profitability and permanent compliance.

The precondition for successful resolution is the structure of the bank's liabilities. The bank must have sufficient debt eligible for conversion into equity. The question is: how much would it cost to issue bonds suitable for bail-in? Demand exists by definition—as long as there are buyers for the bank's shares, there will be buyers for CoCos. CoCos are much less risky than the stocks because the shareholders cover first losses. But the price could still be an issue. Buyers of CoCos do not buy them to become the bank's shareholders. If they consider this possibility likely, they will charge such risks dearly.

For example, there is a significant number of EU banks whose P/E ratio oscillates around 5. It means that investors consider their shares worth taking a risk only if they expect earnings of 20% per year. What would they ask for slightly less risky bonds, it is hard to know. Whatever they will ask, for bonds issued by banks whose P/E is as low as 3, they will ask much more.[4] When looking at the figures, we always must keep in mind that averages or predominant figures, in this case, are not important, extremes are. The weakest bank will fail, not the average one.

Despite all the risks, when the expected return is high enough, investors will buy instruments. However, if the investors perceive the bank as weak, the price could become high. For example, if the price of the bank's shares is 25% of the book value, then issuing CoCos could be quite expensive. If the shares are traded well above the book value, and with P/E above ten, the investors in CoCos will talk about basis points, not percentages of the premium over the senior obligation.

We consider that the bank issued enough CoCos when their conversion can replenish the loss of the whole capital. We already learned that the precondition for a successful bail-in is enough eligible liabilities in the bank. If there is not enough of them, the resolution should use other means, such as the "senior" obligations, or rely on government funds.

If there are not enough CoCos, other liabilities could become eligible for the conversion. Partially eligible, as it would usually be enough to take just a small portion of them. Still, there are clear limits. Insured deposits must not be touched. Also, there is no intention to use uninsured private deposits and corporate transaction deposits.

CoCos and other instruments of MREL will become important when the supervisor notices that the bank is, as an official term says: "failing or likely to fail". Then the supervisor informs resolution authority about the fact, and they jointly initiate

---

[3]Regulatory preconditions required to maintain a bank's licence. Article 2 of Regulation EU 2016/1450.

[4]Some information about dynamics of EU bank subordinate bond yields can be found (Nuevo, 2019).

actions of the bank resolution. From that point on, the resolution authority has a leading role.

If the bank is failing or likely to fail, the only bank's body supervisor could not touch—the general assembly of the bank—lost its authority. By poorly leading the bank, shareholders lost ownership together with ownership rights. Now the resolution authority decides instead of them. The authority first decides about resolution strategy. Though the plan is defined earlier in the process of resolution planning, it needs to be confirmed in a specific situation.

If the strategy is bankruptcy, the bank is simply bankrupted. The court runs the further process.

If the strategy is bail-in, then the resolution authority determines who will be the new shareholders. After making such a decision, the authority uses its powers to turn chosen liabilities into equity. Ideally, the authority completes the process during a weekend, and the affected bank would continue its regular operations on Monday. However, not entirely normal just yet, as the resolution management replaced the earlier bank management. The resolution management will run the bank until new shareholders get the licence and establish a new corporate governance structure.

Establishing the structure means electing supervisory and management board. It could take sometime. Buying CoCos does not require a licence while becoming a significant shareholder does. So, if someone acquired weighty shareholding through the conversion of convertible securities, it needs to be licensed. Besides, all the members of the Supervisory and management board must be licenced. So, the process takes some time. During that period, the resolution management still runs the bank, in line with instructions of the resolution authority.

That is a sensitive, prolonged interregnum period. The bank already has new shareholders, but they do not control the bank yet. First, all new shareholders that acquired significant shareholding must be licenced. In the meantime, the new shareholders should meet to agree on the agenda of the general assembly. They should decide who will be new members of the supervisory board or the Board of directors. Once they choose them, they will request resolution management to call the general assembly meeting. There is at least a month until the GA meeting. Once they elected the Supervisory board, the supervisory board members must be licenced. Then the Supervisory board should meet and appoint the Management board. Then all members of the management board must be licenced. Only then new management can take over the bank.

As the new assembly is probably a big group of small shareholders, who most likely did not work together and never intended to become shareholders, it could take them sometime to agree about strategy and names. Depending on their agreement and administrative efficiency, the process can take anywhere between 2 months and who knows. While shareholders try to get together, resolution authority runs the bank. That is a susceptible period for the success of the process.

The establishment of the new corporate governances finishes the resolution. The bank begins a regular business, and the supervision takes over daily oversight over the bank's operation.

The organisation of the resolution function in the EU is not standardised. In some countries, the resolution authority is an organisational unit in the same institution conducting the supervision. In others, two separate institutions perform those functions. The organisation must be such that resolution and the supervision authority coordinate their work while they retain full independence in decision-making.

It could appear as a bizarre idea that someone is allowed to take other people's money and invest it in shares without the owner's permission. In normal circumstances, bankruptcy resolves situations when a firm cannot pay its debts.

The resolution through bail-in is an exception from that rule, and it only applies to the most critical credit institutions whose failure can send shockwaves through the system.[5] Shocks could potentially cause a considerable loss of value, for example, on the stock or the real estate markets. They could cause people to lose their jobs and income. So, everybody will be at a loss if something like Lehman would happen again. By converting eligible liabilities into shares, those risks are, if not avoided, then notably decreased.

The "no-worse-off" rule prevents a situation where investors suffer excessive damage from a bail-in. If the resolution authority establishes that some investors would be worse off in a bail-in than in bankruptcy, those investors should receive compensation. The value of their assets at the end of the resolution should be at least equal to the one they would obtain through a bankruptcy.

That is at least the principle. Its implementation faces significant challenges. The process of acquiring data for the analysis is not perfect. First, resolution authority undertakes two evaluations: a "going concern" and "gone concern" scenario. Going concern recognises the value of the bank's business, while gone concern observes only the price of the assets and the cost of liquidation. If "going concern" is more valuable, then the principle "no worse off" is, generally, achieved. On the paper, it will almost always be the case.

Achieving it in real life could be challenging. The bank's reputation and business can be hurt during the resolution. It could cause unplanned losses after the resolution. Those losses could make the shareholders worse off. However, the guarantee expired. They took over management of the bank and losses are their problem.

After a comparison of those two scenarios, follows the analysis whether all participants in the bail-in have the same formal position as they would have in the bankruptcy. For example, if some receivables have a higher priority in the bankruptcy, while they suffer a haircut in the bail-in, then this haircut should not be higher then the losses they would suffer in the bankruptcy.

There is some misunderstanding about the application of the "no worse off" principle. The people misunderstand that the relative position of creditors will be the same as in bankruptcy. It is not a case. It is only vital that you get the same or more then you will get in the bankruptcy. Rules do not forbid others to get much more.

---

[5] "The collateral damage, including the domino effects and the potential disruption of the broader economy, would likely be significant even if the direct cost of bankruptcy or resolution were borne by investors or by the banking industry." (Admati & Hellwig, 2014, p. 78).

Also, no worse off does not mean that investors will receive indemnification if the stock of the resolved bank after its flotation falls below the value the investor was supposed to get from bankruptcy. The evaluation takes into account the balance sheet and business plan. Whether the market would agree with the valuation is not relevant.

The resolution plan prepared by the resolution authority beforehand contains the blueprint of the process. Still, specific decisions emerge from a business plan sketched over the weekend, based on unreliable accounting data and put together by the resolution management probably without any experience with this bank. Also, this management will not be responsible for executing those plans. So, after the resolution—Que sera, sera!

Such improvisations and shortcuts are unavoidable in the present institutional framework, as we learned the hard way that it is essential to avoid the shock from the failure of a big bank. CoCos investors were aware of the risk when they bought them, and they received the required premium for doing so. Also, they have the opportunity to restructure their bank and earn handsomely from acquired shares. Therefore, we should shed no tears for them.

The whole structure is based on the decision of the Basel Committee. It decided to establish the so-called TLAC—total loss-absorbing capacity. TLAC is the amount of own funds and junior liabilities eligible to cover losses and make a bank resolvable through a bail-in. The concept of TLAC became a part of the EU legal system through the so-called MREL—minimum requirement of own funds and eligible liabilities. As usual, when applying the Basel Accords, the EU does not fully follow the set requirements. The deviation is insignificant, just big enough to be busy proving that EU is compliant with Basel.

Nevertheless, it is not really a problem as TLAC applies to global systematically important institutions (G-SII) while MREL applies to all systematically important institutions (O-SII). European G-SII will anyway apply TLAC and MREL, as otherwise, the EU compliance with BASEL would be questionable. For O-SII Basel don't care, so the EU can do as it pleases.

MREL is required in a large enough amount to replenish capital fully if a bank loses it. So, if a bank loses all of its own funds, it can still convert MREL and continue regular operations in compliance with the law!

Not precisely in full compliance, as MREL is also part of the legal requirements. Unless the bank had much more eligible liabilities than required, immediately after a bail-in it could not be compliant.

Regulators will give a bank time to rectify the lack of MREL. Issuing new eligible liabilities unavoidably takes time. In the meantime, the bank would be allowed to operate without full MREL.

Minimum authorisation conditions, which the bank should meet at any time to operate legally, are stipulated in Article 2 of Regulation EU 1450/2016. The transition period after the resolution is described by Article 8 of the same regulation, saying that the transitional period will be as short as possible. But during that "short" period, the bank is supposed to collect a certain amount of MREL every 12 months. So, the transition could last for years, until investors forget the unpleasant destiny of the earlier MREL providers.

The law allows the resolution and supervision authority to approve the bank's temporary non-compliance if it is likely that the bank could achieve full compliance in the foreseeable future. The purpose of such exemption is obvious. After performing bail-in, it would be wrong to close the bank just because it cannot collect full MREL immediately. The resolution authority uses discretion to avoid such a mistake and to facilitate the meaningful and sensible application of the law. Therefore, authorities have prerogatives needed to implement the law smoothly. Discretion is required, as the law cannot describe all possible situations, and therefore, flexibility in its implementation is crucial.

Still, there are clear limits to flexibility. Regulations 575/2013 and 876/2019 or CRR I and II, define capital requirements. Regulation 1450/2016 defines the minimum authorisation requirements, i.e. minimum capital bank must have at any time to be compliant. Those regulations govern only equity, not MREL. Therefore, it is not in contradiction with CRR if the bank is allowed to operate without MREL, as long as it fulfils minimal authorisation requirements.

MREL has a very different legal framework than equity. Based on TLAC requirements, the basic MREL requirements defined in Commission Delegated Regulation 1450/2016 as regulatory technical standard supplementing Directive 2014/59. Based on those documents, national laws were applied. They authorise national resolution authorities in coordination with the Single Resolution Board to determine the MREL requirements for individual banks. In that process, the respective national resolution authority and Single Resolution Board have flexibility in applying those requirements. On the other hand, equity requirements are decided by the competent authority and based on CRR and national laws.

If this seems to you as quite a complicated and awkward system of banking regulation, you are not alone. Furthermore, the system is new, and we don't know how will it work under stress. The complex network of involved institutions required to quickly act in a decisive and coordinated manner under high stress gives little ground for enthusiasm.

The ideal type of future resolution would be an "open-bank resolution". The basic design of the resolution is such that, if executed properly, hardly anyone would notice the failure and recovery of a bank. The bank would continue to function normally from the customers' perspective. ATMs, branches and cards would work as usual; all payments would go as ordered. Only the owners of CoCos would notice something strange. They would get a notification about a change in their portfolio. As simple as all that! Of course, a necessary precondition for such a solution would be that the bank has enough MREL. That is the essential requirement of the Single Resolution Board towards the bank.

The idea behind the structure looks promising. Nonetheless, how will that legal structure function in times of crisis is still an open question. The only dynamics we can see, for the time being, are periodical postponements of set timelines. Postponements always indicate the regulators' doubts. Sometimes, as in this case, the doubts appear to be quite reasonable.

Besides the MREL, the success of the process would, as we already said, heavily depend on the reputation of the resolution authority. The status should be deserved one, as, the authority would need exceptional administrative and communication skills to bring the process successfully home.

Success also depends on new shareholders and their attitude towards their shareholding in the bank. If they are, for example, pensioners who kept their "black days" reserve in banks bonds, their behaviour can be pretty unpredictable and volatile, not entirely focused on the establishment of the new corporate structures. Quite different acts, such as demonstrations, the bitter public attack on the process culminating even in suicides, could be expected. Such a situation could pose a threat to the success of the resolution. It could be avoided if the selling strategy of TLAC and MREL instruments, though not formally licenced, are closely supervised and limited to professional buyers.

The next critical phase comes after the completed resolution. Then the bank is required to replace MREL. We already know that it would be a challenging task. The bank should regain the investors' trust before it could collect full MREL. The resolution authority decides every 12 months about a feasible level of MREL the bank should raise. During that lengthy "interim" period the bank would be less robust than legislator sees fit and its stock price will permanently suffer from "MREL overhang".

The question is also why we think that the bank would lose no more than one required capital? MREL replenishes one required capital. So, it appears that the proposed mechanism would not work if the bank loses more.

Except, it would. Once the resolution process spends all MREL without re-establishing the authorisation conditions, the resolution authority has a choice. Either some other liabilities become eligible or, if the resolution authority decides not to use them, it has the legal power to perform a bail-out after the executed bail-in.

In that case, it appears that taxpayers would pay for the bank's resolution. That is precisely what this regulation tries to avoid. Nevertheless, taxpayers will pay much less and much less likely than without MREL. Secondly, the money would come from a resolution fund in which banks would collect money for the purpose. Therefore, the real costs of the bail-out should not influence the execution of the government budget.

Nonetheless, due to formal accounting rules, it still creates public debt. Failed banks sometimes lose more than their entire capital. Therefore, MREL would sometimes be insufficient to recover the failed institution fully. The risks of such massive failure increase if the supervisors are not authorised to intervene in the bank's accounting, as then the problem could cumulate in front of the supervisor's eye until it spirals out of control.

If the bank loses enough to wipe out all its junior liabilities, all MREL will disappear. Then the government can provide capital. After giving the capital, the government would become the owner of a healthy bank. The government can then sell the bank and recover a significant part of the cost or even all of it. For the government, it is better to have two required capitals at stake instead of just one. Also, it comes handy to have money banks collected explicitly for that purpose.

Such a mechanism, in all the cases except the biggest one, protects the government budget from unexpected resolution costs.

The risk of possible government involvement in the bailout of failed banks should not worry us. Such a possibility is unavoidable for all the reasons we discussed earlier. Banks of systemic importance should not go bankrupt. The associated social costs proved prohibitive. Therefore, the modern banking system requires government intervention as the final "backstop" in a situation of unavoidable failure of such an institution.

The principal line of defence against such costs imposed on the government is intrusive supervision and strong capitalisation of banks.

So, the introduction of MREL is a piece of good news. Though it would not formally increase the robustness of banks, it would offer a flexible, though complex and demanding framework for dealing with a failing bank.

Having MREL is a good thing. Still, the cost of MREL in the present environment should bother us. The price of MREL depends on the bank's reputation. Investors at this moment perceive that only a handful of the major European banks are worth their money. In such circumstances, the question is, what will be the price of MREL for the majority of EU banks of systemic importance.

If investors perceive that their shares are worth half of the book, this means that already on the day of signing, they should consider the conversion of their CoCos as possible, even probable.

The same investors invest in shares and CoCos. So, what will they ask for CoCos? We can only guess. It is a new regulation, still in the process of implementation. So, no bank met MREL as yet, although the regulation already has years on its shoulders. The Directive, 2014/59, BRRD, was approved in 2014. It is a directive, not a law. The directive does not apply as a regulation, but it orders member states to make their laws accordingly. That makes the implementation process unavoidably slow. Nevertheless, not so slow.

This directive took quite an extended implementation period. It is a significant and essential change in rules. For such a radical change, a smooth transition is fundamental for its success. Furthermore, the situation on the market is not encouraging for its urgent implementation.

According to the schedule, the amounts of MREL for significant banks and groups were supposed to be defined during 2019. However, it is postponed until the end of 2020.

When the resolution authority makes the decision, banks will issue such instruments on the market. They are supposed to collect all MREL until 2024. That obligation will overlap with phase-in of output floors in Basel III. Therefore, the banks will offer to the market a lot of "quasi-capital instruments" in the following period. Unless something radically changes, that could severely weaken some already weak banks.

Everybody is, as usual, verbally committed to implementing measures that would decrease risks in the financial systems. Still, there is reluctance in the implementation. The hesitation is entirely rational. The market senses it and, as a consequence,

European banks are notably under-priced compared to US banks. The pricing difference is visible in both the ratio between the price and book value (price-to-book) and between the price and performance (price-to-earning).

Those requirements will be a new burden on the banks' profit. For some banks, the charge could be quite substantial.

For example, let us assume there is a bank that barely satisfies the capital requirement of 10 billion EUR. Now, let us assume it makes a modest before-tax return on equity of 8%. Its shares are traded somewhere around the average for EU banks, eight times income, or about 50% of the book value. Now, the MREL requirement is put forward for another 10 billion of capital or CoCos.

Investors already trade their shares at a discount, indicating that they don't believe that the bank is worth as much as the accounts say.

Even if all accounts are fundamentally accurate, the investor's negative expectations could easily become true. As the investors are reluctant to buy new issuances, and the bank is forced by a firm deadline to collect MREL, then the investors would set a high price. Let's say 9%. The bank would have no choice but to accept it.

New money received from investors in MREL instruments in the present situation could only be invested in bonds with low or negative returns or would replace practically free liabilities. The cost of MREL should then burden the bank's operating results. The bank could plunge to marginal profitability or even to operating loss, putting the price of its shares further down. Consequently, the price of CoCos falls below face value. So, by a single bold regulatory action, a perfectly sound bank is turned into loss-maker, cut off from the possibility of new stock issuance, profit retention or MREL collection. The bank suddenly becomes a problem without having done anything wrong.

Furthermore, the requirements would come to all banks at the same time. Their simultaneous pressure on the market would not help. If due to the cost of MREL, the entire industry's performance will decrease, the distress would only increase.

A precondition for successful MREL issuances is strengthening the reputation of European banks. If the enforcement of the regulation would disregard the actual situation, then a request to prepare the banks for resolution could even cause some of them to fail.

Nonetheless, despite all the risks, the process should go on. It is an integral part of the overall banking security architecture.

Again, we move in the circle. MREL collection should improve confidence in the industry, but trust is an unavoidable precondition for the successful collection of MREL without undesired side effects. Here, regulators are facing quite a frustrating experience, a kind of *circulus vitiosus*. MREL increases regulatory overhang, which increases investors' ambiguity. Such worries decrease share prices, increasing further fears and overhang. Alexander is needed to deal with the knot.

That is the problem burdening European banking and the investors' community at the moment. In the US, the prices of bank shares are generally above or close to the book value. If the price of a bank's stock is above the book, then TLAC instruments will be priced reasonably. The higher the stock price is, the easier and cheaper the

TLAC collection should be. Of course, the mechanism is not fully deterministic, but it would best explain investors' expectations.

The stock price represents the belief of shareholders in the bank's future performance. If people firmly believe in the future of the bank and buy its shares with a premium, they would have no reason to set a high price for MREL. The possibility of conversion will not be priced.

Still, in early 2020, stock price indicators of American banks are much lower than those of other large American companies. A request for TLAC could be one of the reasons. Nonetheless, the US handled the regulatory request much better than EU. First of all, they applied TLAC where Basel committee aimed it—on G-SIBs. Majority of US banks, even large US banks, are relieved from that request. The EU designed MREL request for other systematically important banks, while the Americans can afford not to do it. Their banks have, on average, much more capital than EU banks.

The Americans also made a wise regulatory move, directing TLAC requests and resolution planning towards bank holding companies instead of licenced operational banks. In the EU, especially if the resolution strategy is the so-called "multiple point of entry", the entire focus is directed towards operational banks.

Also, the US solved a big problem that the EU ignores, which is the incompatibility of the "single point of entry" resolution strategy with the limited liability of a holding company. The Americans breach the limited liability of the holding company by requesting it to sign a contract promising in the case of distress the support to the banks it holds. Then, in case of peril, the holding company will go bankrupt instead of the operational bank. The beauty of this solution is simple: no one except its shareholders would care. The deposits, payment orders and cards will all perform well.

In the EU, resolution planning does not involve such a breach of limited liability. This means that the SRB performs resolution planning without the formal commitment of the bank involved in the plan. So, if the chosen strategy is a single point of entry, the owner of a bankrupt bank is allowed to invoke limited liability with impunity. After all, the resolution was the Single Resolution Board's plan, not its. The law should be on its side.

References

Admati, A., & Hellwig, M. (2014). *The bankers' new clothes*, Princeton University Press.

FDIC. (2019). https://www.fdic.gov. Retrieved from https://www.fdic.gov/bank/individual/failed/banklist.html.

Kay, J. (2015). *Other people's money*, Profile Books. ISBN 978-1781254431.

Nuevo, I. P. (2019, September). Has the new bail-in framework increased the yield spread between subordinated and senior bonds? Working Paper Series.

Chapter 11
Banking Regulation in the EU

Abstract The EU banking regulation is, as the EU itself, a unique structure in the world. Two unique features of EU banking regulation are single jurisdiction with several legal frameworks and several jurisdictions sharing the same legal framework. The pile of regulation applying to banks is enormous. Such nature of the regulation emerges from the nature of the EU. It is maybe unavoidable but is it useful to apply such a complex regulation on the institutions having literary all the money in the world to pay lawyers? There are promising recent changes, but as politics initially got cold feet the term gradually in their implementation now really means it. Our children will see their full impact.

The EU banking regulation is, as the EU itself, a unique structure in the world. There was nothing like it before, so the regulatory framework develops based on the gained experience and political will of EU member states.

In a single country, the development of banking regulation is complex. There are many interests connected with banking, and they are involved and motivated during the creation of the regulation. Nevertheless, compared with the situation in other jurisdictions, the complexity in the EU increases several times. The process of reaching agreement goes on national and EU level, with multiple iterations and compromises.

EU is not even single jurisdiction. It has eurozone, which is nominally one jurisdiction. Nevertheless, it is hard to claim that it functions as a single unified jurisdiction. NCAs have a relatively wide area of influence within individual countries, and there are significant national discretions in the regulation. Nominally, all the banks are supervised by Single supervisory mechanism, though the majority of banks are, except for licencing, supervised locally. Furthermore, there are countries out of Eurozone, that are separate jurisdictions in any meaning, except that same legal framework apply.

So, those are two unique features of EU banking regulation: single jurisdiction with several legal frameworks due to national discretions and macro-prudential autonomy and several jurisdictions sharing the same legal framework. Nonetheless, that is just a beginning.

D. Odak, *A Political Economy of Banking Supervision*,
https://doi.org/10.1007/978-3-030-48547-4_11

Two main acts regulating EU banking are Regulation No 575/2013 and Directive 2013/36. For simpler orientation in this alphanumerical soup, we usually call them by their nicknames: Capital requirement regulation (CRR) for 575/2013 and Capital requirement directive (CRD) for 2013/36.[1]

There is an essential difference between those documents. The regulations are in fact laws—they apply on the EU level and in each country directly. So, courts and regulators should apply their text, if possible uniformly, across the EU. The uniformity takes care European court of justice, which is the final instance of appeal.

The directive, on the other hand, is an order given to EU parliaments to make laws in line with it. Each national Parliament makes law accordingly and then apply it as domestic law. ECJ can be involved in so-called infringement procedure—the procedure establishing whether the law correctly applied the directive.

Consequently, EU banking regulation consists of single Regulation (575), 27 national Credit institution acts applying the Directive (36) and all bylaws and guidelines implemented by the NCA-s. Making the task of following the regulation more demanding, CRR was frequently amended. Eight regulations changed CRR during the period 2014–2019: three commission delegated regulations and five regulations. Most interesting among them is Regulation 2019/2033, which regulates investment firms. Nevertheless, it also by-the-way changed the definition of the credit institution.

After those small changes, big changes occurred in 2019 when the first significant amendment of the CRR and CRD came—Regulation 2019/876 and Directive 2019/878.

Those changes implemented, among other things, conclusions of the Basel committee from 2017—so-called Basel III and a half.

On top of all that, there is the Directive, 2014/59, BRRD, regulating bank resolution and recovery. Based on that directive parliaments of the member countries made 27 laws.

Implementation of the regulation goes through so-called technical standards. There are two basic types—implementing technical standards (ITS) and Regulatory technical standards (RTS). Those technical standards, approved by EBA, solve some aspects of the main regulation making it easier and more precise for implementation. Then there are guidelines issued by NCA-s and SSM.

It is clear from this description that the pile of regulation applying to banks is enormous. No one knows how big it is, for example, in the number of standard pages. Only the pinnacle of it, CRR and CRD, together with their significant amendments from 2019 have about thousand seven hundred standard pages. Now we should add 27 national laws based on CRD, delegated regulations implementing ITS and RTS, national bylaws, a directive and 27 national laws of the BRRD framework, again regulations implementing it, and so on.

Such a volume of the regulation, obviously makes compliance very demanding. There is a lot of banking groups operating in a lot of EU countries. They should comply with all banking laws and bylaws applicable, so compliance must consider

[1]It is important to remember the way of numberation of documents. Now they all have year first and number last. Until 2015 regulations had number first preceded with abbreviation No.

several thousand pages before making an opinion. Furthermore, part of the legislation consists of large numbers of non-linear mathematical formulas. Handling such regulation requires multidisciplinary compliance function, as lawyers are seldom good in mathematics.

Besides, someone must supervise the regulation. In the Eurozone ECB, while doing supervision, must respect the specific national position of each supervised bank. It should monitor banking groups according to several national legal frameworks. It does not make the ECBs job any easier.

Such nature of the regulation emerges from the nature of the EU. Though it is maybe unavoidable, one can have a reasonable doubt how useful it is. EU applies such a complex regulation on the institutions which, as we earlier said, have all the money in the world to pay for lawyers and advisors. In such a vast pile of paper, it would be a wonder if there is not a lot of non-intended or even silently intended loopholes and contradictions. In such cases, only when ECJ makes a verdict, it is clear what parliament wanted to say. It usually means about 10 years after any dispute began.

Fortunately, there are people whose heart do not faint when they face such a forbidding mountain of the paper. Those able to focus on important things and try to improve them at least a little.

Among them are the first head of ECB supervision, Mrs Danièle Nouy and her team. We said non-performing assets are the murkiest part of the balance sheet, and for the success of supervision, it is essential to keep them under control. Knowing that, they decided to strengthen regulation concerning those assets. To achieve it, they proposed in 2018 an addendum to the Guidelines approved in 2017. It introduced an automatic decrease in the accounting value of the asset as the period of non-performance gets longer. That would strongly motivate banks to solve those loans as soon as practical, before the ticking of the clock pushes their accounting value below their actual value.

The dynamics following that proposal was messy. As usual, verbally everyone supported the noble intentions, but there were a lot of issues preventing the application of such guidelines. However, it was not easy to stop Mrs Nouy and finally, the revised guidelines were published a few months before she finished her mandate. The ECB organised a farewell party, sang a few songs and approved the guidelines. Those guidelines are the first deliberate step intended to resolve the big issue of the magic.

But afterwards, things became complicated again. A year after the guidelines were approved, a similar mechanism appeared in the new Regulation 2019/630. That improved the situation, as the regulation partially removed the constraint created by the formulation from Sect. 6.1, of the initial guidelines: "While this guidance cannot provide specific accounting requirements…".[2] The regulation has a much stronger position. It enables supervisors to decrease the regulatory capital of a bank by the amount of lacking provisions.

The ECB is a supervisor of the EU banking market, but as such, it is not a regulator. Therefore, neither is it allowed to make banking rules, nor it has a vote in the bodies

[2]ECB (2017, p. 66).

approving them—a strange message. Still, the addendum and later regulation went through, and that is good. What is not good is the effort and time spent to implement a much-needed change.

The implementation of Regulation 2019/630, amending Regulation No 575/2013, makes the future supervisory position potentially stronger. Still, instead of solving the issues we discussed here, it opened new questions and uncertainties we will discuss in the last chapter.

Unfortunately, the new regulation imposes a limitation. It applies only to assets acquired after April 2019. It created an awkward situation where supervisors are supposed to treat loans with the same fundamental characteristic in three distinguished regimes.[3] ECB solved the treatment of the loans that became NPLs before April 2018 by public communication from July 2018. Supervision will treat the loans disbursed before April 2019 and becoming NPLs after April 2018 according to the addendum. Finally, the CRR regulates loans granted after April 2019. For readers interested in understanding the obstacles and unnecessary work loaded on ECB supervision, we recommend finding and reading the communication. Available online, footnote 3, URL in the reference.

Now, let us discuss the substance of the problem. The source of all this confusion is an issue of legal certainty. Legal certainty means that once you concluded a contract based on the applicable law, the new law is not supposed to change your rights under the contract. It is an important principle. But it applies to personal and material aspects of the contract. Here we talk about accounting rules.

The accounting rules do not affect material rights. Therefore, the principle of legal certainty should not govern them. They influence the presentation of those rights, not right themself. In the case of Regulation 2019/630, we do not even talk about changing the accounting value, but about the decrease of regulatory capital. Therefore, whichever way the bank presents an asset in its accounts or its regulatory capital, the shareholders will finally receive a cash flow attached to those assets. Altering the accounting presentation does not change the material rights in any way.

Accounting of fundamentally similar assets should be consistent. Same things must have equal value, despite a year of origination. They are either worth 100 EUR, or not. A statement that the bank has 100 million of capital because those loans were defaulted in 2017, while it would have no capital if those mortgages were originated in 2020 is by its nature the abrogation of the syntagma "banking supervision".

The incorrect application of the standards leads to a double absurd. The addendum applies legal certainty not based on the contract date but the date of the contract breach. The principle of legal certainty does not work that way. At least, it did not work until this innovation.

Now insufficient provisions on assets becoming NPLs before April 2019 cannot be subtracted from a bank's capital. Or maybe they can. In its introduction the regulation says the following under item 6: "The prudential backstop should not prevent competent authorities from exercising their supervisory powers in accordance with Directive 2013/36/EU. Where competent authorities ascertain on a case-by-case basis

[3] ECB, www.bankingsupervision.europa.eu (2019, p. 8).

that, despite the application of the prudential backstop for NPEs[4] established by this Regulation, the NPEs of a specific institution is not sufficiently covered, it should be possible for them to make use of the supervisory powers provided for in Directive 2013/36/EU, including the power to require institutions to apply a specific provisioning policy or treatment of assets in terms of own funds requirements. Therefore, it is possible, on a case-by-case basis, for the competent authorities to go beyond the requirements laid down in this Regulation for the purpose of ensuring sufficient coverage for NPEs."

Does this "go beyond" involve the ability of the competent authority to decrease regulatory capital for insufficient provision of exposures originated before April 2019? Some would say "Obviously!". Others would tell: "No way!". It is not explicitly solved in item 6. So, what now?

Therefore, if supervision finds out that a bank would fail due to its legacy NPL portfolio, they must decide whether the bank has failed or not. Whichever way they decide, they run an enormous legal risk. The invoice for this risk could amount to billions—quite a lot of them. There is no better way of preventing supervision from acting than serving it with obvious legal risk.

Finally, there is a possible situation when accounting rules become a matter of legal certainty. They become so in the case of moral hazard. Than material right do not refer to the fundamental value of the enterprise, but on the amount of dividends and other material benefits shareholder can enjoy before ..it hits a fan. That is an actual material impact. It is hard to believe that it is the reason why regulators consider the rules as material right. Nonetheless, it is also hard to find an alternative explanation.

Notwithstanding everything we said, the fact is that present regulation re-established the stability of the banking system after the crisis. Why then contemplating its change again? Every change bear risks and risks associated with the shift in the banking regulation are, because of everything we discussed earlier, huge.

One reason is—it is just too complicated. Such level of complexity unavoidably creates unintended costs and consequences.[5] In the European case, it is written frequently as a compromise not only between regulators, politics, and industry but also among countries. So, its language in the process of reaching agreements is sometimes vague or deliberately ambiguous. Regulation 575/2013 and Directive 36/2013 together have 270.000 words, which is equivalent to about 1000 standard pages. The risk reduction package approved in April 2019 is about 60% that size. It is just the pinnacle on the heap of regulation we earlier described.

Regulations 575 and 876 also contain pages of complicated non-linear mathematical formulas taken from the Basel accord. The purpose of a law is not to be interesting for mathematicians, but to be transparent and predictable, enabling compliance officers to give a clear answer to the board. It is unlikely that any of the

[4]NPE—non-performing exposure.

[5]"We should put an end on seemingly endless proliferation of complex rulebooks which are even now beyond comprehension of far too numerous regulatory professionals." p. 8.

"A few minutes at a meeting of regulatory professionals leave one crying out for someone who can see wood from the trees" (Kay, 2015, p. 305).

compliance officers are masters of mathematics. They probably studied law precisely to avoid mathematics they did not like. Same goes to judges that are supposed to ensure enforcement of the law. The law without enforcement or with unpredictable enforcement is not good.

If, for example, the proper application of the article 280b imposing so-called Capital AddOn for credit risk through the following formula:

$$\mathrm{AddOn}_j^{\mathrm{Credit}} = \sqrt[j]{\left(\sum_k \rho_k^{\mathrm{Credit}} \cdot \mathrm{AddOn}(\mathrm{Entity}_k)\right)^2 + \sum_k \left(1 - \left(\rho_k^{\mathrm{Credit}}\right)^2\right) \cdot \left(\mathrm{AddOn}(\mathrm{Entity}_k)^2\right)}$$

become subject to the legal dispute, the outcome of that dispute appears to be very unpredictable.

Besides, the text offers a few from the supervisory point unusual solutions. For example, a bank was allowed to give an unlimited amount of loans to its major shareholders and related companies for real estate development projects.[6]

That is a slightly exaggerated statement: the amount is not unlimited. If we take into account the leverage limit and liquidity requirement, depending on the structure of liabilities, it is about 20–25 times the capital. Just apply articles 402 and 395 in connection with 126 and the hocus-pocus is there. It also helps if you have the friendliest appraiser money can buy.

We should keep in mind that financing real estate was the primary source of the most post-1929 banking troubles in developed countries. Therefore, real estate financing, both mortgages and commercial, should be an area of special attention. How could this be achieved when such a gaping hole was open in the primary law governing the area?

Strange enough, such a solution is not the lawmakers' mistake, but rather their intention. Lawmakers even placed built-in "switches" enabling countries to decide whether they will apply this possibility or not. Some states required it, as they wanted their banks to finance real estate projects without regulatory hindrances. As such, compromise was acceptable to those who did not want it to happen. They chose not to do it and let others do it.

The situation now is somewhat different. In the meantime, the European Central Bank took over the supervision of the most important banks in the Eurozone. So, it is now supposed to have the major say how the law will be applied. Nevertheless, national authorities have national discretions, and the banks have legal remedies for actions of ECB.

Furthermore, as we already learned, the ECB has to have a political background for each new set of rules. In the EU, political context means mingling through an uncertain and long decision-making process.

That is not the only example where this regulation put regulators in the position requiring them first to create a defendable legal ground and then to act. Such an approach sometimes takes quite a lot of resources, imagination and courage to achieve

[6]Glossary: CRR—real estate treatment.

the desired objectives. As we all know, the most imaginative and courageous people in the world usually do not become public servants.

The law must clearly demonstrate lawmakers' intentions. In the case of EU banking regulation, it is hard to feel those intentions. In many areas, bankers got the upper hand. Speaking in military terminology, instead of on hilltops, lawmakers positioned supervision in the valleys. Instead of comfortably holding the high ground, regulators are in a position to fight expensive, difficult and risky uphill battles.

Many battles over the regulation go on as we speak. The interesting thing is that almost all fierce battles finally bear on the treatment of real estate. The most important topics are risk weights and asset quality.

Banks were until recently very successful in those battles. Conditionally successful—future will teach us whether low resilience of the banking system is anyone's success.

In some EU jurisdictions, by applying IRB, banks are allowed to use risk weights below 10% for mortgage loans. The capital requirement is 8% of the risk-weighted amount for mortgages. Therefore, if a bank's balance sheet is a combination of mortgages, cash and government bonds, the overall capital requirement could be much below 1% of total assets. Without additional measures, such a bank could support a portfolio over 100 times its equity. We already said that all recent banking crises emerged from real estate financing. Such low-risk weights for mortgages certainly do not provide a guarantee that another one is not possible.

The recent change in regulation, mostly Regulation 2019/876, made limits to such excesses. It introduced leverage and output floors for IRB. It is good, while relatively long implementation period, until 2027, is not so good.

Nonetheless, in this regulation, the purpose of the leverage is not to obstruct the "normal" functioning of risk-sensitive measures. Therefore, any methodology producing leverage above 3% is "normal".

If there is a long period of permanent increase in real estate prices, then obviously non-performance would be rare, and LGD very low. The increased value of real estates covered all losses, and expected loss will practically tend towards zero. Consequently, IRB risk weights would be very low. Does this tell us anything about the future?

We can answer "yes" only if we expect that the growing trend of the prices will be permanent. This assumption reminds us of our earlier discussion about price bubbles. On the other hand, if we assume the possibility of a reversal in real estate prices, such an approach could create extreme systemic risk.

The European real estate market recently proved to be a robust one. Except for a few southern countries, in the EU there was no sharp decrease in housing prices. Nevertheless, we should be aware that it tells us nothing about the future.

It is essential to recognise that, by allowing low and extremely low-risk weights, banking supervision helps people to get cheap housing loans. Despite its unquestionable independence, considerations about public reactions silently influence supervisory actions. The approach to housing and commercial real estate loans is the most obvious example. While developing the regulation, supervisors pushed aside negative experiences and allowed the IRB approach based on favourable mid-term data to demonstrate how robust this portfolio is.

Still, we should be careful when calling that beneficial to consumers. It could easily prove to be quite the opposite—consumers could find themselves subsidising the banks' risk-taking.

Consumers take a fully secured loan with recourse for purchasing real estate on the market in an extremely low-interest environment and with an ageing and potentially decreasing population. What are the odds that this market will experience continual growth? We know the rule: low-interest rates—high real estate prices. If market rates are negative, as they are today, their future change could push real estate prices only downward. The influence of demographics could easily be similar. Banks offer a fairly asymmetric risk distribution when they motivate clients to take such loans.

As opposed to the American approach, European lending is "with recourse". That means that the borrower bears all risk of future developments in the real estate market. Despite all, unless the client is financially ruined, the loan will be entirely repaid to the bank. It is not possible to "give keys to the bank" and walk away. Therefore, by offering highly leveraged and readily available loans, the bank motivates the consumers to bet on future real estate prices. Those risks could become significant in the case of declining housing prices.

Fortunately, in Europe north of Alps, there is no recent history of a sharp fall in the housing prices. So, hopefully, this risk would remain only hypothetical. However, there was also no history of the sharp rise of the Swiss Franck against EUR or DM before 2010. The old rule says, "What can happen, eventually will happen". When it does, we should better be ready.

In the US, there were cases of abandoning entire neighbourhoods or even towns. Houses there lost all of their market value. In those circumstances, "walking away" was the only viable solution for the debtors, enabling them to honour the contract with a bank, maintain their credibility and have a fresh start in a new environment. In Europe, a radical fall in prices did not happen. At least not on the housing market.

Still, in the existing environment, even a relatively moderate price oscillation could bring a serious number of consumers, using high leverage, "underwater". In the case of any adverse change in their income, those consumers would have meagre options. They cannot continue repaying their debt, but also, they cannot sell their flat and fully repay their debt. Today, in a bank's books, such loans sometimes require less than 1% of the capital. Is this a reasonable approach?[7]

But let us put aside the concern about risks in banking and take a look at the clients' position. What would happen to those people in case of an unfavourable development on the real estate markets and economy? They would lose their credibility and dwelling while remaining indebted.

Enabling such debtors to slip out of the debt trap without losing credibility and getting an unsound credit history would be a better solution. However, the precondition to contemplate such a solution is that banks have much more capital. So, for the

---

[7] "The result of extreme leverage is predictable, though its timing never is." (Blinder, 2013).

time being, EU citizens will, by giving full recourse, continue subsidising the banks' risk-taking in housing real estate.

Maybe it is a good deal. This subsidy, together with low capital requirements, enables banks to offer incredibly affordable interest rates for housing loans. So, everything is ok if everything is ok. Otherwise, as it was in the case of Spain, consumers will pay dearly.[8]

By 2012 in several countries, the portfolio of non-performing loans reached well above 10% of gross loans. Furthermore, in many jurisdictions, the average Texas ratio was close to or higher than 100%. The net value of the bank was smaller than the net worth of the non-performing loans. The net value of the non-performing loans is the nominal value of those loans decreased by the expected loss.

The champion is one institution declaring this ratio over 700% and remaining solvent. At the end of 2012, six EU countries boasted that the average weighted Texas ratio in their banking system exceeded 0.9.[9]

Now let us go back to the earlier mentioned "holy grail". Formally, the answer whether the banks are solvent is clear: yes, they are solvent. Solvency is an accounting category, and their accounts demonstrated that they were solvent.

The real question is would they be solvent if the banks applied different accounting policies? Now, the answer is not so simple and straightforward. We can be confident that it was possible to design quite reasonable accounting policies which would result in the insolvency of some of those banks.

Some EU regulators did not exactly encourage the application of conservative accounting policies. The perceived lack of consistency in reporting asset quality created an overhang, depreciating the price of EU bank shares. Unfortunately, such lack of confidence was not limited only to the banks using optimistic accounting policies. All the banks were affected, despite the actual quality of their reporting.

A significant number of EU regulators would disagree with this statement, claiming that such a cautious approach saved the day, enabling EU banking to finance the real economy and therefore support its recovery from recession.

Maybe it served the purpose, but it also severed the confidence of investors in EU banks. The politics appreciate and encourage such a cautious and balanced approach of regulators. Investors have difficulty to understand such arguments! They focus on the expected cash flow from the investment and the likelihood of receiving it. Today they notice problems in both areas, and that has consequences.

The destiny of European banking, its growth and ability to support the real economy is in the hands of investors, while the fate of regulators is in the hands of politicians. Unfortunately, it appears that in this particular case, those two groups of people do not understand each other.

Through the valuation of EU banks, the market explicitly expresses doubts about European banking reporting and oversight. If the market perceives supervisors as

---

[8]"Spanish housing in the 2000s was the US experience on steroids." p. 119.

"Government officials say Spain's system of personal guarantees saved its banks from the turmoil..." (Atif Mian, 2014, p. 121).

[9]Mody and Wolf (2015).

reluctant or restrained, then investors could conclude that the banks' accounting is too optimistic. In such a situation, only bold moves should convince them otherwise.

One thing must be clear—the ECB supervision is not the culprit for the situation. The problem mainly emerges from the restraints this young organisation suffered from the very beginning. These restraints are constraining the authority of the SSM more than any other banking supervising authority in the world. The ECB supervision faces constrained judgement, the inability to order accounting adjustments and restrictions on the scope of the new guidelines. How to fight with legs and arms restrained?

As we already mentioned, Mrs Nouy managed to push through a very good addendum to the guidelines. The primary requirements of the addendum are now made compulsory by the new regulation. It should gradually improve the situation. However, politics initially got cold feet and restricted the scope of those guidelines in Regulation 630 in such a way that the term gradually now really means it. Our children will see their full impact.

References

Atif Mian, A. S. (2014). *House of debt*, University of Chicago Press. ISBN 978-0226081946.

Blinder, A. S. (2013). *After the music stopped*, Penguin Books. ISBN 014312448X.

ECB. (2017). Guidance to banks on non-performing loans. Retrieved from https://www.bankingsupervision.europa.eu, https://www.bankingsupervision.europa.eu/ecb/pub/pdf/guidance_on_npl.en.pdf.

ECB. (2019, August). www.bankingsupervision.europa.eu. Retrieved from https://www.bankingsupervision.europa.eu/press/letterstobanks/shared/pdf/2019/ssm.supervisory_coverage_expectations_for_NPEs_201908.en.pdf.

Kay, J. (2015). *Other people's money*, Profile Books. ISBN 978-1781254431.

Mody, A., & Wolf, G. B. (2015, July). The vulnerability of Europe's small and medium sized banks. Bruegel Working Paper.

Chapter 12
European Banking—Yesterday and Today

Abstract US financial market is "the market". It tells you the price, whether you like it or not. European financial markets are different. EU and Euro-area are very much bank-centric. The bulk of the assets is here immersed in stagnant pools of "hold to maturity" and "historical cost". In the EU, everything is slower and exposed to judgement and discretion. The reality always catches up at the end, but it takes a while before it shows up. The crisis 2008–2009 demonstrated the difference very convincingly. While American banks had two terrible years and remained profitable ever after, EU banks were profitable throughout the crisis. However, from 2012 onwards they desperately try to crawl away from the grasp of reality going after them.

EU and Euro-area are very much bank-centric. When we talk about Euro-area and EU banking, besides the regulation, the banking itself is also huge. It is among the relatively biggest in the world. Assets of the euro-area banking are more than 2, 5 times the GDP. As such, it dwarfs some other large jurisdictions, for example, the US which has a banking system with total assets barely above GDP.

Another difference is in the structure. While in the US and some other developed countries, significant market shares hold specialised financial institutions, in the EU, almost all commercial banks are the universal bank.

European banks have by far leading position among financial firms. Consequently, banking credit is, also by far, a dominant mean of financing for all except the largest borrowers. Financial markets of EU are much timider and smaller than the US financial markets. Also, they are less liquid.

For example, capitalisation on New York stock exchange oscillates around 30 trillion US$ while NASDAQ has another ten. Two largest stock exchanges have joint capitalisation over two times US GDP. Total capitalization on the two largest European stock exchanges, Euronext and Deutsche Börse does not reach 6 trillion EUR, or slightly above one-third of EU BDP.

Those ratios nicely illustrate the differences, which exist not only in structure but also in the spirit of the market.

D. Odak, *A Political Economy of Banking Supervision*,
https://doi.org/10.1007/978-3-030-48547-4_12

US financial market is "the market". It tells you the price. Whether you like it or not, there is hardly any place to hide. The legal and regulatory framework supports such market. Very important for that structure is the institute of non-recourse lending. It removes a significant part of downside risk from the borrower and concentrates risk management where are people who learned in school how to do it-in banks.

The valuation of the European financial markets is different. The bulk of the assets is in the banks. The market does not permanently check its value. Those assets are immersed in a stagnant pool of "hold to maturity" and "historical cost". They are protected by a buffer of housing lending "with recourse". In the EU, everything is slower and exposed to judgement and discretion.

This discretion is always transitional and temporary. The reality always catches up at the end. However, as we will soon see, in the US finance it is quicker, while in the EU it is not in a hurry. It takes a while before showing up.

The crisis 2008–2009 demonstrated the difference very convincingly. American banks started the crisis with average leverage close to 10%, then increased it to 12% during the crisis, and they ended the crisis with leverage somewhere above 11%. EU banks started with average leverage below 6%, while some large jurisdictions were reporting less than 4%. Americans accounted for losses of roughly 25% of their initial net value for 2 years, about 3% of total assets.

An interesting difference in the performance of US and EU banks occurred during the last crisis. They both suffered losses, but in a different way and at different times. While the profitability of banks listed on the S&P 500 and Eurostoxx was quite similar in 2007, already in 2008, they were a world apart.

In the period 2008–2011 EU banks lived in the wonderland. Although the EU had 2008/2009, a deeper recession than the US, the banks appeared as if they live in the alternative reality. In 2008, American banks were up to their necks in losses. They lost almost 20% of their net value in that one year. In the same year, European banks declared small aggregate losses. Almost a break even. Next year American banks lost another 5% of their equity, while the European banks, despite a deep recession that year in the EU, were profitable. Both American and EU banks remained profitable from 2010 until 2012.

In 2012 something even stranger occurred: European banks reported aggregate losses, and continued doing so until 2016, while American banks remained profitable with RoE about 10% throughout the whole period.

Europe experienced another recession in 2012, but that one was shallow. It is unlikely that such a shallow recession created much more losses than the sharp slowdown in 2009. Therefore, it appears that the losses fundamentally attributed to the downturn in 2009 found their way into the financial statements only in the period from 2012 to 2015. If true, that would alone tell us volumes about the reliability of corporate governances, risk management and accounting policies of EU banks.

How is it possible then that US banks recorded such a horrendous loss, while EU banks reported almost a break even in 2008, and then a profit during the recession year? The difference was asset structure, the legal environment, and the capital strength of the banking system. The capital strength was the primary factor which determined the regulatory and supervisory reaction to the crisis.

The Americans reacted swiftly. They aggressively re-established confidence in the banking system shaken by the Lehman bankruptcy. They forced the managements of major banks to accept government investments in their capital. The structure of the investment was very similar to what we now call CoCos—equity and loans convertible to equity if the banks become non-compliant. So, the banks received support, but they were not nationalised unless they declared that they lost all their funds. Confidence returned. From the clients' perspective, the government funds would protect a bank's solvency even if it would lose all its earlier equity. Leverage was pushed up to 12%, making the system even better capitalised than before the crisis.

Then US banks used their high leverage to perform radical value adjustments. They did not have a choice. The balance sheets of American banks are much more exposed to the market than the balance sheets of EU banks. Postponing the recognition of losses and evergreening the non-performing portfolio was not an option.

Legal differences yielded very different results. A significant difference was non-recourse mortgages typical for the US, and lending with recourse in the EU. In the US, highly leveraged clients returned their flats and houses to the banks. The real estate market depreciated sharply. Change of the prices forced the banks to recognise the market price of the repossessed real estates. At the peak of the crisis, the value was sometimes zero, or even negative. The cost of disposal was considered higher than the expected price of the house.

The second reason for the immediate recognition of losses was derivatives—asset-based securities (ABS) in the banks' portfolios. As the housing loans lost a significant part of their value, the same thing happened to ABS in the banks' portfolios. As the market price of ABS was substantially below parity in 2008 and 2009, banks recognised the loss of their market value. An interesting fact is that a significant part of the losses reported by EU banks in 2008 was, in fact, also a consequence of the depreciated value of American derivatives purchased by the banks.

All those facts forced US banks to recognise losses, digest them and go on living. They had 2 bad years, but after that, they liquidated the repossessed portfolio above its accounting value. ABS also proved more valuable than they appeared in the depth of the crisis. Consequently, the banks became profitable and were able to repay their debt to the government while retaining a strong balance sheet. The crisis was still in their memory, but no longer in their balance sheet. Their shareholders, until now forgot losses and enjoy almost 10 years of continuous profitability.

In Europe, the situation evolved quite differently. As we already noticed, reality comes to EU with some delay, for better or worse. At first, it appeared that the crisis does not concern the EU. While the US experienced a severe economic slowdown in 2008, the EU economy grew. Impact came a year later. When the recession began in the EU, it was a big hit—4%.

As we said, banks were in the wonderland. So much so that they were profitable in 2009. Neither housing nor corporate loans indicated any troubles. They did not have any "proof of loss" required to reclassify loans and adjust their value. Banks were not the only ones reacting slowly to the crisis; their clients were also slow to demonstrate weaknesses. As we said, everything moves in slow motion here.

Housing loans in the EU are debtor's obligation. It is not possible to repay them by merely giving the flat to the bank. Consequently, debtors had no initiative to declare a default and hasten the recognition of non-performing loans. While the recognition was slow, value adjustments proved to be even slower.

In corporate banking, bad loans recognition was also very slow. In Europe, the most significant part of real estate development continued. Real estate prices were generally much more stable than in the US. In some markets, the recovery of housing prices and liquidity was quick. In other markets, the banks reacted to the crisis mostly by adjusting the repayment schedules to the "new environment". In countries where real estate prices recovered, banks did not have high non-performing loans.

Slowly moving processes started to boil after the crisis was already over. The level of non-performing loans and the Texas ratio nicely indicated it. The Texas ratios were exceptionally high, as their own funds were low. The consequence was the very reluctant adjustment of the value of the non-performing loans.

Initially, everybody was happy. No recovery actions took place. People lived in their houses although they were overdue on mortgages; banks reported profit and shareholders had nice dividends. It was so lovely and harmonious that we could ask ourselves why in the world would anyone ever pay any debt? Only in 2012, the harmony fractured.

Where recovery stalled, there was a delay in recognition of difficulties. According to the then valid IAS 39, the value of non-performing loans was equal to the net present value of its expected future cash flow. The cash flow was estimated based on real estate valuation. The collateral valuation usually exceeded the debt, triggering no value adjustment despite the duration of the non-performance.

All the factors we discussed so far had consequences. EU banks were generally not in excellent condition after recent crises. Initially, low net value made the banks vulnerable. Then, the losses generated in the crisis depleted their equity even further.

Consequently, some of them kept the losses from the crisis in their balance sheets for a prolonged period. The evergreening affected their profitability, ability to raise fresh capital and worse of all distorted their corporate governances. It appeared as a moral hazard in the making, long-lasting, omnipresent and quite visible.

It was, of course, noticed. However, fragile equity and lost access to the capital market kept supervisors from radically challenging the bank's assets. If EU banks had encountered a similar level of losses relative to assets as the US banks did, it would have undoubtedly made some large banks insolvent. The whole system could have become technically insolvent. Such a dynamic loss-taking, which would quickly mop up all consequences of the crisis from the banks' balance sheets was out of reach for European banks. They did not have enough net value to do that and continue with the business.

Under banker's influence, politicians and regulators delayed the measures aimed at strengthening the banks' capital. They also continued with the application of "risk-sensitive approach". The bankers managed to convince policymakers that such an approach is reasonable. The long period of relatively stable economic growth resolved part of the problem, but overhang remained.

Those were times before the introduction of a single supervisory mechanism. Some among the supervisors tolerated the accounting policies allowing the calculation of future cash flows based on the estimated value of the collateral, without proof that the collateral was collectable within a reasonable period, and that the bank can sell it. That created a kind of a circle: the collateral secures the value of the loans. Not exposing the collateral to the market protects the collateral price (or maybe an illusion about it). The approach was justified by its purpose—avoiding fire-sale.

In the end, the approach proved to be successful. It saved a lot of the value, most of all for debtors stricken by the crisis. The crisis subdued and NPLs were gradually resolved. Such success opens a fundamental question: should the bank have, at all times, the capital it can use to cover losses, or it is acceptable if the bank reports the capital it expects to have 5 years from now? Grammatically reading the law, it appears that the first answer is correct, while some supervisors relied on the second. This time it turned out well.

This example teaches us that it could be reasonable to allow banks operating with lower capital once a significant crisis struck. Nevertheless, it should be a deliberate and transparent decision, based on the regulation, not improvisation achieved by an innovative reading of the regulation. How to do it, we will discuss in the last chapter.

The conclusion: the recession was deeper in the EU than in the USA. Typically, banks in the more troubled economy take more losses. That wasn't the case here. Were the Americans too conservative, overshooting losses? Were the Europeans understating theirs because of too thin capital? Were the problems of EU banks digested fully over 4 years of loss-making?

It appears that there are no convincing answers to those questions with which bankers, supervisors and, most of all, investors would agree. However, the fact is that during the crisis, American banks always had the required amount of the capital, while European hoped that they would soon have it.

The non-performing loans are a significant part, but only a part of the problem. Today it is a lesser, and a more straightforward issue. The price-to-book ratio nose-dived below 1 for the first time at the beginning of 2009, and never recovered since. Whatever was hidden in those reports then, already found its way to banks' financial statements until 2018. Accounting can be tricky, but not that tricky. Most of all, it cannot hide such large amounts for such a long period and under so much scrutiny. A more credible explanation is a chain of events, one following the other, and keeping investors under pressure and uncertainty.

The most significant four Eurozone banks are in countries that have an aggregate level of non-performing loans comfortably below 5% and quite reasonable average Texas ratios. Still, in early 2019 their average price-to-book ratio was below 50%.

The reason could be a lack of profitability, which troubles one of those banks. However, the other three, although profitable, also have a low average price-to-book ratio of only 60%, less than half compared to the biggest American banks. Their earnings are also heavily discounted. If they have a price-to-earnings ratio similar to the four American largest banks, then their average price-to-book ratio would be 80%. It would partially resolve the issues of the price of capital.

US banks are priced much lower than other enterprises included in the S&P 500. Still, the investors' perception of European banks is even worse. Much worse. Moreover, even if the pricing indicators improve to the US level, many issues will remain. Several important EU banks have unresolved operational profitability problems, now persistent in the mid-term. Those banks could remain a critical regulatory challenge even if all issues of the profitable banks were solved. Those banks are big enough to rock a boat pretty hard.

We see that even the modest ambition to move stock prices near the book value proved too much. There must be a reason for it. A lot of investors invest in both the American and EU stock markets. Arbitration between the exchanges is quite efficient. Therefore, the permanent price gap indicates that it has rational reasons behind. As these doubts have persisted for years, it seems that they will not subside without someone doing something about it.

Let us try to analyse what brought us here. Despite resolved NPL crisis and several profitable years, markets remained cautious, and banks' shares continued to trade with a substantial discount.

In the investment community, now prevails consensus that banks, with few notable exceptions, digested the consequences of crises from 2009 to 2012. Still, investors feel that there are reasons for caution.

The first source of ambiguity is resistance to stress. As average leverage of Eurozone banks is half of the world average, investors have reasons for doubt how resilient they are. Besides, the share price during stable economic conditions indicates that, in the case of stress, it won't be possible to strengthen banks with private capital. If they prove frail, then investors in MREL will become owners of the bank instead of present shareholders, or even bite the dust and cover losses after depletion of insufficient capital. The investors' awareness about that risk influences current prices.

Second is the regulatory overhang. The essential element in it is the implementation of MREL.

GSII will, therefore, collect TLAC and MREL, to be fully compliant to BASEL requirements, while OSII will collect MREL. Obtaining TLAC and MREL is not a double request. They almost completely overlap. It is just an issue of checking whether both standards are fully satisfied.

Collection of MREL is required by 2024. Earlier it was meant to be in 2022, but Regulation 877/2019 postponed the deadline.

The overhang causes the fact that MREL is supposed to be almost as big as present capital of the bank, and quality of applicable instruments should be better than tier 2 instruments presently are. Therefore, GSII should until 2024 collect almost whole new capital. If their average P/B will still be 0, 5, it is quite intriguing which price they should pay for it. Some of them are dragging feet with their profitability; the cost of TLAC could make them even less profitable.

Other large banks would need to collect a certain amount, but we still do not know how much. Whenever the market waits for critical news, it tends to be cautious. Besides, it is hard to figure out what would encourage investors. High MREL would frighten them due to the cost and risk of the collection, while low would be an indicator of relinquishing policy of improving resilience.

The overhang also creates the implementation of Basel III hard floors for IRB. Many EU banks implemented so-called advanced approaches, and those banks decreased their risk density radically. For example, in the Euro-area, capital adequacy is 2, 5 times higher then leverage, while in the US, the ratio is 1, 25. Therefore, Euro-zone (SSM) banks require half of the capital requirement per unit of assets compared with US banks. Implementation of the IRB floors will change it.

On the level of the banking system, the situation appears to be manageable. Declared level of total capital adequacy is 18%. So, even if the application of the Basel III increases the risk density to the American standard, capital adequacy will remain above a minimum of 8%. However, what is valid for the system is not valid for each bank. From available public data, it is not possible to predict the situation in individual banks with certainty.

No bank until now declared its roadmap to fully loaded Basel III. Again, the market waits and becomes cautious.

On top of it, EBA churns out a steady flow of new regulation, increasing operative burden and compliance risks. Public perception of banking is negative, and consequently, political and judicial moves on banks are uncertain and possibly extremely expensive.

This situation generates the complex vicious circle: banks can't collect capital as their shares are sold with a discount, while the shares are sold with a discount because the market expects that the banks will not be able to collect capital and meet regulatory requirements. Decreasing the requirements will not help, as all are aware that without strengthening capital banks are too sensitive to shocks.

Relatively low profitability of some banks, sensitivity to stress and present legal risks do not improve the situation. A lack of confidence created by a combination of all the mentioned reasons causes the high price of capital and potentially a harmfully high cost of MREL.

During the crisis, while they were still shouting "Never again", bankers explain to the politicians what the consequences could have what they called "unreasonably high capital requirements". In one moment "unreasonable" meant more than 2% leverage—own funds in some banks were less than 2% of total assets. Politicians immediately took it seriously, warning regulators to be careful while designing rules. So, EU regulators applied two strategies to improve the situation: a flexible approach to risk density and a slow, gradual push on asset quality.

This strategy sweeps below the carpet the problem of low leverage. Capital adequacy of the banks improved without any dynamics of the leverage. So, time passed while we were all looking in the wrong direction. The EU missed the chance to use a period of growth preparing for troubles ahead. Who misses an opportunity to solve big problems in good times will need to deal with even bigger issues in bad times. It will not be easy.

The real problem is the equity shortage, and it should be addressed and resolved by opening the banks' access to markets and requesting them to use it. If that proved difficult, it was always possible to strengthen banks by retaining profit. That possibility was also dismissed.

The reasoning behind the approach was the fear that if banks retain their profit, the prices of the banks' shares would further fall. Issuing additional capital instruments would become even more difficult. It appears to be the wrong reasoning.

Share prices are for most banks already too low to make new issues. Retaining profit would, in most cases, raise enough money to solve the problem, or at least to diminish it. The paradox is that if banks collect capital through profit retention, the stock price is irrelevant. However, profit retention proved as quite a hot topic and almost all troubled banks still pay generous dividends. Instead of solving the problem, regulators let it be. Understandably, the market remained unimpressed.

To make sure that, despite scarce capital, banks continue with their usual activity, regulators implement new rules very gradually and with long delays. At the same time, they allow fragile banks to pay their profit as dividends!

Whether investors are too cautious, or they understand the situation better than regulators? After all, the EU banking system survived 2008 and the sovereign debt crisis, and it now appears more resilient than at the beginning of those crises. Still, except dividends, investors did not have a lot of joy from that. Index Stoxx Europe banks were at the beginning of 2020 at 140, compared with 330 twenty years earlier. On average, there was no earning on bank stock in the period 2000–2020. Looking ahead, investors do not see a lot of reasons to expect better.

As the Lehman example teaches us, the beginning of a big mess does not require the whole system to collapse. It is enough to break one relatively important part. The consistency and practicality of regulations are the essential preconditions for preventing the disorderly failure of a strategic institution. We cannot entirely dismiss doubts whether those preconditions are fulfiled in the EU.

We saw in the previous chapter that thousands of pages of documents, mostly written and approved in the last 7 years, regulate EU banking. It is extremely demanding to follow and implement all those rules. Even if you continuously monitor the regulatory development, you still face legal uncertainty. Such an environment does not help banks to enhance their business.

Ultimately, by following instructions from those countless pages, at the end of 2018, Eurozone achieved leverage (fully loaded) of 5.28%,—one of the lowest in the world. According to the World Bank, on that date, the global average is 10.75%, while in the US it is over 11%. The ratio between declared capital adequacy and leverage is 1.27 in the US and 2, 5 in the Eurozone. It feels awkward.

Demanding more on own funds and pursuing a detailed oversight of accounts could be a better way to strengthen EU banking. With such an approach, it would be possible to relax rules notably, decrease the compliance burden and let banks do their business. Most likely, in the long run, the alternative approach would serve us better.

As we already said, the present approach proved successful in retaining the consequences of the crisis. It also improved the stability of the system. Nevertheless, it falls short of preparing the system for a possible future severe financial crisis. Such a crisis in the present situation would almost certainly require significant government backstop.

The reason for such situation most likely is the focus of regulators on short-term limitations. Refocusing on the long-term ones would not only probably increase the value of banks, but also better protect our well-being.

We can summarise regulatory developments in the EU during the last several years in three points: low risk density improved appearance of resilience, leverage stagnated and profits were paid out. While doing that, the regulators constructed a capital requirement cliff consisting of TLAC and hard floors just a few years ahead, most likely facing some economic slowdown in the meantime.

The best way to encourage investors is to explain them in plain language the grand idea behind such apparently myopic policy. After hearing the reasonable explanation, they will probably show more enthusiasm for the bank shares.

The question we are facing is: "What would happen with EU banking once the storm hit?" Do not believe people who say they have the answer, whether reassuring or frightening one.

It depends on a lot of factors we cannot know ex-ante. For example, when and what kind of storm? Banks survived the last two crises, which hit them when they were in a weaker position than they are now. The first crisis was the biggest in 80 years. Banks are much more robust than they look! Very likely, most of them could survive the usual economic downturn using only own resources. The price for the resolution of the others would probably be bearable.

Still, it would be good to omit "it depends". Also, it would be good to say "severe" instead of the "usual" downturn. Regarding banking, we recognise two alternative definitions of stability. First is the stability of the system as a whole and second is the stability of important institutions and critical groups of institutions.

Figuratively, we distinguish the robustness of a rope from the robustness of a chain. The difference is that the rope would snap when the last string snaps, while the chain would crack when the weakest link split, bringing in all the nasty consequences we call asymmetry.

The banking system usually behaves like a rope. It stands firm while the weakest strings snap. If we observe today's EU financial system through this optics, it is robust and reliable. Its reliability comes, despite low leverage, from slow adjustment and low volatility on EU markets, especially of the housing market. Besides, the bank receives massive hidden risk subsidy from consumers through borrowing "with recourse", and the EU industry proved robust and able to withstand the crisis. All those factors indicate that there is no ground for anxiety.

However, we must remember that, under extreme stress, the financial system is capable of performing a "quantum leap", figuratively turning from a rope into a chain. Though it seldom happens, it usually occurs when the least expected and needed.

Lehman is the best-known example. It was neither the first nor the last bank creating severe shock by its failure, but it was the first and hopefully will be the only bank that created a global trauma.

In such an environment, we saw that the failure of a single institution, not necessarily the biggest one, sends shockwaves through the system, generating a destabilising process. Such a shock, emerging from the financial system, could invalidate the assumption of robustness. For such a situation, it would be much safer to have higher leverage.

After a more or less successful overhaul of the system, a priority now should be strengthening the weak spots. It is hard to remain convinced that the rules governing supervision in the EU today are the most suitable to achieve that.

Of course, nothing prevents supervision from strengthening banks. Now is a good time to do it. The economy is growing, and the banks are mostly stable and profitable. It is the best possible time to address the weaknesses of significant institutions—the best, and maybe the only time to do it.

But it does not happen. Leverage stays low and indicates no dynamic. The increase in capital adequacy is driven mainly by a decrease in risk density.

Supervision should also not tolerate the fact that the market value of some of the most important EU banks has been stable around one-third or even one-quarter of their accounting value for years. Either the market is irrational, or the supervisors are reckless.

In both cases, supervisors should act. In the first case, to remove irrationality from the market by increasing the credibility of the bank's reporting, in the second case by recognising and correcting errors in the reports. The action which could achieve both objectives is the same: strong oversight.

Formally, the stock price is not a supervisory concern. But in reality, it could easily become. The price of the stock determines the ability of a bank to raise new capital. There are two ways to motivate shareholders to issue stock: the stock prices must increase, or the book value decrease.

Such a situation indicates a different perception of the risk by market and regulators. Until now, we have at least learned that, except in the very short term, no one can outsmart the market. Surprisingly little regulatory action emerged from that knowledge.

We will see that there was a strong connection between the activity of the supervision and the current level of the stock prices. Despite that, it feels that at this moment, the regulatory community lacks the will to act more decisively. As if the community is relatively happy with what it had achieved, the feeling prevails that the coalition resisting the further strengthening of supervisory powers is too strong.

Switching to the "for-further-action/wait-for-the-new-crisis" mode seems like a more reasonable option at the moment. If a new crisis comes, it would again invite politicians to shout "Never again". That would be a good time for bold steps.

If it will be no crisis on my watch, so much the better. The decision to avoid stricter regulation then proved to be a good one—it wasn't needed!

Because of such reasoning, an opportunity could be wasted to make the next crisis less likely or less severe. That would be a pity! Having strongly capitalised banks, EU regulators could shout this out every day: "The banks we supervise would be able not only to withstand a shock but also to act as a stabilising factor in any realistically possible scenery."

Today, EU regulators can only make a more cautious statement.

From 2009, the shares of an average EU bank traded permanently below their book value. That initiated a discussion about the high "price of capital".[1] If a bank can sell shares for only 50% of the book, the placement of the stock is profitable for existing shareholders if it enables generating a portfolio which brings twice the average profitability to the bank. As this is not likely, the bank typically will not issue new shares.

Still, the term "price of capital" was introduced to obscure the real problem. Talking about expensive capital makes no sense when the average SP 500 investors require only a 5% annual return. Not extraordinarily low, but it is well below the US 150 years average[2] of about 7.5%.

A suitable name for this issue is quite straightforward: "the price of the banks' shares". The apparent discount in the prices of a bank's shares compared to other stocks indicates the market concern about the quality and future of the banking business. The fact that during the last 20 years long-term investment in EU banks was not profitable additionally reinforces such feeling.

The low market value of a profitable bank raises investors' doubts about the bank's reports. The low value of a non-profitable bank is a consequence of the investors' disbelief in the ability of its management. Investors are pricing the predicament of lousy management.

Another source of low valuation of the banking stock could be the market perception of the regulatory environment. For example, the impression that the supervisor is weak would have an impact on the price of the bank shares. If an investor thinks that the supervisor handles banks with kid gloves, they will have doubts about the credibility of their reports. There are good reasons to believe that the tougher the supervision is, the higher the pricing indicators will be. But it is crucial to understand that pretending does not help. Markets quickly recognise the difference between what someone says and what they do. Actions speak louder than words.

Allegedly, higher capital requirement decreases the interest of shareholders to invest in bank stock. Let us test it empirically: buyers are willing to pay for shares following percentages of the reported book value in mid-2019: for the four biggest Eurozone banks the average is 50%; for the four biggest American banks, it is 120%.

The price-to-book ratio of banks is generally much lower in the EU than in the US. Also, there is a persistent difference in valuation between banks with similar performance. Average leverage in the EU is 5,28%, while in the US, it is 11%. Despite it, the investors in US banks appear more convinced then investors in EU banks.

If a bank reported losses, then it is no surprise if its shares are below the book. Nevertheless, even the losses would not justify those ratios well below 50%. If the bank is properly run, a rational investor should expect a quick turnaround and the

[1] "The fact that the market value is lower than the book value suggests that investors believe the book value is overly optimistic. This discrepancy between book values and market values is of immediate practical importance if the bank wants to raise new equity by selling shares in the market." (Admati & Hellwig, 2014, p. 87).

[2] S&P 500 chart.

establishment of a sustainable business model within a year or two at the most. After all, we talk about commercial banking, not about nuclear physics.

Such low ratios indicate much deeper concerns of the investors. They doubt not only present profitability, but also the bank's reports, the bank's ability to perform a turnaround, and especially its ability to withstand shock. The market discarded entire business models and the corporate governance of some banks. The question is, should supervisors tolerate what the market rejected? Supervisors have access to non-public documents and data in banks exactly to do things in another way—to recognise what the market cannot see.

Solving the issue of trust by intrusive supervision and by imposing conservative accounting, but also by establishing resilience standard acceptable for investors, in other words, regaining market confidence, should be the focus of EU regulators. For the time being, they hardly excel at it.

However, we should note that even profitable and confident American banks are traded at a discount in both the price-book and price-earnings terms, compared to blue-chip companies from other US industries. Strangely enough, a banking licence and all the benefits it brings are not such a feat anymore.

Reference

Admati, A., & Hellwig, M. (2014). *The bankers' new clothes*, Princeton University Press.

Chapter 13
What Now?

Abstract What is the purpose of the extreme complexity of the banking rules? It creates a smokescreen for loopholes left there for good purposes. To help banks to finance the economy and abundantly shower homeowners and government with almost free financing. The strategy works well. Banking is stable, interest low, inflation almost non-existent. However, the approach is reasonable only if we are confident that no significant systematic event would happen soon. Summarising earlier chapters, this one tries to offer ways forward in the specific EU regulatory environment. It proposes regulatory reset, not as a radical change of the rules, but through adjustment of the parameters in the existing regulation. The purpose is single-minded, an increase in the resilience of the EU financial system.

Why are the banking rules so complex? What is the purpose of the complexity?

They are sophisticated, complex and they appear strict. Nevertheless, as we have already seen, the rules are not as severe as they pretend to be. Their volume and complexity more act as a smokescreen for loopholes left for good purposes.

The prevailing rules and the ways that banks implement them make many people happy. They motivate banks to provide ample and affordable funding to government and citizens, especially for mortgages. What happened during the last 10 years is more or less the following: banks continued to provide the economy with loans and to flood citizens and governments with cheap loans. Supervisors gradually strengthened their capital requirements and asset quality, but in some cases, quite slowly. They do not want to hamper the banks in their activity, which makes everybody happy.

At the same time, the endless provision of money by a central bank supports liquidity. All three sides: the banks, politics and the citizens then caught the beat and waltzed together. Regulators in the process try to improve the sustainability of the banking system. While doing that they take care to avoid changing the rhythm and spoiling the dance.

Evaluating the results of such an approach, we can even admit that the strategy has worked well so far. Banking is stable, interest low and inflation almost non-existent. Banks serve the real economy and citizens well, without significant incidents. Credit

D. Odak, *A Political Economy of Banking Supervision*,
https://doi.org/10.1007/978-3-030-48547-4_13

grows at a sustainable pace, resolution of NPLs is mostly completed and interest rates are very affordable.

Maybe from a risk point of view, the approach was not optimal. It has weaknesses and undesired consequences. Nonetheless, it proved reasonable in the given circumstances. After all, the risk point is only one of the possible points of observation.

However, the strategy is reasonable only if we are confident that no significant systematic event would happen soon. So far, we have been lucky. Still, the present situation is unique in history. As it is innovative to the core, we cannot know the risks it could create. We do not know whether we live in a new normal or we still wait for "normalisation" after quantitative easing.

If it is a new normal, it is confusing. Efficient individual optimisation in time requires positive discount rates. Such optimisation is impossible within a framework of negative discount rates. The underlying reason is simple: when the market uses negative interest rates as discount rates, money becomes more valuable the later you get it. It is not in line with our nature and preferences. Market parameters, to be useful, should reflect our preferences. Unless the textbooks we learned from are all wrong, the distortion of the optimisation mechanism by negative nominal rates should cause disbalances. This means an increased sensitivity of the economy. Therefore, despite all successes of policy towards the financial sector, accepting unknown risks without significant space in fiscal and monetary policy, with high public debt and low leverage in banks could be very brave.

Fortunately, we still can say: "Don't nag, you see that everything ended well". However, nothing ended! Like in the joke about a man falling from the 15th floor. Somewhere around the fifth, he said with relief: "So far, so good".

The economy is in a period of growth, and banks are mostly performing fine. We will be able to judge regulatory achievements once the banks come under stress. Then they will not be subject to a stress test, but reality. The reality will be, as always, different.

The good news is that this time the general direction of the regulatory development brought forward by the Basel Committee is reasonable. Still, its slow application and specific elements in the EU approach towards dividends and asset quality could become a matter of concern. In time, the approach will strengthen the system. The question is: do we have time?

In this game, time is of the essence! We don't know when the banks will need every cent in their capital buffers to withstand a new flood. Nevertheless, we can safely guess that they will eventually need it! At the moment, it would be priceless if they would also have it.

In other industries, harsh security rules could obstruct economic activity, increase costs and decrease output. In banking, this is not a case. It could even be the opposite, as stricter capital requirements could reduce the compliance burden on banks and remove regulatory overhang. A higher capital requirement for banks can influence the long-term return on investment rather than any daily activity of profitable banks.

Temporarily, it could make an investment in them less attractive. We have already seen that American banks, having much more substantial leverage than EU banks, are priced higher in terms of both the price-to-book and price-to-earnings ratio. There could be a rational reason for that. Despite the almost linear decrease in profitability, higher capital steeply decreases the likelihood of total loss of investment.

If we assume that possible shocks are normally (Gaussian) distributed, then twice as sharp shock could have a much lower likelihood. For example, in the normal distribution, a negative variation of 1.5 or more standard deviations from mean has a probability of 6.7%. Twice that variation, three standard deviations, has about 50 times lower likelihood. Though we cannot know the distribution of future shocks, still investors feel that it is worth paying some profit to move from the top towards the bottom of the bell. Those insisting on staying on the top will be priced accordingly. Though we know today that strategic banks should not bankrupt, that is not good news for their shareholders. They will almost certainly pay dearly for bank's bravery.

The risks for shareholders progressively decrease as the leverage increase until they reach a zone where a further decrease in risk is tiny. At least theoretically. The problem for the optimisation of capital is the same one IRB faces from the very beginning: we do not know the distribution of future losses, and then we do not know their standard deviation. Last but not least, in reality, regulation should allow for "fat tails" not calculated in the theoretical models. Those are the reasons why we face ambiguity instead of risk.

If we knew the standard deviation of future losses, the solution would be simple. Just define the distribution of expected losses, and then calculate its integral for a specific interval. Where the decrease in profitability equals the reduction of expected loss, the capital request is optimal. Precisely—optimal from the shareholders' position.

Nonetheless, we should keep in mind that optimisation from shareholders position is not the same as optimisation from a social perspective. The regulation should keep asymmetry in mind, and make sure that the likelihood for a significant bank to fail is beyond the point shareholders would choose as optimal. Higher leverage protects the payment system, economy, budget and political order. Setting more stringent requirements means a safer future. Only a small price needs to be paid for it today.

Doing two things: requiring higher leverage and ordering adjustments of accounting value would significantly improve the safety of the system within a relatively short period. The shareholders of banks would be relatively unhappy during the transition period because they would have more money in their shares and less on their checking accounts than they desire. Once perceived improvement into the safety of the investment pushes the market price of the banks' stock up, they would just have more money. Then, they would be happy again.

Such an approach could create perils for some banks. Still, this means that those banks are also suspectable on troubles in case of adverse events. Reasonable people face difficulties when they are ready for them, instead of when they cannot avoid them.

Let us now make a simplified summary of what we learned about EU banking regulation.

From previous chapters, we learned that banking supervision is all about preventing banks from destroying the government budget or society as a whole. Repeatedly in the past banks proved that they are capable of achieving it.

With a forbidding mission comes a Herculean task: while attempting to save us, supervisors should not disturb banks in their business. If they do, the banks could stop financing the real economy. In their actions, supervisors walk a tightrope between the abysses of financial instability and credit crunch.

The essential job of supervision is deciding how much capital a bank should have and checking whether the capital exists. Banks should have the capital to pay for their mistakes without losing the depositors' or government money. If a bank does not have its own money, it relies upon a government guarantee to get cheap liabilities, and then it tends to be brave and reckless, accepting excessive risks. We call that moral hazard.

The most crucial difficulty with checking the capital of banks in Europe today is the fact that supervisors are procedurally constrained from checking it. They cannot change the valuation of assets established by management and confirmed by auditors. As they cannot adjust the estimate to what they believe is realistic, they cannot say how much money the bank has. So, management decides how much capital the bank has, and supervisors can only state their expectations and complain in case of non-compliance.

On the other hand, a bank's management has the right to use econometric models based on historical data to decide which risk weights it will apply to the bank's assets. Once approving the models, supervisors should not interfere with them. Therefore, banks are entitled to calculate how much capital they need.

Thus, banks are free to decide how much own funds they have and how much capital they need. The supervisors' main job is supposed to be doing precisely that.

As they are relieved of their primary duties, the supervisors now have enough time to do SREP, stress tests, anti-money laundering and consumer protection.

The further problem is that, without ordering an accounting adjustment, it is very hard to fail a bank orderly. The only way for a bank to fail is to admit that it does not have enough capital. Banks, especially those plagued with moral hazard, would be extremely unlikely to do it. So, failure, when it finally comes, could be quite badly timed, disorderly and big.

Though the description above summarises the major problems we discussed earlier, it is an oversimplification. It makes the presentation very clear, but fortunately, not realistic.

Banks and banking are much older than supervision, and they functioned very well for centuries without it. Before deposit guarantees, the market was a more convincing corrective than regulation. The market typically reacts more vigorously than supervision. Also, there is no legal remedy for the actions of the market. The market, knowing everything we discussed before, makes pressure and impose market discipline on banks. This pressure is not as efficient as it will be without deposit insurance. It is OK; we do not want it to be so strong!

As we have seen earlier, market characteristics, reinforced by the lack of transparency of banking, made the market too trigger-happy to be an effective corrector of banking behaviour. Recognising that, politics created the present structure, more as a replacement than a reinforcement of market discipline. So, to be effective, supervision must have a powerful punch as the market does. It should be able to fail a bank without waiting for the bank to admit its failure.

Despite all imperfections, EU supervision is very present and active. It significantly influences the actions of bankers. Due to the obstacles it is facing, it spends more resources than necessary and, when dealing with non-cooperative bankers, it faces excessive legal risks.

Consequently, as we will later demonstrate, the supervision has not so far been successful in convincing the market that supervised banks are in good shape. Certainly, that is not the consequence of a lack of effort.

Concerning the development of banking regulation, on the high international level, things generally go in the right direction. Basel III and a half would help. IRB would remain, but its adverse impact will gradually diminish until 2027, after introducing significant limitations and the "output floor".

The lengthy application period will not offer excessive respite, as "frontloading" would soon reach the banks. Their shareholders would like to know how far they would be once "fully loaded" requirements will apply. Management will make plans to get there. The content and perceived quality of those plans will influence share prices, and soon afterwards, ratings. However, we should be aware that, although its implementation will improve the situation, the requirements of the Basel accord are still minimal, especially in terms of leverage.

The EU finally reached an agreement and approved the so-called risk reduction package. It introduces 2017 modification of Basel III, and together with earlier changes of CRR, it will gradually strengthen the formal position of supervision. Unfortunately, those processes would be painfully slow, too slowly closing the gap of uncertainty.

The reason for discomfort is the fact that all those processes are slow and gradual, while the recent business cycle now enters its 12th year. The usual duration of business cycles is 10–15 years. This cycle, due to the already mentioned negative interest rates and quantitative easing has very particular characteristics. It has the potential of developing innovative risks and market distortions. Also, both monetary and fiscal policy have a very narrow space to act.

However, risks are growing, and now the time is right for banks to be ready for the storm, sails set, decks clean and hatches closed. Some of them are, but some quite important ones are still partially dismasted and leaking seriously from the damages inflicted by the last crisis.

They can afford it, as we are now in the period of economic stability and growth. When the weather is nice, all ships are seaworthy. Also, their shareholders are surprisingly tolerant of the state of affairs. The only way shareholders let us know what they think is by determining the price they ask for the bank's shares.

A storm will hopefully never come. However, there is no reasonable alternative but being ready for it. If it hits EU banking in its present shape, there is no guarantee that some of the important institutions would not fold.

There is a strong consensus today that important institutions will not be allowed to disorderly fail. Nonetheless, we can never know what will be financial and, even more importantly, political circumstances. Mr Paulson certainly did not plan to let Lehman in bankruptcy, but events got it there. The political power sways in the crisis in unpredictable ways. People opposing bail-outs sometimes get their moment of glory. Therefore, the idea not to push banks hard because they will be bailed out if the need arises is not necessarily a good one.

The rules in banking should be as light and as simple as possible without compromising the safety of the system.[1] They should allow banks to do their business freely in the best possible way. However, such regulation would require banks to have enough money to pay for their possible mistakes. When they have enough own money, they do not create externalities. Remember—if an entrepreneur pays costs with his own money, it isn't an externality. Removing the risk of creating externalities also diminishes the risk of moral hazard. The primary task of supervision is the prevention of the risk of moral hazard generated by the government guarantee. If capital is high, such a threat is low. Then, the supervision could be simplified.

It is easy to make mistakes in finance; therefore, banks should have a lot of money. Their own money. Banks generate a significant part of their profit from borrowed government credibility. Safety is the least we should ask in return.

Everyone makes mistakes in life. It is unavoidable. Bankers' mistakes could be expensive and could have devasting consequences for others. The best way to keep bankers from the temptation of over-risking is by making the risk expensive. Risk becomes costly when one expects to pay all the bills potentially emerging from it. Therefore, if banks have enough capital to cover risks, they have less enthusiasm to take risks.

The reason for being non-profitable in banking is past mistakes. The mistakes could emerge from strategy, asset and liability structure and most commonly, credit approval. The bank will regain profitability once it redeems and pays its mistakes. It can pay them only from the equity. To be safe, a bank must have enough capital to sustain a period of loss-making without stoping credit growth and compromising regulatory compliance.

On the other hand, we already know that if banks were not profitable enough, they would not entice investors to buy the banks' shares and provide the needed capital. High capital requirements could decrease the attractiveness of investment in stocks and force banks to lower risk-weighted assets—meaning to reduce the financing of the real economy.

Here we notice a conflict between two objectives: higher equity increases safety but decreases profitability, while low profitability decreases interest to buy shares. As we said in the beginning, banking regulation is an art to find a balance between safety and profitability. Still, if a bank is obviously positioned on the top of the Gaussian

[1]"So heuristic …they live within the radical uncertainty instead rather than assuming it away. In applying coarse and robust rules, they don't try to capture all the nuances of the possible states and their probabilities. They use simple approaches that are robust to changes…" (Bookstaber, 2017, p. 70).

distribution of risks, it requires little intuition to recognise that the way down is a good idea. Once it comes down, then fine art of balancing takes place.

While doing so, we should keep in mind that capital is today cheap. Besides, different from most other industries, profitability in banking does not require any particular skill and knowledge. It comes by default. If a bank is of critical size, takes deposits, gives loans and most of all—makes payments, ever faster, ever more convenient, safer and cheaper, it will be profitable. The crucial question is: How profitable should a bank be to attract investors?

The banking industry is a mature industry with captive clients. Banking is almost like a utility: readily available on-demand to their clients. In the EU, all those colourful adds that banks put on TV do very little to reposition them on the markets. Unless a bank is very reckless or poorly managed, it retains most of its clients as long as they live. Operating utilities is not a risky business and does not require much profit. The safety of the market and the income should offset less than average profitability.

Despite all that, today, investors in banking stock are very conspicuous about the risks. It is easy and cheap to lead a bank astray, but hard and expensive to get it back on track. That is the reason why strict risk management and a conservative approach have always been key to long-term success in banking. Or instead, it was. In early 2000, consolidation spree triggered by the implementation of Basel II changed the face of traditional European banking. The consolidation led the bravest, not the most cautious bankers.

Since then, it appears to us that banks are always in trouble. Therefore, they are a risky business. That isn't so! Indeed, we did not notice them when they did not face problems and when they did not create problems.

Consequently, the perception of banking is negatively biased. In the Western world, banks had, until 2008, a seven decades-long period of more or less continuous profitability. Local banking crises were very few and wide apart. Among 40 banking crises recognised by the BIS in the period from 1980 to 2007, developed countries participated in only four.[2] That means four countries in two crises: Scandinavia in'91 and the Far East in'97. Just for the sake of comparison, Argentina alone has four crises on the list.

As we have already said, if banks do a lot of innovative things, then they face creative risks. On the other hand, if a bank understands its place in the world, it will do only good old things. It will do them slightly better each year. If doing so, it will face only the risks it is familiar with.

It is possible to challenge such a view. Granting mortgage loans is also one of those good old things. Mortgages were the source of the last big shock. Based on that, we could conclude that such reasoning is flawed.

If we look carefully at the sources of the 2008 crisis, mortgages were not the source of the predicament; innovation was. Of course, every mortgage has an element of risk, as the housing market has inherent volatility. The oscillation of market interest rates is its primary source. When the rates are low—housing prices go up. When

[2]Cecchetti, Kohler, and Upper (2009).

the rates grow—housing prices go down. Banks can easily protect themselves from such volatility by a substantial down payment and by selecting reliable clients. That would, of course, limit the size of the business, but it would also eliminate excessive risks. Setting the risk acceptance policy right is the most important decision for any bank.

Too much innovation[3] caused difficulties in 2008. Banks ceased to be banks, and they became originators. Producers of loans to sell, without any concern about their future. This removed all safety nets and caused an unnoticed accumulation of risks. The bottom line was their reckless credit policy. The widespread practice of aggressively selling mortgages without a down payment, credit history and recourse now seems quite lightheaded. Such practice, conducted long enough and with enough zeal, unavoidably accumulates enough risk to shake any banking system to the core.[4]

If banks give mortgages as they used to for centuries, selectively and with a significant down payment, expecting to hold them until maturity, it is quite a safe business.

For example, if during the last 50 years, housing prices adjusted by inflation oscillated close to 30%, then 30% of the down payment solves that risk. That would probably be too much, and the bank would sell too few mortgages. Accepting some risks is necessary for commercial success. In this case, a 15% down payment for credit with recourse appears to be a practical measure of acceptable risk. Not very complicated.

The risks faced by banks are much, much lower than the risks faced by other industries. Even other mature industries, such as the car industry. If you are a car producer, every 2 years you must present a new design of a complex machine of a few thousand moving parts with 130 years of history of redesigning. You should find buyers, produce for a competitive price, avoid and take care of technical complications, observe and react to competition. So, every step is an enormous risk, with the possibility of critical losses. While you are doing it, your creditors watch you like hawks, instead of sleeping on the government guarantee.

On the other hand, if you are a banker, your only real concerns are whether debtors will repay the loans and whether you will have a proper structure of funding to keep the loans profitable through market rate fluctuations over 20 years. You have your clients; competition is harmless, products are boringly the same, government guarantees make deposits stable.

Now, let's go back to the subject of the required profitability. Mid 2019, the average S&P 500 PE ratio was 20, while it was 11 for the four largest US banks. That means that people are willing to invest in an average large company for an expected return of 5%, while they would invest in the four largest banks if they hope to earn 9%. In the EU, things are even worse; investing in the stock of the largest banks would

---

[3]If we look at it from the proposed perspective: "The utility of financial innovation is measured by the degree to which it advances the goal of making payments, allocating capital and handling risk." (Kay, 2015, p. 6), it is obvious that innovations in the period preceeding crisis were excessive and not useful.

[4]"Sadly, this was the case in America during the boom years, when regulators stopped regulating, underwriters stopped underwriting, and financial engineering ran amok." (Blinder, 2013, p. 56).

require a return of around 12%. So, banks are considered a riskier investment than the average S&P 500 company. Substantially riskier. There is at least one large EU bank having a P/E ratio stable during 2019–2020 in the region of 3. For expected annual earnings of 33%, people usually need to invest in blood diamonds, not in the banking shares. If the price is stable in that region, it means that the perception of the risk is also persistent. It would be strange to doubt the rationality of investors, but if we do not do it, the only possible conclusion is a crisis of confidence.

In a typical environment, banks are not risky, and they should be able to convince the market so. If they are considered just an average risky investment, let alone less than average risky, investors would be happy with the same profit on twice the investment. Before 2008 they required even less. A thing that substantially changed since then is not the banks' profitability, but the perception of their risks.

A part of that problem is still a vivid memory of recent issues, including the feeling of investors that balance sheets are murky as well as the fear of frequent regulatory changes. The uncertainty about future regulatory changes keeps investors on the edge of their seats. They are ambiguous whether the banks will be able to comply and at what cost.

As usually, to decrease the perception of the risk, the best possible approach is to reduce the risk. Low capitalised banks are risky. They offer high earnings in good times, but with a clear option to lose everything in bad times. The explicit and implicit guarantee does not cover shareholders. The consequence is that shareholders require a high return while they have it.

Increasing capital would decrease profitability, but it would, even more, reduce risk. The usual outcome is that banks with leverage above 10% typically have significantly higher P/B then banks with leverage below 5%.[5]

Some banks could feel uncomfortable concerning the concept of simpler rules and more capital. The implementation of such an approach would on a one-time basis decrease the rate of return for shareholders of weak banks. Shareholders of healthy banks would get rid of regulatory overhang practically without any dilution. Many banks already have a relatively high leverage ratio and can adjust to new requirements quite easily. Though strongly capitalised, those banks should also follow the complex and demanding requirements designed as a kind of protection for their weaker colleagues.

The required leverage should undoubtedly be higher than the minimum required by Basel III. Three percent equity on the overall portfolio protects banks from risks equivalent to a 0.3% interest increase on ten-year government bonds. It does not appear to be a reliable risk coverage.

Still, it would be good to reinforce leverage with a capital requirement based on standardised approach risk weights. Most importantly, to be sure that the bank adequately meets those two requirements, supervisors should interfere in accounting.

High capital alone, though increasing banking resilience, is not enough to consistently achieve objectives of the supervision. Its protection requires permanent and

[5]Glossary: "The resilience of the alternative regulatory structure" demonstrated difference in risk exposure between high and low capitalised bank.

vigilant supervisory measures making sure that the bank manages its risks appropriately. From a supervisory perspective, the issue of non-performing loans is relatively simple. If supervisors have unconstrained judgement and the power to interfere in accounting, they will resolve the problem quickly.

The more challenging part is the recognition of the concentration risks. For example, the accumulation of uncertainties in the run-up to 2008 was very difficult to identify, while there was no tool adequate for preventing it. Everything was perfectly diversified on paper, while the real correlation of risks was strong and well hidden.

Today, macro-prudential supervision addresses this part of the problem. We can only hope that it will be successful. Available tools and applicable procedures are untested and not always promising.

However, strong equity could be a remedy for the issue. With capital at least 20% of risk-weighted assets (standardised approach), a bank will stay afloat in all circumstances except total disaster. Also, being aware of the considerable worth of their bank, entirely independent of its business, the owners would do their best to prevent losses and the accumulation of risks. So, internal corporate governances could adequately cover both—micro- and macro-prudential tasks.

The best approach would be a combination of leverage and a standardised approach. Leverage alone would also be reliable enough; only, in that case, it should be somewhat higher.

Historically, we saw banks going bankrupt with leverage as high as 50%. Such cases should not concern us, as those were particular banks. They did not apply reasonable limits for single and connected risks. Those banks were focused on financing the owners' oversea voyages or real estate developments. Today, regulation and oversight would hopefully prevent such things from occurring. Of course, necessary precondition to achieve this is that the EU Parliament removes from CRR the possibility of giving such loans.[6]

A more straightforward, simpler and business friendlier regulation would also make the supervised rules simpler, making oversight more efficient and less uncertain for both banks and supervisors.

We will now forget the state of affairs in banking regulation and create from scratch a model of sound banking regulation. Let us now summarise the hypothetical regulatory structure:

(a) Leverage—fully loaded 10%.
(b) Capital adequacy—20% on standardised RW.
(c) Minimal conditions for authorisation:
    - Leverage 5%
    - Capital adequacy 10%
(d) The SSM issues compulsory resolutions requiring accounting adjustments.
(e) The ECB independently issues guidelines in line with applicable Regulation (today: 575/2013, 2019/630, 2019/876) and other relevant acts.

[6]Glossary: CRR, large exposures and treatment of commercial real estates.

We would not call this a proposal.[7] It is a kind of picture of an alternative structure. Things apparently must go the way they do until they reach a logical conclusion. However, ideas must stay alive. Who knows, maybe one day their time will come?

First and foremost, let us avoid misunderstandings. A request for a 10% leverage and 20% capital adequacy does not assume TLAC or MREL of 20% and 40%, respectively. The structure encompasses them.[8]

From that perspective, it is much closer to the mainstream. CAR[9] of 20% is proposed on risk-weighted assets, while TLAC in the context of BASEL brings us to at least 16%. With buffers, and from the capital adequacy perspective, the actual requirement could easily be above the proposal. Therefore, the idea is not to increase TLAC, but rather to restructure it.

Considering all this, the structure could appear so close to the mainstream that someone could ask "Why bother?". However, there are several significant differences.

Primarily, within the proposed structure, TLAC would not significantly change for banks using the standardised approach. For IRB banks declaring capital adequacy four times the leverage, it would be quite a radical change. In the EU, such a ratio between leverage and adequacy is not only possible but also rather the market standard.

The second difference is leverage. It is now very low, even including MREL. If MREL were about twice the capital, the minimum overall leverage would be 6%. That is still too low. With such leverage, a bank could not absorb any significant shock while remaining solvent and compliant. Therefore, it is necessary to push it at least to 10%. It is still below the world average, but not for the present order of magnitude.

The third difference is the approach used in the case of an emergency. There is no failing and resolution if TLAC can solve the issue.

In such cases, it would be simpler if we would call things by different names. There is no reason to do the fancy footwork of failing and then resurrecting a bank. Why? Just because part of its equity consists of CoCos? What is wrong with CoCos, from the perspective of the government and senior lenders?

The story about resolution understandably confuses people. They would ask over and over again, "Will they take my money?" and "Will my credit card work?". Besides, the public announcement that the bank failed does not establish confidence in it. As mentioned earlier, the bail-out indicates that the government will give its credibility to the bank. Bail-in will be much more confusing process. So, it is advisable to avoid it.

On the other hand, if a bank's regulatory capital requirement would equal TLAC, while the minimum requirement for the authorisation would be half of that amount,

[7]In the last few years, many proposals have been made to address the risks that the banking system imposes on society. Very few however, have been implemented. Most proposals have been rejected, diluted, or delayed, some of them endlessly it appears, because the banks have convinced policy-makers, regulators and sometimes the courts that the regulations might be too expensive (Admati & Hellwig, 2014, p. 82).

[8]Glossary: The resilience of the alternative regulatory structure.

[9]Capital adequacy ratio.

then the bank could execute fundamentally the same process without failing and being resurrected. The drama will play within boardrooms and assembly, between the bank and supervisor, while the public will remain out of it.

If the bank is unable to meet its full regulatory requirement, while it is above minimum requirements for authorisation, it is subject to supervisory measures instead of resolution. When the shortage of own funds becomes apparent, the bank's assembly will decide on covering losses. No one will jeopardise their constitutional rights by making decisions on their behalf in the messy and improvised resolution process. The actual resolution would occur if the bank's capital went below the minimum requirement for the authorisation. If that happens, and the bank is that essential, a bail-out is possible. The present resolution procedure renders substantially the same results through a more complicated and riskier process.

The proposed structure also gives macro-prudential flexibility. After significant event generated losses, the regulator can decide to tolerate all of the bank staying above minimal conditions for the authorisation but below the required capital. That would enable banks to continue business as usual providing all their services to the economy without regulatory hindrances until conditions improve enough to raise new capital. That is equivalent for allowing temporary partial waiver of MREL. Naturally, during that period, the bank will not pay out dividends.

That would be substantially the same reaction as the one applied by some EU jurisdictions in the period 2012–2015. However, there will be one crucial difference. This way, everything can be transparent, and no corporate governances should be bent to achieve it.

In the real world, to do their job, supervisors must have the authority to adjust accounts through a simple and straightforward process. Without such powers, how would they conclude that a bank is not compliant? The new remedy—decreasing of regulatory capital in case of improper accounting—is confusing. It means that regulators can decide that regulatory capital is too low, while official accounts demonstrate that it is not. That could open attractive legal options for the shareholders.

Ordering accounting adjustments also should not create problems. No one could have material consequences from that. On a transparent and well-functioning financial market, such a problem cannot exist. If a bank considers the supervisory request unreasonable, it can sell the doubtful asset during the supervisory process. As supervisors are not allowed to require any value adjustments on cash, the problem would be easily solved. If the asset cannot be sold for more than the supervisor thinks it is worth than the bank has no reasonable choice but to accept it.

At this moment, practically the entire NPL stock is older than April 2019. Therefore, the only way to fail a bank is that the bank declares failure itself. Banks, especially banks plagued with the moral hazard issue, would do anything to avoid it. For example, they could report being solvent while reporting a Texas ratio of 700%.

The structure assumes abandonment of present resolution regulatory framework. It seems like the logical thing to do, by merely turning TLAC-MREL into the capital requirement. However, it would and should not mean abandoning a resolution fund and structure of management for that fund. It is always handy to have some money if needed.

Such proposal simplified administrative, legal and management perspective of stabilisation of weak banks. Present resolution structure is a consequence of some confusion in the process of developing it. The initial idea was that a resolution would grasp deeper into a bank's liabilities. An authority which would do that requires a broad institutional and legal framework. The owners of uninsured liabilities, even retail depositors, were seen as potential providers of equity and future shareholders of a bank in distress.

However, after experiencing the consequences caused by several such resolutions, it became obvious that this approach did not serve the purpose. The conversion of subordinated instruments owned by retail customers created too intense reactions. Its political and legal consequences are comparable to the disorderly failure of a bank, if not worse.

After learning that, authorities became hesitant to perform such bank resolution. Still, instead of redesigning the regulation in a more meaningful direction, the process of resolution planning continued as initially designed, and got stuck in delays.

It is better to base the recovery strategy on CoCos and similar instruments owned by professional counterparties, instead of taking a broader liability base, including liabilities of retail customers. However, we should be aware that such a solution, although much better in case of conversion, increases difficulties during the phase of MREL collection. Professional investors are more suspicious and require more information and assurances than retail investors. Especially now when retail investors are desperate to get any return on their savings.

Today it is apparent that, except maybe in some nightmarish scenario, the only liabilities qualifying for a bail-in would be those capable or almost capable of being tier 2 capital. However, if the bank meets MREL requirement with equity, then, in all the situations potentially resolvable through a bail-in, there would be no reason to fail a bank.

If the regulation made only one step further, requiring the approval of CoCos as tier 2 capital, the whole "resolution" framework would be redundant. Instead of deep government involvement in corporate governances of private companies, there would only be one simple and straightforward decision if a bank fails—either bankruptcy or bail-out. A bail-out can, if the conditions permit, be performed through bail-in, or at least contain an element of it.

Finally, but very important concerning the resolution strategy, the obligation of the holding to support subsidiaries needs to be formalised at least on the level of the SSM. As holding typically has full control over corporate governances of the subsidiary, operate under the same brand, it is unacceptable that it can invoke limited liability in the case of difficulties. If the holding does not have full control, then this requirement should not apply.

We should be aware that, even if it were practically possible to introduce the earlier presented regulation, it would not be any kind of silver bullet immediately solving the problems aggravating the present EU banking.

The problem is a vicious circle in which low prices of shares create the self-fulfilling hunch among investors that a higher capitalisation of the system is not possible due to the reluctance of present shareholders to alow cheap dilution. If the banks are weak, they are risky for shareholders, therefore cheep.

The solution to the problem would require a significant transition period during which the banks will find strategies to comply. The availability of both—the equity or CoCos—depends on the same factor, i.e. the investors' trust in banks. So, the question is, what could this structure do to improve the perception of EU banks on the market?

The most important achievement would be confidence in the balance sheet. If SSM acts uniformly and strictly, consistently adjusting values, then investors will have no doubts whether they subsidise legacy losses. That is necessary, but not sufficient condition for their investment in banks.

Sufficient conditions would be a demonstration of stable and robust profitability. No one can achieve it except bankers. The regulator should remove all excuses they have now for poor performance, and leave CEOs in front of their boards facing clear and unflexible roadmap. Some will achieve it, while others will be replaced or their banks acquired.

There is already a quite extensive history of attempts to encourage investors. So far, they were not successful. Nonetheless, that should not discourage us. Their task was extremely demanding.

One such attempts was the stress test performed in 2011. It was an attempt to reinforce, the good old, but seemingly not very successful, supervision as a confidence builder. As the supervision, not yet integrated into the banking union, failed to convince the markets that the banks' financial statements are accurate, the stress test was supposed to persuade reluctant investors.

The stress test applied the so-called bottom-up approach. The banks were required to simulate the consequences of the stress in their balance sheets and profit and loss accounts. Then, based on those results, their ability to withstand stress was measured. The results were encouraging, but as we said, the banks provided the results.

Then, just months after publishing the results, a bank passing the stress test with flying colours, with capital adequacy over 10% in adverse scenario[10] went down in flames and received government bail-out of 6 billion EUR.[11] It is easy to grasp why the stress test was not a success in encouraging the market, especially in the middle of turmoil caused by the sovereign debt crisis.[12]

The following attempt was much more elaborate. It was an asset quality review with a stress test. The narrative was that the modest success of the first stress test had emerged from the fact that banks based the stress test on their balance sheets without previously checking their accuracy.

[10]EBA stress test (2011).

[11]The curriosuity is that the same bank, Dexia, was already bailed out in October 2009 with 6.4 EUR billion.

[12]Such outcome is not a consequence of mistakes in stress test procedure. It is fundamental design flaw of the stress test as a tool. The stress test is not main supervisory tool, it does not follow standard procedure of major supervisory tools and publishing its findings on the individual level bear significant risk.

Design of the new procedure rectified that issue. It was the review of the asset quality of all banks involved in the future "single supervisory mechanism" before the ECB will accept responsibility for them. The whole program was far too demanding to complete it through the regular oversight procedure.

Besides, the ECB could not do it alone. It did not have completed the organisation yet. The competent national authorities had the capacity, but the ECB wanted to check their findings independently before becoming responsible.

Therefore, an external advisor was employed to design the stress test, while ECB hired the auditors to perform the review. The whole exercise was massive, and it gave the ECB an initial idea of what they were taking over.

Auditors in charge of auditing large banks performed the review. There are no other accounting firms sufficiently able and competent for such a big job. However, if an auditor was in charge of auditing a bank, then it was not permitted to review that bank.

The auditors reviewed under close ECB oversight and instructions. After completion of the review, the balance sheet emerging from the analysis created the basis for the stress test. The test was prepared by the advisor and run by ECB. After finalisation of the process, detailed findings were published.[13] This time there were no surprises, at least no unpleasant ones.

The process initially appeared convincing. The average share price for EU banks, having a steady growing trend from Mario Draghi's speech "Whatever it takes!" in July 2012, increased nicely. Price book ratio exceeded 0, 9 in the first quarter of 2015, the first time in 5 years, indicating that investors took asset quality review seriously. Besides, it seemed they like it!

The credibility of the system improved significantly. Unfortunately, it did not last. Already in 2015, confidence was weakening, and prices went down again.

As the stress test and the subsequent asset quality review with the stress test were not a great success in boosting confidence, the EBA organised another one. That one was supposed to be uncompromising and trustworthy. As we see from the present situation, it did not help either.

The negative market sentiment appears too stubborn to be only sentimental. It behaves as if something material stands behind it. Still, as we described in the last chapter, no one can put the finger on it.

Let us now move back to square one. To appear credible, one must be convincing, for example, as the masks in Kabuki theatre. When you see one, you know its character.

The convincing regulator should be allowed to regulate. If the regulators must push all documents through an endless and demanding political maze, they certainly do not leave such an impression. They appear more like Sisyphus.

The Supervisory Review and Evaluation Process, SREP, now a central piece in the oversight of banks, takes considerable resources, especially in the examination of international groups. The outcome is quite a small difference in capital requirements

---

[13] ECB (2014).

between banks. Much work for a little, more symbolic result. Supervisory judgement in the process is, as the ECB manual clearly states, constrained.[14]

Notwithstanding the need to retain an understanding of the whole institution, it would help to use part of the resources used for SREP for a permanent in-depth analysis of asset quality.

The supervisors should issue compulsory resolutions. They should not find themselves in the position of invoking "supervisory expectation" in vain.

Discussing PowerPoint presentations of the strategic plan is relatively easy. However, checking whether the principles mentioned in the presentation represent guidelines for operational procedures is an important task. Furthermore, examining whether a bank executes all transactions in line with operational procedures is the most crucial task. Failing to turn strategy into working documents and especially making sure that everyone follows those documents in daily work, transaction by transaction, is the most frequent reason for a bank's demise. Therefore, the examination should be most focused on details and transactions. While doing so, the supervisory judgement should be constrained only by common sense.

The fact that supervision needs to perform a complex exercise, such as "comprehensive assessment", to evaluate missing value adjustments does not help to resolve distress created by the "cost of capital". The vast and widely discussed SREP reports also will not decrease the cost of MREL. Only credible risk-based supervision, establishing and enforcing the realistic value of equity on a daily basis can do that. Investors in new shares do not want to give their money for covering the bank's historical losses. Credible supervision is an implicit guarantor in that respect.[15] When reports are trustworthy, and a bank is profitable, the value of its shares exceeds the book value. So, there is no problem to collect as much capital as the regulator requires.

How credible would supervision appear to the investors if it would have the power to decrease regulatory capital only for loans originated after April 2019, is quite an interesting question. Furthermore, even this power would not interfere with the accounts. So, the decrease in regulatory capital is a supervisory, not an accounting transaction. It does not cover losses and provides no comfort to investors. Besides, it does not stop the bank from declaring profit and paying out the dividend. The payout can be forbidden. However, it creates one more formal act the bank can challenge.

Could supervision become credible consistently using a soft but firm hand? Possibly, but so far, it does not look promising. That should not surprise us if we understand how daunting the task is.

A fully and convincingly implemented automatic value adjustment could, in time, become a robust supervisory tool. Still, we should be aware that such automation cannot replace intensive on-site and off-site oversight, specific and backwards-looking, instead of holistic and forward-looking. The control focused on inconsistencies, peculiarities and unrecognised risk concentrations. Will the ECB manage to

[14]"Departing from constrained judgement not allowed as a rule" (ECB, www.bankingsupervision.europa.eu, 2019a, 2019b, p. 16).

[15]ECJ tends towards understanding that supervisor should be explicit, even personal guarantoor (Praag, 2018).

achieve it in the present regulatory jungle using constrained judgement? However, if someone has the skill and experience to wriggle through this, it is Mr Enria. To what end remains to be seen.

Once supervision became more convincing, the banks would quickly recognise the problems themselves, and investors would become more confident in the banks' reporting.[16] We can see how successfully the process of creation of SSM and asset quality review initially improved the market perception. Adding substance to the form this time could make improvements durable.

If the perception of EU banks improves, the collection of MREL and movement towards a "fully loaded" Basel III would not be a problem. When existing shareholders get a premium for selling new shares, they are pleased to sell them.

Another major predicament is the regulatory overhang. At some point, the EU should announce the end of intensive regulatory development. Once banks have proper MREL in place, the undoing of some rules and requirements could also help. A kind of regulatory reset might also be a good idea, especially if authors would one more time read Liikanen report.[17]

Europe still awaits a credible decisive step towards re-establishment of confidence in EU banking. Unless convincingly addressed and put under control, the tensions in the EU financial system could have consequences in all aspects of life in the EU.

Probably nothing short of allowing the regulator to regulate and supervisors to supervise would keep the asymmetry at bay. That will certainly not bring us to heaven, but might save us from hell.

References

Admati, A., & Hellwig, M. (2014). *The bankers' new clothes*, Princeton University Press.

Blinder, A. S. (2013). *After the music stopped*, Penguin Books. ISBN 014312448X.

Bookstaber, R. (2017). *The end of theory: Financial crises, the failure of economics and the sweep of human interaction*, Princeton University Press. ISBN 9780691169019.

Cecchetti, S. G., Kohler, M., & Upper, C. (2009, September). Financial crises and economic activity. NBER Working Paper.

EBA stress test. (2011). Results of the 2011 EBA EU-wide stress test: Summary (pp. 1–3). Retrieved from https://eba.europa.eu, https://eba.europa.eu/sites/default/documents/files/documents/10180/15935/f42af5f4-a7ed-446d-afb7-89941904f612/BE004.pdf.

ECB. (2014). Assessment of 130 euro area banks in 2014. Retrieved from https://www.bankingsupervision.europa.eu, https://www.bankingsupervision.europa.eu/banking/tasks/comprehensive_assessment/html/2014_index.en.html.

ECB. (2019). www.bankingsupervision.europa.eu. Retrieved from SSM SREP Methodology Booklet—2018 edition—to be applied in 2019 https://www.bankingsupervision.europa.eu/ecb/pub/pdf/ssm.srep_methodology_booklet_2018~b0e30ced94.en.pdf.

[16] "...public confidence in the industry is the outcome, not the purpose, of effective regulation." (Kay, 2015, p. 237).

[17] High-level Expert Group on Bank Structural Reform (2012).

ECB. (2019, August). www.bankingsupervision.europa.eu. Retrieved from https://www.bankingsupervision.europa.eu/press/letterstobanks/shared/pdf/2019/ssm.supervisory_coverage_expectations_for_NPEs_201908.en.pdf.

High-level Expert Group on Bank Structural Reform. (2012). Report of the European Commission's High-level Expert Group on Bank Structural Reform (Liikanen report).

Kay, J. (2015). *Other people's money*, Profile Books. ISBN 978-1781254431.

Praag, E. V. (2018, October 7). EU Court of Justice rules on liability of national banking supervisor. Retrieved from https://www.linkedin.com, https://www.linkedin.com/pulse/eu-court-justice-rules-liability-national-banking-emanuel-van-praag.

Chapter 14
Glossary

Abstract This chapter contains materials needed to understand other chapters if the reader is not familiar with the theory of economics, or is interested in going deeper into the mathematics behind some subjects. This chapter is not intended for reading as single integral text, but its parts are given as the references in the other chapters.

Bubble

Despite all historical experiences, we should keep in mind that according to the mainstream economic theory, there are no bubbles. There are no valid theoretical explanations for the possibility to form a bubble. It has practical consequences on economic policy. Without a theoretical interpretation, it is impossible to recognise ex-ante an underlying pattern of a bubble.

Being practical, we recognise that the phenomenon exists. History did prove wild and unexplainable oscillations of the price. However, those oscillations are almost always explainable. Unfortunately, it does not mean predictable.

The book Bubbleology[1] brings amusing discussion between two fictitious characters: Shareholder and Philosopher, indicating that there was strong economic reasoning for excessive prices of some tulip bulbs even in the famous tulipmania 1638. Quote:

> Shareholder: See- that little onion-like bulb just sold for 5.500 guilders. That's almost 110 oz of gold!
>
> Philosopher: It's an impressive price- and it should be. That bulb is a Semper Augustus. Its flower is one of the most beautiful ever seen.
>
> Shareholder: But that can't be a reasonable price! The poor fellow is going to lose everything! Let's fast forward and see how it turns out.

---

[1] Hassett (2002, p. 128).

D. Odak, *A Political Economy of Banking Supervision*,
https://doi.org/10.1007/978-3-030-48547-4_14

...

(100 years later – author's comment)

Philosopher: This shop is selling a large bundle of Semper Augustus bulbs for 5 guilders.

Shareholder: I knew it! Now you can purchase a bucket full of bulbs at a fraction of the auction price. That poor fool lost everything. The bulb is now worthless.

Philosopher: On the contrary, that "poor" man is quite rich. And all because of his daring purchase of a Semper Augustus.

It turned out that the man bought a bulb that was one of its kind—a mutation. As tulips reproduce slowly, one double every year, he went out of the market and doubled his stock every year. After 20 years he had about a million bulbs giving flowers as no one has ever seen. He launched bulbs on the market and got extremely rich.

Therefore, if one is extraordinary lucky (or knowledgable) and outstandingly patient, he can profit even from the so-called bubble. Does it prove that there are no bubbles? Was the price offered for Semper Augustus a bargain at the moment it was delivered, as it proved to be 20 years later? Given example is literary "one of the million". Most of the people purchasing bulbs during the mania lost their investment unless they found a buyer while the craze lasted.

Those are difficult questions, and it is hard to get a firm answer. It is practical to ignore theory and recognise the existence of "bubbles" in the real world. The price patterns indicate their presence. Radical corrections mostly occur without any significant new information that would explain it.

Nevertheless, such a pragmatical way of discussing bubbles does not bring any value. Those bubbles can be recognised only ex-post, making their recognition futile from the policy perspective.

Concentration risk

Concentration risk emerges from a combination of individually recognised risks if they have a visible or hidden correlation. That means that realisation of one risk, could increase the probability that another will also activate. In the case of a hidden concentration, the bank accepts apparently independent risks, only to find out that it was, in reality, one single risk.

For example, if companies have a common controlling shareholder, they are considered as a single risk. Therefore, all limits applicable to a single exposure should apply to a joint exposure of the bank to those companies. That is an example of visible concentration risk.

However, in the case when the companies have a significant common shareholder who does influence but does not control them, the situation is less clear. Formally, they can still represent independent risks, but not if the shareholder de facto establishes control using his influence on the company. Therefore, in such case, the bank must perform due diligence and form an opinion whether those risks are connected or not.

The most challenging case of concentration risk is a hidden connection of independent risks. That is the case when independent borrowers are all exposed to the same market risk to the extent turning them into a single risk. A large group of citizens in some cases can behave as connected persons, though they have no mutual relationship. They even do not need to know each other. When affected by adverse developments on the market, they tend to react in the same way. Then, instead of independent risk, the bank faces a single risk.

In the case of 2008, it was the case with mortgage borrowers. In the case of 1929, those were investors on the stock market.

Through such a mechanism, a bank with an apparently properly diversified portfolio without any excessive single risk exposure may find itself exposed to a risk it had never decided to accept.

The bank should make an effort to recognise the potential concentration of the risks and prepare for the possible accumulation of individual risks. It is sometimes a challenging task.

CRR, large exposures and treatment of commercial real estates

Regulation 575/2013 set limits to large exposures in Article 395. The ceiling is, as agreed in the Basel Accord, 25% of its own funds. However, also partially in line with the Basel Accord, the limit should be observed after decreasing the amount of exposure for the value of specific items according to Articles 399–403. Such exclusion is reasonable. It avoids setting a regulatory burden on transactions bearing no real risk. Article 400 excludes all claims having, directly or indirectly, risk weight 0 and gives the competent authority the discretion to approve the exclusion of certain other items. That means that there is no limit on exposure towards cash, receivables from the central bank and government. It also excludes all exposures collateralised by such items.

Such exclusion is logical, as a loan given by a bank with cash or similar collateral does not represent credit risk and therefore should not be limited. However, now Article 402 moves in. In paragraph one, it excludes loans collateralised by housing real estate eligible according to Article 125 up to 50% of the collateral value. In paragraph 2 it excludes all loans collateralised by commercial real estate according to Article 126, also up to 50% of the real estate value. The collateral should be eligible for applying the 35% RW in case of housing, and the 50% RW in case of commercial real estate.

Therefore, exposure collateralised by such assets is not part of large exposures; neither is limited by limit for the largest possible exposure.

Putting a housing mortgage in this context is a bizarre but harmless idea. Just imagine how should look house with a value exceeding 25% of the capital of a bank. Versailles and Schönbrunn would hardly qualify.

Nevertheless, let us assume that a company controlling a large number of commercial real estates has a significant shareholding in a bank. In this case, the regulation allows the bank lending to the owner all its assets, well above the capital. The requirement is that the collateral value is twice the loan value. The leverage and liquidity consideration would limit the amount to less than 30 times the capital.

Such treatment equals cash and real estate as collateral. The experience with collecting loans collateralised by real estate certainly does not confirm such a solution. Furthermore, there are no additional limits for financing the connected party (licenced shareholder, board member). That could open space for an irresistible temptation.

On the other hand, the competent authority can prevent such application of Article 402 by merely prohibiting the use of the 50% risk weight on commercial real estate.

Deleveraging

The bank can choose to increase its capital adequacy by decreasing its risk-weighted assets. Therefore, they deleverage by collecting or selling assets having high risk weights attached. Then they use proceeds to repay creditors or to acquire assets bearing no or low risk (zero or low risk weight).

High risk weight assets are corporate and un-collateralised consumer loans. Typically, they generate a significant income stream in the bank and create additional business for a bank (payments, accounts). Therefore, such strategy weakens the market position and income stream of a bank but enables it to maintain compliance without an infusion of additional capital.

Deleveraging is the most challenging and potentially risky strategy a bank can pursue to achieve regulatory requirements. The requirement emerges from the bank's asset structure and business profile. Therefore, it could be decreased only by changing the bank's structure.

Asset securitisation is one of the possible strategies. During the securitisation, the bank sells assets with high risk weights for cash. Cash creates neither risks nor income. A similar effect could be achieved merely by collecting loans without granting new ones.

Widespread deleveraging can obstruct "financing the real economy". If the majority of banks were pressed hard against the wall to get additional own funds while there is no market to issue stock, and the banks' profitability is low, the banks have little choice. Issuing new shares is not attractive for investors, and debt eligible to supplement equity would be too costly. The only way out would then be to decrease the risk-weighted assets.

In the given circumstances, the choice would be wrong on a systemic level, but it could seem like the right solution for a single bank, provided that other banks would not do the same. If one bank collects loans without giving new ones, others can replace its loans easily. However, if the majority of banks are in a similar situation, they will create a condition called "credit crunch". The shortage of credit could be so severe that it would hurt the functioning of the economy as a whole.

Risk weights could further complicate the issue. When banks focus only on capital requirements, risk weights commence producing undesired consequences. They can trigger a selective credit crunch for segments of the economy.

Replacing an asset having a risk weight of 100% with an asset weighting 50% would decrease the capital requirement in half. Such a change could easily solve the problem of capital increase. But, in a situation of capital shortage, all banks could focus on the optimisation of capital requirements. They will dispose of the assets with higher risk weights and acquire the assets with lower weights. If most banks start doing that, the market segments requiring higher risk weights would be starved of loans, while the banks would overflood those requiring lower risk weights with credit.

Loans to industry and trade companies typically have the highest risk weights, while housing mortgages and government debt require the lowest. Due to risk weights, in the case of scarce equity in the banking system as a whole, loans would be limited and expensive for the economy, while abundant and cheap for housing loans and government debt. The final consequence of such development would be overinvestment in real estate and excessive public debt.

Risk weights create such a distortion in motivation if equity is tight that sometimes supervisors are willing to (ab)use them as a policy tool, motivating banks to give loans for specific purposes. However, that would be wrong. The only purpose the risk weights should be calibrated for is setting a standard of the expected risk for certain assets. If we abuse them to achieve other goals, such as directing the flow of credit, we seriously distort the system.

It is important to notice that, from shareholders position, the increase in capital is, in most cases, a superior strategy to the one based on decreasing risk-weighted assets. The most profitable part of a bank's portfolio is loans with higher risk weights. We can do a back-of-the-envelope calculation: if the capital requirement is 12% of the risk-weighted assets, each unit of equity supports roughly eight units of the loans with a 100% risk weight. If by reallocating those assets to a lower risk weight, a bank annually loses only 1.5% of the risk-adjusted income per unit of the loan, such restructuring would result in a loss of almost 12% of the revenue per unit of capital. In other words, it is better to pay 12% for the tier 2 liabilities than to restructure the portfolio. Therefore, such restructuring makes sense if, and only if, the pricing is extreme, or there is no interest in the market for new issuances. It is better to share the profit with others than to keep all the losses for yourself. In fact, in real life, there is no banking strategy with more undesired consequences than the one focused on the decrease in risk-weighted assets.

It practically blocks the generation of the corporate and consumer loans portfolio. Those portfolios are the most profitable for the bank. Besides, when clients cannot get a loan, they transfer their business to another bank. We already mentioned that banks are natural monopolies. Having more clients for a bank means less cost per client. The decrease in the number of clients would increase average costs, impacting the bank's competitivity and profitability.

The permanent push on costs, inevitably accompanying such a strategy, could further weaken the bank's development and market performance.

Therefore, no reasonable banker having any choice would ever apply such a strategy. Such an approach is feasible only if there is no choice.

Having no choice in a developed market economy with strong financial markets could only mean a strong aversion of investors towards the bank. Such an aversion, if it lasts, is probably reasonable. Therefore, if a bank applies a strategy of decreasing risk weights, it should be an alarming sign for the supervisors. The usual suspect is called "asset quality".[2]

If the market believes that the bank overvalues its assets, investors would be very reluctant to join before the existing shareholders cover the perceived losses.

There are two ways out: convincingly address worries and, if required, adjust the accounting value of the assets. Such a move should convince the investors that the shares are now a profitable investment.

Alternatively, strong supervisors with a good reputation can use their reputation to improve the bank's reputation. That is a hazardous strategy, and only a supervisor performing diligent and intrusive supervision should dare do it. If the strategy goes wrong, it is very troublesome for the supervisor.

Widespread deleveraging creates macroeconomic risk and negatively influences economic growth. While the credit expansion does not have a significant impact on the growth, net collection of loans create liquidity problem making it difficult to continue with the same or increased level of economic activity.

Difference between investment and commercial banks

We call both—commercial and investment banks—"banks". They both have the following significant characteristics of banks: customer accounts, the ability to accept a deposit, grant loans and execute payments. Nevertheless, the business models of commercial and investment banks are very different. Consequently, the skills and character of commercial and investment bankers are different. Commercial banking is a "plain vanilla" activity. Bankers take deposits, make payments and give loans. The essential thing about commercial banking is that it deals predominantly with unprofessional clients—those that are not experts in finance. They offer services to the general public, enterprises and other banks, including investment banks.

Commercial banks represent the economy's infrastructure, almost like utilities. A vast number of small transactions cleared through them enable participants in the marketplace to successfully, safely and efficiently do their daily business. Clients do not worry about the safety of their money, and they have a source of credit if demanded. The functioning of commercial banks in normal times is so smooth, and the cost of using them is so low that people forget about them.

Commercial banks tend to be relatively large. If they are small nationally, they are frequently large regionally. That is because they are "natural monopolies", meaning that the cost of serving the new client is almost always lower than the average cost per client. As such, large banks have an advantage over smaller ones, and they tend to become even larger.

Investment banks are entirely different. They are focused on transactions on the capital markets. Their primary business is generating and trading securities on behalf of the bank's clients and the bank itself. That means that clients use bank accounts to issue, buy and sell stock and bonds, derivatives and commodities on regulated

---

[2]"The bank management may have incentives, of course, to delay such recognition so as to present the bank's assets to investors and regulators as being more valuable than they actually are, which also overstates the value of its equity." (Admati & Hellwig, 2014, p. 86).

exchanges or over the counter. Their assets consist of such items as stock and derivatives. Their value is more volatile than at commercial banks. Also, investment banks usually do not collect retail deposits on the market, but they finance themselves by own and wholesale funding.

Consequently, their income and liabilities arise predominantly from professional clients and financially proficient clients. Instead of the vast number of small fees earned by commercial banks, investment banks make a relatively small number of substantial fees. Instead of repeating simple transactions, such as payments, they are focused on a lower number of tailor-made deals explicitly designed according to their clients' demands.

As a consequence, their business model is much more sensitive than at commercial banks. Also, the risks of investment banks are higher than the risks of commercial banks. The assets in their balance sheets are of very uncertain and volatile value. Therefore, their net worth is exposed to vivid oscillations unless it is appropriately hedged. That means that an item on the assets side should have its opposite item in liabilities to cancel the volatility of prices.

For example, if an investment bank owns 10 General Electric shares, the simplest way to hedge is to owe 10 General Electric shares to a client. That means that to close the balance, the bank does not pay the specified amount of money, but merely gives the client 10 GE shares. A complex structure of positions and hedges lays within each investment bank, sometimes quite opaque even for their management.

Furthermore, commercial banks have a structural surplus of cash. As people bring money to them for safekeeping and transacting, banks are typically unable to invest all of it. Paradoxically, even when they give a loan to someone, money "physically" stays in the banking system. So, they have a permanent cash surplus. On the other hand, investment banking is very imaginative about the uses of cash. By integrating the two, a situation is created in which investment banking operations are "oiled" by the liquidity of commercial banking. Such integration tends to create an environment in which not only supervisors but also bank managers lose track of the risks they are taking. The connection between those risks becomes too complicated to understand and manage. Furthermore, those risks are sometimes entirely obscured and hidden, only to appear suddenly out of the blue.

To safely manage a commercial bank, the management must understand its business and the risks it faces. If its business model is limited to "classical" transactions, meaning liabilities are deposits and assets are loans and cash, it is relatively easy to manage. The value of loans is stable, and the deposits are fixed obligations, while fee flow and cost level are also predictable.

If properly managed, a commercial bank provides no notable surprises to its management. If it ensures a strict observation of internal governances, accounting rules and good practices, around June, the management already knows how the year will end.

In an investment bank, things look entirely different. As it earns its income mainly from relatively large fees and large transactions, its earnings are more volatile. Also, in some deals, the bank assumes a considerable part of the risk in its books without any hedge. So, its profitability and value of its assets are more sensitive than in the case of a commercial bank.

Until 1970 US laws prohibited investment banks from floating their stock publicly. Typically, management was the dominant owner of the bank, forming a partnership similar to the present structure of law firms or auditors. That was an additional check on risk-taking.

Efficient-market hypothesis (EMH)

One of the most fundamental, most counterintuitive and most challenging assumptions in Economics. The premise is simple and logical—it claims that market price represents all relevant public information. However, formalisation of that principle creates several counterintuitive consequences.

First one is that expected price tomorrow $E(p_1)$ equals price today p_0. If the $E(p_1)$ would be different from p_0, then p_0 would already change to benefit from the expectation. As we know that, on liquid and deep markets almost always $p_1 \neq p_0$. It means that public information changed between days 0 and 1. As the new public information cannot be foreseen before it becomes public, it means that the information changes randomly and p_i should follow suit. Therefore $p_1 = p_0 + r_1$, where r_i is the change in the price between days 0 and 1. If the change is random, then it should flow several rules.

The first one is $E(r_i) = 0$. Expected change in the price between 2 days is zero. Though it never is, the claim can be proven by further proving several rules. If the distribution of r_i is not significantly different from the normal distribution grouped around zero, its time-series do not exhibit autocorrelation, significant runs[3] and average r_i is not significantly different from zero in any series with a high number of observations; we can claim that $E(r_i) = 0$.

Actual analysis of r_i distribution, especially in deep and liquid financial markets, clearly indicated that those conditions are fully met in all analysed series. Even the series taken during obviously one-sided market dynamics, for example, during strong market rallies or falls, exhibited those characteristics.

That is "weak form" of EMH—one that is never successfully challenged based on the observation of the actual data.

There are several consequences of the EMH which proved counterintuitive. The first one is that it is not possible to outperform the market systematically. It means that any price paid for asset management is, on average, a waste of money. The best performance is expected from random buy and hold strategy, as this strategy avoids the cost of fund management and trading costs. That is, of course, the reason for numerous fund managers relentlessly attacks EMH.

It is easy to challenge that conclusion, as there are investors systematically outperforming the market. Nonetheless, it cannot be proven. There are a vast number of investors, and runs are randomly distributed. In the overwhelming number, it would unavoidably be some very long runs of positive outcomes. As only those people hit

[3] A run is a string of values r_i with same sign. As $E(r) = 0$, then actual r_i are expected to alternate betwen positive and negative values randomly. Therefore, runs should also follow random rules.

front pages, we never learn about those with numerous runs of adverse outcomes. Experiments proved that historical results do not predict well future results of asset managers.

In a funny experiment, the chimp got a task to make the portfolio selection by throwing darts on the page of the Wall Street Journal. He consistently outperformed at least half of experts choosing competitive portfolios.[4]

The second strange consequence of EMH is that there can be no market bubbles.[5] The bubbles are supposed to be irrational changes in the prices. If the prices change in line with EMH, then its variations should be rational. Rational means that there is a rationally expected course of future events justifying the price. The only reason why the ex-ante rational ex-post appears irrational is that expectations did not fulfil.

The consequence is that it is not possible to recognise market aberrations and market trends, offering ground for the superior investment strategy. Famous J M Keynes summarised his experience in a sentence: "Markets can stay irrational longer than you can stay solvent."

The third consequence is that economic policy measures are mostly ineffective, as they meet opposite rational expectations. For example, increased public spending to boost demand causes an increase in savings to prepare for future austerity due to high public debt.

The ultimate paradox of EMH is that it is valid only if the majority do not take it seriously. Its principal finding is that, because everyone is vigilant and watchful, the best strategy is doing nothing. If everyone accepts it as fact, they will cease to be vigilant, and the hypothesis will become false.

Numerous researchers have disputed the efficient-market hypothesis, both empirically and theoretically. Behavioural economists recognise as a source of the financial market imperfections a combination of predictable human errors in reasoning and understanding of the information, such as overconfidence, overreaction, information bias and others.

Nonetheless, weak form EMH (different from the strong form) remained empirically untouchable. Therefore words "efficient market" in EMH do not necessarily mean the rational market, but most of all, the unpredictable market.

So, EMH can be a useful guideline for trading and investment strategies. However, it proved as a disastrous foundation for economic policies. The initial reaction of US politics on the crisis of 1929 was entirely in line with EMH (though EMH was not yet formally formulated), and we know the consequences.

---

[4]For example: http://www.stockinvestor.com/35446/beating-market-surprise-surprise-monkeys-win/.

[5]Glossary: Bubble.

Internal rate based (IRB)

The IRB approach relies on a bank's assessment of its counterparties and exposures in calculating capital requirements for credit risk. The introduction of IRB was in 2001 in a consultative paper issued by the Basel Committee for Banking Supervision (BCBS). IRB was made eligible for practical use based on the Basel Accord agreed in 2004.

Two primary objectives of its introduction were declared as follows:

Risk sensitivity—Capital requirements are sensitive to risk, meaning that the amount of the capital required is a consequence of the quality of the credit portfolio;
Incentive compatibility—The Bank is motivated to choose better risks, as such risks decrease the required regulatory capital.

A precondition for using this approach is a categorisation of exposures into asset classes as defined by the Basel II Accord and an assessment of the following risk parameters:

- Probability of default (PD)—represents the likelihood that the exposure would default during a single year;
- Loss given default (LGD)—a percentage of the expected loss in the accounting value at the moment of default. Loss given default considers economic loss, not accounting loss. It fundamentally corresponds with the methodology applied in IAS 39 with a difference that IRB LGD should be calculated and documented by historical data instead of evaluated. LGD takes into consideration the value of the collateral adjusted by the historical rate of collection from that collateral;
- Exposure at default (EAD)—the remaining exposure at the expected moment of default;
- Maturity (M)—the remaining loan duration until the final collection;

Risk parameters are used in risk-weight functions to define capital requirements.

Risk-weight functions—the functions provided as part of the Basel II regulatory framework,
Minimum requirements—Banks must meet the core minimum standards to use the internal ratings-based approach. That means that the ratings must be used internally in the banks' credit approval and monitoring practices. A rating system solely devised for calculating regulatory capital is not acceptable. Banks are required to demonstrate the use of risk parameters for risk management for at least 3 years before obtaining a licence.

A bank may choose between two IRB approaches:

- Foundation IRB: the bank calculates PD for its exposures, while the national competent authority gives other risk parameters (this approach is possible only for corporate, sovereign and bank exposures);

- Advanced IRB: the bank calculates all risk parameters in line with general guidelines. That is the only acceptable approach for retail exposures.

Definition of default: a material amount of exposure is 90 days overdue or unlikely to pay.

The probability of default should not be lower than the long-term annual default rate for that group of exposures, except for retail customers.

Cross-default is mandatory for corporate and banking exposures. That means that the default of one exposure automatically defaults all exposures towards the client. In retail exposures, the bank has no obligation to use cross-default.

For the calculation of the risk parameters, at least one downturn should be taken into account, and LGD should be calculated based on adverse economic conditions.

Econometrics is used to evaluate PD from historical data, which is a crucial parameter in the evaluation of capital requirements, together with LGD.

IRB offers significant benefits for banks with exposures towards clients with a lower PD. For example, clients with an internal rating equalling BBB-require ¾ of the standardised approach, while a rating equivalent to A + requires only ¼. Here internal ratings are involved, not ratings provided by rating agencies. Therefore, it is (theoretically) possible to have a group of retail clients with a rank equivalent to Luxembourg's rating. Also, it is very practically possible to have retail clients with a rating equal to Ireland.

For a detailed description and mathematics, please refer to:

Basel III: A global regulatory framework for more resilient banks and banking systems, Bank for International Settlement, December 2010 (rev June 2011), available online:

https://www.bis.org/publ/bcbs189.pdf.

Criticism:

What is wrong with IRB?

It is a very sophisticated, numerically based, formally tested and mathematically refined approach. It passed all formal tests with flying colours. It enables banks to reward themselves for better risk management. The less risky a portfolio they take into the balance sheet and off-balance sheet, the less capital they need. Such methodology enables banks to support better their most important clients: strong and reliable customers bearing small credit risk.

Despite all that, it is fundamentally and thoroughly wrong. It is wrong not only from a technical aspect. It is fundamentally flawed beyond recovery.

Fundamental flaws:

The capital of banks is a buffer against the unknown. Well-run banks cover all known risks by pricing their products. For example, the long-term loss rate on consumer loans is the first building block put on top of the funding cost when preparing an offer for such loans. Long-term loss is exactly historical PD * LGD * EAD. Therefore, if risks remain the same as in the past, a bank needs no capital to bear those risks. They are all covered by the bank's operating income, as long as the circumstances remain unchanged.

Capital is needed to weather an unexpected event—moments of discovering risks unknown until then. These are times when invisible correlations surface and collateral become a burden instead of a relief. Major profit-making low-risk products turn into financial black holes. Such moments are few and far apart, but we can easily recognise them. Those are moments when the banks' capital makes a difference.

Under pressure, the behaviour of the banking system and public finance becomes a watershed between an accident and a disaster. The more capital banks have and the lower the public debt, the easier it is to manage the situation. Small capital and high public debt seem like a safe recipe for turning stress into a crash.

Therefore, a bank's need for capital has no logical connection, and especially no statistical connection with the quality of its credit portfolio. On the other hand, the capital requirement is highly dependent on the size of the portfolio as, in times of turmoil, all parts of the credit portfolio create losses or risks. For example, cash, deposits in a central bank and the best banks and public debt will not create credit risk, but they could be a source of significant market risk.

Almost any asset could in a future event cause a capital decrease. The likelihood of such events cannot be recognised using IRB methodology. History tells us that, apart from a few people considered as freaks before the events, no one was able to identify incoming problems timely. The same will happen in the future: a crisis will come precisely at a time and in a form almost no one expected.

If IRB had been used back in 1929, there could have been no safer exposures than margin loans. A decade without any loss! Pure AAA—no need for capital at all. Which IRB portfolios could be more reliable than housing loans in the USA in 2008? Over ten years without material losses.

Still, those risks, though invisible for the IRB methodology, resulted in events destroying 3000 banks (and a lot of other things) in the first case and wiping out a quarter of the banks' share capital in the second. Therefore, the IRB methodology proved to be potentially counterproductive if we want banks to remain stable in an adverse environment. Such an environment is the only one potentially creating the only situation when banks need their capital. Earlier two examples clarify that, based on IRB, banks would conclude they need no capital exactly for those products which would explode into a losing spree just a few months later. If IRB had been used in 1929, it would make things even worse.

Furthermore, IRB is very unpractical. A practical man solves a problem when the problem can be solved. Deliberately creating a situation in which a problem will arise when you cannot solve it is very unpractical. An alternative term is—procyclical!

Banks can quickly increase their capital in good times. So, it is practical to require them then to do so. Bad times typically come after good times. A transition from good times to the bad absorbs capital to cover realised risks. Once the accumulated risks cause a major harmful event, those risks cease to exist. Empirically, the post-crisis portfolio is much better than the pre-crisis one. Therefore, it is both practical and reasonable to allow banks to operate with less capital in the post-crisis environment, replenishing capital as good times return.

IRB does precisely the opposite. It decreases capital requirements during good times while increasing them once growth of PD and LGD becomes apparent. So, it gives an unneeded respite in good times, while imposing an unrealistic and unnecessary regulatory burden once the situation worsens. Who would buy bank shares a year after a significant event?

There are also valid technical issues which, compared to the problems of IRB being risk increasing and procyclical, are much less important. Those fundamental reasons tell us quite clearly that the IRB methodology has such fundamental flaws that it is not a good supervisory tool.

Basel III will much improve the situation by implementing output floors in the 2022–2027 period. Still, it is hard to grasp why to retain a complex and demanding tool offering nothing useful, other than increasing risks in an upturn and procyclicality in a downturn?

Model of optimisation of a bank's profitability

Let us assume that the management of a bank has a perfect understanding of the market, involving expectations of future risks. Based on those assumptions, we can define their optimisation strategy and its consequences.

Initially, let us focus on the role and influence of the capital requirement on the optimisation process. The capital requirement is frequently regarded as the major factor affecting the banks' propensity to lend.

First, we shall define profit as a function of the credit volume generated during a year:

$$\pi_i = \phi(C_i, r_i) + K \tag{14.1}$$

where the following is defined:

ϕ—a function of profit

K—constant, in fact, a function of C_j, r_j, where j represents $i-1, i-2, \ldots, i-n$ for the years of a bank's operation. Still, as a change in C_i, r_i cannot influence K, we can consider it as a constant.

C_i—credit generated in the observed year ($C_i \geq 0$)

r_i—risk measured as an annual percentage of the expected loss of C_i.

We will assume that the credit portfolio has cumulative growth. Loans are serviced but not repaid. Therefore, the whole credit portfolio is

$$C = \sum_{i=1}^{n} C_i$$

We can recognise that

$$r_i = g(C_i) \tag{14.2}$$

where

$$\frac{dg}{dC_i} > 0, \frac{d^2C_i}{dC_i^2} > 0 \quad \text{and}\, g(0) = 0 \tag{14.3}$$

meaning that the riskiness of loans is a function of loan growth such that the increase in growth of C_i increases riskiness of given loans.

Then

$$\pi_i = \phi(C_i, g(C_i)) + K \tag{14.4}$$

and

$$\pi_i = f(C_i) + K \tag{14.5}$$

where f consists of ϕ and g

Here we introduce a function of profitability $p_i \rightarrow \pi_i$ divided by E_i.

$$p_i = \frac{\pi_i}{E_i} \tag{14.6}$$

$$p_i = \frac{f(C_i) + K}{E_i} \tag{14.7}$$

The equity of the bank is defined by the equity in the previous period $(i - 1)$ and credit growth in the period iCi multiplied by the capital requirement ε.

$$p_i = \frac{f(C_i) + K}{\varepsilon C_i + E_{i-1}} \tag{14.8}$$

$$p_i = \frac{f(C_i)}{E_i} + \frac{K}{E_i} \tag{14.9}$$

The maximisation of profitability would occur at $\frac{dp_i}{dC_i} = 0$

Therefore

$$\frac{dp_i}{dC_i} = \frac{f'(C_i)E_i - f(C_i)\varepsilon}{E_i^2} \quad \left(\text{as } E_i = (\varepsilon C_i + E_{i-1}) \text{ then } \frac{dE_i}{dC_i} = \varepsilon\right) \tag{14.10}$$

$$\frac{dp_i}{dC_i} = \frac{f'(C_i)E_i}{E_i^2} - \frac{f(C_i)\varepsilon}{E_i^2} \tag{14.11}$$

$$\frac{dp_i}{dC_i} = \frac{f'(C_i)}{E_i} - \frac{f(C_i)\varepsilon}{E_i^2} \tag{14.12}$$

$\frac{dp_i}{dC_i} = 0$ if $\frac{f'(C_i)}{E_i} = \frac{f(C_i)\varepsilon}{E_i^2}$ and therefore, p_i would reach its maximum at the point where

$$f'(C_i) = \frac{f(C_i)\varepsilon}{E_i} = \frac{\varepsilon(\pi_i - K)}{E_i} \tag{14.13}$$

Let us assume perfect competition. Therefore, the interest rate on loans and deposits would not change if Ci changes in the bank. We would consider costs as fixed in the optimisation period. As in such an environment income becomes a linear function of C_i and we already defined in Eq. (14.3) that if $g'' > 0$ then $f'' < 0$.

The maximum of π_i occurs at

$$f'(C_i) = 0 \tag{14.14}$$

As π_i and E_i are both positive, obviously in the case of $\varepsilon > 0$ the maximum of p_i would be reached sooner than the maximum of π_i.

But let us explore the Eq. (14.13) in more detail. A possible explanation could be that, given the same profitability $\left(\frac{\pi_i}{E_i}\right)$, an increase in capital requirement ε decreases C_i. But that conclusion would overlook the fact that $E_i = \varepsilon \sum_{i=1}^{n} C_i$. Including that, the point of maximum profitability becomes

$$f'(C_i) = \frac{\pi - K}{\sum_{i=1}^{n} C_i} \tag{14.15}$$

$C = \sum_{i=1}^{n} C_i$—the bank's entire credit portfolio.

Therefore, the bank's propensity to lend would (other things being equal) increase, as the average profitability of the bank's portfolio would decrease. The capital requirement does not influence that.

That is also intuitively logical, as shareholders would be willing to dilute as long as new capital would achieve at least average profitability. Therefore, all other things being equal, a bank with a more profitable credit portfolio would stop lending sooner than a bank with a less profitable one.

But such conclusion holds only in the case that new capital is collected at parity—if the profitability of the bank does not influence its stock price. But if the stock price depends on the profitability of the portfolio, then the conclusion would be much less obvious. Now it depends on the assumption describing how profitability would influence the stock price.

From the shareholders' point of view, the capital requirement ceases to be ε, and it becomes $\lambda\varepsilon$. λ is the ratio between the book value and the market price (inverse of $\frac{P}{B}$). Therefore, Eq. (14.13) now becomes

$$f'(C_i) = \frac{\lambda\varepsilon\pi_i}{E_i} \tag{14.16}$$

Consequently (14.15) changes to

$$f'(C_i) = \lambda\frac{\pi_i}{\sum_{i=1}^{n} C_i} \tag{14.17}$$

Therefore, in the case that the stock price is twice the book value, $f'(C_i)$ would be optimal when reaching 50% of the average return. That is rational, as the participation in profit is determined by the number of shares held, not by the money paid for the shares. Therefore, existing shareholders would readily accept a decrease in marginal profitability of the portfolio by 50%, as from their point of view such a return on new loans would still increase the performance of their shares.

Therefore, without making assumptions about the relation of a bank's portfolio profitability and λ, we cannot make any conclusion about the influence of profitability on the propensity to lend. We can reasonably assume that the share price would increase with an increase in the portfolio's profitability. Therefore, based on the assumption about such a relationship, it would significantly decrease, cancel or invert such influence.

The conclusion above depends on the availability of capital on the market. The unavailability of capital would indicate a failure of either the bank or the market. In the ordinary course of the events, we should rule out the assumption of capital unavailability.

Therefore, the examination confirms that the capital requirement does not influence the propensity to lend. The profitability of the portfolio could have an influence, but most likely, in reality, it would not be significant. Therefore, we should look further to find the source of such influence. Let us explore now the following part of the Eq. (14.2) $r_i = g(C_i)$.

Function g cannot be empirically recognised. It is a mathematical formalisation of an expectation. The decision-maker cannot know the level of future losses that will be associated with newly disbursed loans. Using historical experience and expectations about the future, in the planning process, the decision-maker explicitly or implicitly evaluates function g.

Therefore, the estimation of $g(C_i)$ and then $g'(C_i)$ could radically vary among planners. Such a difference would strongly influence the optimisation process of banks.

Let us now assume that two competing planners assume function $g - g_1(C_i)$ and $g_2(C_i)$ such that $g_1'(C_i) > g_2'(C_i)$ for every C_i.

Then we have two systems: $\pi_{i1} = \phi(C_i, g_1(C_i)) + K$ and $\pi_{i2} = \phi(C_i, g_2(C_i)) + K$.

Those two systems then create two functions of profitability $f_1(C_i)$ and $f_2(C_i)$.

Then $f_1'(C_i) < f_2'(C_i)$ for any $C_i \geq 0$. The consequence is that $f_1(C_i) < f_2(C_i)$. The decrease in π_i increases the propensity to lend, but the elasticity of $f'(C_i)$ would be higher than the elasticity of $f(C_i)$. Also, we demonstrated that share prices decrease or cancel the influence of π_i. Furthermore, when we look at the structure of Eq. (14.4), we see that, except in the first year of operation and some unlikely cases of extreme growth, K generates most of π_i—income on credit portfolio created in the past. Consequently, a more pessimistic g necessarily decreases the propensity to lend.

If we assume that

$$f'(0) \leq \lambda \frac{\pi_i}{C}$$

then optimally $C_i = 0$. So, if a bank expects the profitability of new loans to be lower than the profitability of the whole portfolio adjusted with λ, then the bank would not grant any loans this year.

We can conclude that, under the above assumptions of the model, the size of the optimal C_i in year i would be strongly influenced by the market price of the bank's stock and expectations of future losses. The variation of capital requirements has no influence, while the profitability of the credit portfolio has some impact. A relationship between the profitability of the portfolio and the stock price further decreased, cancelled or even inverse this influence.

The resilience of the alternative regulatory structure

Compared with the present capital requirement and Basel III standards, the proposed requirements could appear excessive. They are certainly not, and we will demonstrate it here using the simplified methodology of stress-test.

The requirement behind the design of the proposed regulatory structure is the creation of resilient banking able to finance the economy throughout the financial cycle without the need to increase the capital or stop credit growth in the crisis. To achieve it, we will push the hypothetical bank to maintain a credit growth rate of 5% annually.

The design of flexible regulatory requirements enables the bank's unconstrained activity throughout the cycle. The flexibility should follow the logic that realised risks decreased cumulated risks. Regulatory requirements should also respect the limitations of reality. For example, the collection of the new capital on the bottom of the cycle is not a realistic possibility, so it should not be assumed.

The assumption is that, after the bank recognises losses and go below capital requirement, the regulator would approve the bank to continue with the business, as long as minimal conditions for authorisation are fulfilled.

The model used for simulation is attached at the end of the section.

It begins as a profitable bank, earning 10% ROE, with CAR 21% and leverage of 11%.

Then it is exposed to a crisis turning 30% of its loans in NPL-s. Those NPLs do not generate income, and also they are subject to value adjustment of 10% of the exposure on default annually. Assumed LGD is 40% value adjustment that occured over 4 years. After that, provisioning stops and recovery begins. Also, the risk-free interest rate increases by 1%, decreasing the value of bond holding for 3% in the year one. Operational costs are assumed fixed.

In the first year after the shock, the bank has losses. Its capital decreases for one fifth, and CAR falls to 14% and the leverage to 9%. Declared Texas ratio is 180%. Losses continue during 3 years, depleting capital and bringing bank on the minimum authorisation conditions, CAR 10% and leverage 6% with Texas ratio 164% in the year 4. After year four, the bank recovers profitability, and the recovery of NPLs begins.

We see that despite the gradual recognition of losses, the capital requirement is not excessive. It barely saves the bank from the resolution in case of the loss of 12% of the bank's credit portfolio. More dynamic provisioning, for example within 2 years, would make bank non-compliant in both CAR of 7% and leverage of 4%. The difference is the lack of operating income from the years of 3 and 4. Despite "excessive" capital, the bank can maintain regulatory compliance only if there is an understanding of the regulator. It cannot recognise the whole LGD immediately but need to account for it gradually.

The bank declares and maintains the Texas ratio above 150% for 4 years in a row, which is exceptionally worrisome for supervisor, especially in combination with indicators dangerously close to minimal conditions for authorisation.

So, we see that even "excessive" capitalised bank has limited loss absorption capacity. For example, maximal portfolio loss of the bank can swallow in a single year while maintaining minimal conditions for the authorisation is 7.5% of the loan portfolio (not total assets). It is high, but not excessively high.

We will now compare that loss bearing capacity of our bank, let us call it the Alternative bank with fully loaded Basel III bank, well capitalised, with more than required MREL and very profitable. The Basel III bank has CAR of 15% and Leverage of 5.4%. Therefore, the bank is comfortably compliant. We see that Basel III bank becomes non-compliant after the loss of less than 3% of the loan portfolio. It is significantly less then US banks suffered in 2008–2009.

The difference is not so much in real resilience, but the fact that the Basel III bank would have a significant part of the capital in the TLAC instruments. We will assume that it has 100 million in the junior debt. Instead of withstanding the loss and going on with business, as the MREL would still be enough to satisfy minimal authorisation criteria, the present regulatory structure would "resolve" bank. We should also note that the bank we simulated was not marginally compliant. For a barely compliant bank, any losses can cause resolution, because it is not possible to get new capital in the crisis.

Therefore, we have two alternative situations in the case of the same losses. If we begin with Basel III bank and impose losses of 3% credit portfolio a year through 4 years, it would come under the resolution at the beginning of the second year. Then it will again become non-compliant 2 years later.

Therefore, the regulatory framework is such that the bank's management will be replaced in the second year by resolution management. The resolution management will be replaced with the new management of the bailed-in bank during the second or third year, after an extended interregnum in the resolution.

In the fourth year, the new management would be replaced one more time with resolution management. Finally, the bank will be saved by the bail-out with public money. Unless all this management change ruined the bank, the government would harvest excellent profits. Unfortunately, the profits will come only after angry public uproar because of saving bank with public money. A most impressive feature in this situation is that, basically, all those managements can do a little to change anything. The markets are closed for new issues while the destiny of the bank writes in its balance sheet. Any attempt to sell NPL would require accepting additional losses, and the bank cannot do it.

In the alternative scenario, the bank continues business without sudden changes in the corporate governances (unless shareholders want some) while digesting loss of 12% of the portfolio. All profits from recovered bank belong again to the same shareholders, and government money stays in the government coffers.

From the real economy perspective, the Alternative bank provides all services, including loans without any limitations or distress. It is not likely that the Basel III bank would be able to grant any loans. More likely, it would try to decrease RWA by collecting or selling a loan portfolio.

We see that in the year 7 Alternative bank recovered most of the losses, and its shareholders enjoy profit and receive dividends. On the other hand, in the same case in Basel III bank, not only shareholders lost everything, but also TLAC providers are wiped out throughout bail-out. We see the difference in the risks shareholders are exposed too. In the Alternative bank, due to 7 years of the lost dividend, shareholders lost maybe even 50% of expected share value before the crisis. In case of the Basel III bank shareholders and TLAC providers lost everything.

Furthermore, we see that shareholders of Basel III bank will lose everything, even in the case of one-quarter of the loss the Alternative banks survived. One-quarter of the loss is many times, maybe even hundreds of times more likely.

We should also remind that the Basel III bank is not a picture of the present EU bank, but the bank that completed the transition now recognised as very demanding. Nonetheless, it has an average leverage of Eurozone bank today.

Another difference in the models is that Basel III bank will before the crisis have ROE of 19%, while Alternative will hardly reach 9%. People would today gladly invest for 9% return. They will willingly invest for 5% return if they perceive the investment as safe. Therefore, earning per share of the Alternative bank would be high enough to mobilise the equity before the crisis.

If they are rational, they would much rather accept less then 1% of the risk for 50% of the return. The whole recovery process of the bank is much smoother then multiple resolutions crowned with bail-out of the Basel III bank. As all the dynamics in the Alternative bank will be private, occurring behind closed doors of boards and between the bank and the supervisor, it will preserve its reputation throughout the crisis. It would retain its clients and business and would be able to return on capital markets soon to mobilise needed capital.

The public would very much notice the distress of Basel III bank. Its reputation would be tarnished, clients upset and business harmed. The capital market will open to it reluctantly and late.

The final question is how realistic stress was? Twelve per cent of lost loans during 4 years is an extreme assumption. Nonetheless, it is not impossible. "Fat tails" of observed distributions make theoretically impossible events unlikely but possible. So, it is nice to be ready even for it.

Loss in the region of 6% of credit portfolio in one year is also unlikely, but much more likely than 12%. Nonetheless, 3% becomes practically possible, even likely within a few decades. When we talk about 1%—something that could harm marginally compliant bank, that occurs almost certainly in a decade. Therefore, the shareholders of the weakly capitalised bank are not irrational at all if they sharply discount future cash flow and require high P/E.

Model of Alternative and Basel III bank in the crisis

Assumptions: The crisis begins in year one and makes 30% of the bank's loans NPL
During the following 4 years, 40% of defaulted loans will be lost. Remaining loans will be gradually recovered, beginning with year 4
Interest rates on riskless assets will increase in the first year for 1% and a decrease in the fourth year on the earlier level. It would have an impact on the value of the reserves of 3%
NPLs will create no interest in income and no non-interest income
Loans will continue growth with a steady rate of 5% a year
All other parameters stay the same

Year 0	**Alternative bank**							
Assets			Liabilities					
Cash	100		Current accounts			1000		
Liquid reserves	1000		Term deposits			1000		
Short term loans	1000		Issued bonds			650		
Long term loans	900		Equity			350		
Total	3000		Total			3000		
C&I	Average rate		Income		**Capital adequacy**		RW	RWA
			Cost		Cash		0%	0
Cash	0,00%		0		Liquid reserves		20%	200
Liqid reserves	1,50%		15		Short term loans		100%	1.000
Short term loans	5,00%		50		Long term loans		50%	450
Long term loans	4,00%		36		**Total**			1.650
Interest income			101					
Current accounts	0,00%		0		**CAR**			**21,21%**
Term deposits	2,00%		20		**Leverage**			**11,67%**
Issued bonds	4,00%		26					
Equity	0,00%		0					
Interest cost			46					
Net interest income			55					
Non-interest income			17					
Total income			72					
Operational costs			25					
Operative earnings			47					
Risk cost			10					
Profit before tax			**37**					
Profit tax 15%			**6**					
Profit after tax			**31**					
RoE			**9%**					

Year 1 of the crisis			**Alternative bank**					
NPL 30%								
Provisioning 10% of initial NPL EOD								
NPLs earn 75% of interest								
Increasing bond rate 1% cause loss of 3% of the value of the liquid reserve.								
Assets			Liabilities					
Cash	100		Current accounts			1000		
Liquid reserves	1013		Term deposits			1000		
Short term loans	700		Issued bonds			650		
Long term loans	630		Equity			306		
NPL	513							
Total	2956		Total			2956		
C&I	Average rate		Income		**Capital adequacy**		RW	RWA
			Cost		Cash		0%	0
Cash	0,00%		0		Liquid reserves		20%	203
Liqid reserves	2,50%		25		Short term loans		100%	700
Short term loans	5,00%		35		Long term loans		50%	315
NPL	3,40%		17		**NPL**	513	150%	770
Long term loans	4,00%		25					1.987
Interest income			103		**CAR**			**15%**
Current accounts	0,00%		0		**Leverage**			**10%**
Term deposits	2,00%		20					
Issued bonds	4,00%		26					
Interest cost			46					
Net interest income			57					
Non-interest income			17					
Total income			74					
Operational costs			25					
Operative earnings			49					
Risk cost			64					
Profit before tax			**-15**					
Profit tax 15%								
Profit after tax			**-15**					

Year 2 after the crisis		**Alternative bank**		
Provisioning 10% of initial NPL EOD				
Credit growth 5%				
Assets		Liability		
Cash	100	Current accounts		1.000
Liquid reserves	995	Term deposits		1.028
Short term loans	735	Issued bonds		650
Long term loans	662	Equity		270
NPL	456			
Total	2.948			2.948

C&I	Average rate	Income / Cost		Capital adequacy		RW	RWA
Cash	0,00%	0		Cash		0%	0
Liqid reserves	2,50%	25		Liqid reserves		20,00%	199
Short term loans	5,00%	37		Short term loans		100%	735
Long term loans	4,00%	26		Long term loans		50%	331
Interest income		88		**NPL**		1,5	684
							1.949
Current accounts	0,00%	0		**CAR**			**14%**
Term deposits	2,00%	21		**Leverage**			**9%**
Issued bonds	4,00%	26					
				Texas			**169%**
Interest cost		47					
Net interest income		42					
Non-interest income		12					
Total income		54					
Operational costs		25					
Operative earnings		29					
Risk cost		64					
Profit before tax		**-35**					
Profit tax 15%							
Profit after tax		**-35**					

Year 3 after the crisis		Alternative bank	
Provisioning 10% of initial NPL EOD			
Credit growth 5%			
Assets		Liability	
Cash	100	Current accounts	1.000
Liquid reserves	995	Term deposits	1.026
Short term loans	772	Issued bonds	700
Long term loans	695	Equity	235
NPL	399		
Total	2.961		2.961

C&I	Average rate	Income	Capital adequacy	RW	RWA
		Cost	Cash	0%	0
Cash	0,00%	0	Liqid reserves	20,00%	199
Liqid reserves	2,50%	25	Short term loans	100%	772
Short term loans	5,00%	39	Long term loans	50%	348
Long term loans	4,00%	28	**NPL**	1,5	599
Interest income		91			1.917
Current accounts	0,00%	0	**CAR**		**12%**
Term deposits	2,00%	21	**Leverage**		**8%**
Issued bonds	4,00%	28			
			Texas		**170%**
Interest cost		49			
Net interest income		43			
Non-interest income		13			
Total income		56			
Operational costs		25			
Operative earnings		31			
Risk cost		64			
Profit before tax		**-34**			
Profit tax 15%					
Profit after tax		**-34**			

Year 4 after the crisis			Alternative bank					
Provisioning 10% of initial NPL EOD								
Credit growth 5%								
Assets			Liability					
Cash	100		Current accounts			1.000		
Liquid reserves	995		Term deposits			1.026		
Short term loans	811		Issued bonds			700		
Long term loans	730		Equity			204		
NPL	295							
Total	2.930					2.930		

C&I	Average rate		Income		**Capital adequacy**		RW	RWA
			Cost		Cash		0%	0
Cash	0,00%		0		Liqid reserves		20,00%	199
Liqid reserves	2,50%		25		Short term loans		100%	811
Short term loans	5,00%		41		Long term loans		50%	365
Long term loans	4,00%		29		**NPL**		1,5	443
Interest income			95					1.817
Current accounts	0,00%		0		**CAR**			**11%**
Term deposits	2,00%		21		**Leverage**			**7%**
Issued bonds	4,00%		28					
					Texas			**145%**
Interest cost			49					
Net interest income			46					
Non-interest income			14					
Total income			60					
Operational costs			25					
Operative earnings			35					
Risk cost			65					
Profit before tax			**-30**					
Profit tax 15%								
Profit after tax			**-30**					

Year 5 after the crisis		Alternative bank	
Credit growth 5%			
Assets		Liability	
Cash	100	Current accounts	978
Liquid reserves	995	Term deposits	1.000
Short term loans	852	Issued bonds	700
Long term loans	767	Equity	235
NPL	200		
Total	2.913		2.913

C&I	Average rate	Income Cost
Cash	0,00%	0
Liqid reserves	2,50%	25
Short term loans	5,00%	43
Long term loans	4,00%	31
Interest income		98
Current accounts	0,00%	0
Term deposits	2,00%	20
Issued bonds	4,00%	28
Interest cost		48
Net interest income		50
Non-interest income		15
Total income		65
Operational costs		25
Operative earnings		40
Risk cost		8
Profit before tax		**32**
Profit tax 15%		
Profit after tax		**32**
RoE		**14%**

Capital adequacy	RW	RWA
Cash	0%	0
Liqid reserves	20,00%	199
Short term loans	100%	852
Long term loans	50%	383
NPL	1,5	300
		1.734
CAR		**14%**
Leverage		**8%**
Texas		**85%**

Year 6 after the crisis		**Alternative bank**	
Credit growth 5%			
Assets		Liability	
Cash	93	Current accounts	978
Liquid reserves	1.008	Term deposits	1.000
Short term loans	893	Issued bonds	700
Long term loans	805	Equity	272
NPL	150		
Total	2.950		2.950

C&I	Average rate	Income / Cost	Capital adequacy	RW	RWA
			Cash	0%	0
Cash	0,00%	0	Liqid reserves	20,00%	202
Liqid reserves	2,50%	25	Short term loans	100%	893
Short term loans	5,00%	45	Long term loans	50%	403
Long term loans	4,00%	32	**NPL**	1,5	225
Interest income		102			1.723
Current accounts	0,00%	0	**CAR**		**16%**
Term deposits	2,00%	20	**Leverage**		**9%**
Issued bonds	4,00%	28			
			Texas		**55%**
Interest cost		48			
Net interest income		54			
Non-interest income		16			
Total income		70			
Operational costs		25			
Operative earnings		45			
Risk cost		8			
Profit before tax		**37**			
Profit tax 15%					
Profit after tax		**37**			
RoE		**14%**			

Year 7 after the crisis		**Alternative bank**						
Credit growth 5%								
Decreased interest on liquid reserves for 1% increases the value of liquid reserves for 3%								
Assets			Liability					
Cash	117		Current accounts			978		
Liquid reserves	1.008		Term deposits			1.000		
Short term loans	938		Issued bonds			700		
Long term loans	845		Equity			330		
NPL	100							
Total	3.008					3.008		
C&I	Average rate		Income / Cost		**Capital adequacy**		RW	RWA
Cash	0,00%		0		Cash		0%	0
Liqid reserves	1,50%		15		Liqid reserves		20,00%	202
Short term loans	5,00%		47		Short term loans		100%	938
Long term loans	4,00%		34		Long term loans		50%	423
Interest income			96		**NPL**		1,5	150
Current accounts	0,00%		0					1.712
Term deposits	2,00%		20		**CAR**			**19%**
Issued bonds	4,00%		28		**Leverage**			**11%**
					Texas			**30%**
Interest cost			48					
Net interest income			48					
Non-interest income			14					
Total income			62					
Operational costs			25					
Operative earnings			37					
Risk cost			9					
Profit before tax			**28**					
Profit tax 15%								
Profit after tax			**28**					
RoE			**9%**					

Year 0			**Basel III bank**					
Assets			Liability					
Cash	100		Current accounts			1.000		
Liquid reserves	800		Term deposits			1.000		
Short term loans	1.000		Issued bonds			650		
Long term loans	900		Equity			150		
Total	2.800					2.800		
C&I	Average rate		Income		Capital adequacy		RW	RWA
			Cost		**Cash**		0	0
			0		Liqid reserves		0%	0
Liqid reserves	1,50%		12		Short term loans		70,00%	700
Short term loans	5,00%		50		Long term loans		35%	315
Long term loans	4,00%		36					1.015
Interest income			98		CAR			15%
Current accounts	0,00%		0		**Leverage**			**5%**
Term deposits	2,00%		20					
Issued bonds	4,00%		26					
Equity	0,00%		0					
Interest cost			46					
Net interest income			52					
Non-interest income			16					
Total income			68					
Operational costs			25					
Operative earnings			43					
Risk cost			10					
Profit before tax			33					
Profit tax 15%			**5**					
Profit after tax			**28**					
RoE			**19%**					

Year 1 of the crisis			**Basel III bank**					
NPL 30%								
NPLs earn 75% of interest								
Provisioning 10% of initial NPL EOD								
Increasing bond rate 1% cause loss of 3% of the value of the liquid reserve.								
Assets			Liability					
Cash	112		Current accounts			1.000		
Liquid reserves	799		Term deposits			1.000		
Short term loans	700		Issued bonds			650		
Long term loans	630		Equity			104		
NPL	513							
Total	2.754					2.754		
C&I	Average rate		Income		**Capital adequacy**		RW	RWA
			Cost		Cash		0%	0
Cash	0,00%		0		Liqid reserves		0,00%	0
Liqid reserves	2,50%		20		Short term loans		70%	490
Short term loans	5,00%		35		Long term loans		35%	221
Long term loans	4,00%		25		**NPL**		150%	770
NPL	3,40%		17					1.480
Interest income			98		**CAR**			**7,06%**
Current accounts	0,00%		0		**Leverage**			**3,79%**
Term deposits	2,00%		20					
Issued bonds	4,00%		26		**Texas**			**491%**
Interest cost			46					
Net interest income			52					
Non-interest income			15					
Total income			67					
Operational costs			25					
Operative earnings			42					
Risk cost			64					
Profit before tax			**-22**					
Profit tax 15%								
Profit after tax			**-22**					

Year 2 after the crisis		**Basel III bank**						
Provisioning 10% of initial NPL EOD								
Resolution by converting 100 million bonds in equity								
Assets			Liability					
Cash	100		Current accounts			1.000		
Liquid reserves	781		Term deposits			1.000		
Short term loans	700		Issued bonds			500		
Long term loans	630		Equity			167		
NPL	456							
Total	2.667					2.667		
C&I	Average rate		Income		**Capital adequacy**		RW	RWA
			Cost		Cash		0%	0
Cash	0,00%		0		Liqid reserves		0,00%	0
Liqid reserves	2,50%		20		Short term loans		70%	490
Short term loans	5,00%		35		Long term loans		35%	221
Long term loans	4,00%		25		**NPL**		150%	684
Interest income			80					1.395
Current accounts	0,00%		0		**CAR**			**11,98%**
Term deposits	2,00%		20		**Leverage**			**6,26%**
Issued bonds	4,00%		20					
Interest cost			40		**Texas**			**273%**
Net interest income			40					
Non-interest income			12					
Total income			52					
Operational costs			25					
Operative earnings			27					
Risk cost			64					
Profit before tax			**-37**					
Profit tax 15%								
Profit after tax			**-37**					

Year 3 after the crisis			**Basel III bank**					
Provisioning 10% of initial NPL EOD								
Assets			Liability					
Cash	100		Current accounts			998		
Liquid reserves	800		Term deposits			1.000		
Short term loans	700		Issued bonds			500		
Long term loans	630		Equity			131		
NPL	399							
Total	2.629					2.629		
C&I	Average rate		Income		**Capital adequacy**		RW	RWA
			Cost		Cash		0%	0
Cash	0,00%		0		Liqid reserves		0,00%	0
Liquid reserves	2,50%		20		Short term loans		70%	490
Short term loans	5,00%		35		Long term loans		35%	221
Long term loans	4,00%		25		**NPL**		150%	599
Interest income			80					1.309
Current accounts	0,00%		0		**CAR**			**10,01%**
Term deposits	2,00%		20		**Leverage**			**4,98%**
Issued bonds	4,00%		20					
Interest cost			40		**Texas**			**305%**
Net interest income			40					
Non-interest income			12					
Total income			52					
Operational costs			25					
Operative earnings			27					
Risk cost			64					
Profit before tax			**-36**					
Profit tax 15%								
Profit after tax			**-36**					

Year 4 after the crisis			**Basel III bank**					
Provisioning 10% of initial NPL EOD								
Assets			Liability					
Cash	100		Current accounts			997		
Liquid reserves	821		Term deposits			1.000		
Short term loans	700		Issued bonds			500		
Long term loans	630		Equity			96		
NPL	342							
Total	2.593					2.593		
C&I	Average rate		Income		**Capital adequacy**		RW	RWA
			Cost		Cash		0%	0
Cash	0,00%		0		Liqid reserves		0,00%	0
Liquid reserves	2,50%		21		Short term loans		70%	490
Short term loans	5,00%		35		Long term loans		35%	221
Long term loans	4,00%		25		**NPL**		150%	513
Interest income			81					1.224
Current accounts	0,00%		0		**CAR**			**7,85%**
Term deposits	2,00%		20		**Leverage**			**3,70%**
Issued bonds	4,00%		20					
Interest cost			40		**Texas**			**356%**
Net interest income			41					
Non-interest income			12					
Total income			53					
Operational costs			25					
Operative earnings			28					
Risk cost			64					
Profit before tax			**-36**					
Profit tax 15%								
Profit after tax			**-36**					

Resolution strategies: Single point of entry (SPE) and Multiple points of entry (MPE)

When a resolution authority initiates the resolution of a bank, it does so based on a previously prepared resolution plan implementing a chosen strategy. Though resolution plans can widely vary in details, the plan is always fundamentally determined by the selected strategy.

The single point of entry strategy focuses on a group of licenced banks and bank holding companies. The purpose of the strategy is to stabilise the entire group. The single point of entry resolution re-capitalises or liquidates the entity controlling the whole group. The flow of the capital from the controlling entity towards the group members perform such resolution. Depending on the situation, the resolution of individual group members can be declared, but the strategy usually focuses on the resolution of the group owner. Then the overall resolution can be performed by applying normal corporate governances, as the controlling entity has all necessary powers to make all relevant decisions.

The multiple point of entry strategy triggers the resolution of single operating entities separate from the group. That means that after the bank's failure, the resolution authority initiates a decision in the group member without involving the group in the resolution process. The resolved bank ceases to be a group member. The resolution authority and resolution management appointed by it then make all decisions required to complete the resolution.

Both strategies have advantages and weaknesses. Legally, the single point of entry represents a challengeable situation, as it nullifies the limited liability. Therefore, if such a strategy is applied, the controlling entity can be placed in resolution because of the failure of its limited liability subsidiary. If a resolution strategy is decided on by resolution authorities, without the commitment of the controlling entity, the strategy application could be legally challenged. Without having confirmed any wrongdoing, the owner should not suffer the consequence of a limited liability company's failure above the value of invested capital. Therefore, a single point of entry legally depends on the owner's good will.

The federal reserve board recognised this correctly, and the US resolution authority decided to involve the controlling entity into resolution planning, requiring it to waive limited liability and sign a support contract with the controlled companies.

The most significant advantage of the SPE strategy is that it can function within the framework of existing corporate governances, minimally obstructing the operation of the banks involved. Only the controlling entity has the obligation of collecting TLAC/MREL instruments, while subsidiaries entirely rely on the owner in the case of failure. Regulators in the USA decided that the SPE strategy would resolve bank holding companies, entities not performing banking operations. Therefore, the group can be resolved without the resolution of banks, but by providing them with liquidity and capital support from the owner.

The advantage of MPE is, in the case of international groups, preventing the crisis from spilling over from the host to the home jurisdiction. Therefore, in the case of subsidiary failure, the owner suffers a loss of their investment, without any further obligation, while host authorities, both competent and resolution, deal with the situation based on the previously defined plan. Of course, the owner always has the option to support the subsidiary, but in this case, there will be no need for resolution. Also, for the host authority, the MPE is safer, as it is entirely under its control. It does not involve unresolved legal issues concerning the limited liability we discussed earlier. But the MPE requires that each subsidiary collect MREL and prepare a resolution plan.

Executing the MPE strategy is more demanding and requires better preparation compared to the SPE. Each group member participates in group corporate governances, shares the group brand and standard group technologies. Activating the resolution causes the resolved bank to abandon the group. It should create its corporate governances, management structure, find a technically and legally acceptable solution concerning brand and standard group technologies.

A successful conclusion of all those processes is possible, but they would extend and further complicate the already complex resolution process.

Risk weights

The first Basel Accord introduced risk weights in 1988. Those are numbers used to multiply certain items on the asset side of a bank's balance sheet to adjust (weight) the assets for assumed risks. After applying risk weights, the size of the balance sheet significantly changes (decreases), and those risk-weighted assets are the denominator for calculating the bank's capital adequacy.

The performing portfolio has risk weights between zero and one attached. The least risky assets are weighted 0, requiring no capital. That is understandable as, for example, cash in hand or deposits in the central bank, are assets without any credit risks. Therefore, the bank need not keep capital to support such risk. Risk weights encourage banks to keep extensive reserves, as they do not influence the bank's capital adequacy.

If the bank acquires risky assets, such as corporate loans, the loan generates risk. The Basel Accord requires 8% capital on risk-weighted assets. A 100.000 EUR deposited in the central bank requires 0 EUR capital. In contrast, the same loan amount to a company without rating requires 8.000 EUR capital.

The changes in the Basel Accord implemented in 2004 allowed banks to calculate risk weights of certain assets based on the historical performance of similar loans given to similar clients. A detailed description is in the glossary item: Internal rating based.

Criticism: While the reasoning behind introducing a 0% risk weight is reasonable and understandable, the further sophistication of risk weighting through adding intermediary risk weights of 50, 35 and 20% are much less straightforward. Those risk weights are attached to assets bearing risks, but still representing a kind of reserve of the bank, for example, bonds of rated companies, deposits in lower rated banks. Also, those risk weights are attached to loans, historically creating fewer risks, such as retail mortgages.

Applying intermediary risk weights significantly increases the supply and decreases the cost of loans with such risk weights attached, especially in an environment characterised by a capital shortage. Therefore, risk weights unavoidably become policy tools affecting availability, pricing and distribution of loans.

Standard microeconomic model

That is a fundamental model of the so-called neoclassical analysis. Though the model is not a realistic representation of economic activity, it illustrates the predominant forces shaping an economy. Still, we cannot criticise it for being unrealistic, as it never had an intention to be realistic. It is an extension of classical political economy with the application of modern mathematics. It relies on the usage of differential calculus, assuming a continuous change in observed variables.

The core of the model is the supply-demand diagram, where two lines cross in a point representing an equilibrium defining the price of a product that will enable the production of the quantity precisely needed to satisfy demand.[6]

Technology dictates the shape of the supply curve, and it represents a production function. On the other hand, the demand curve represents the "taste" or utility function limited by disposable income.

The production function indicates the production price for a certain quantity of a product. The demand function determines how much of the product will consumers buy for that price. The entire model is observed under the "ceteris paribus" assumption, meaning that nothing else except the observed price on the market changes.

The assumptions needed for a smooth optimisation is that both curves are continuous, derivable on the whole relevant range (quadrant I, negative values are not applicable). That means that any change in price (however small) will affect both supply and demand.

The first derivative of the supply function should be positive and of the demand function, it should be negative on the whole relevant range. That means that supply will increase and demand decrease while the price increases.

The model has an optimal solution, with the largest quantities produced and consumed when all market activities are unobstructed by any discrete external intervention. Any such intervention "pushes" the supply curve up or the demand curve down. That decreases the quantity produced and consumed, therefore negatively affecting the utility for the population.

The element of the neoclassical analysis appeared in the second half of the nineteenth century with different authors, and the first textbook involving all elements of the theory was Alfred Marshall's "Principles of Economics" (1890).

[6]For example: https://en.wikipedia.org/wiki/Supply_and_demand.

References

Admati, A., & Hellwig, M. (2014). *The bankers' new clothes*, Princeton University Press.
Hassett, K. (2002). *Bubbleology*, Crown Business. ISBN 0609609297.

The manufacturer's authorised representative in the EU is Springer Nature Customer Service Centre GmbH, Europaplatz 3, 69115 Heidelberg, Germany. If you have any concerns regarding our products, please contact ProductSafety@springernature.com

Printed and bound by CPI Group (UK) Ltd, Croydon, CR0 4YY
30/09/2026
02225510-0002